ACCA

PAPER F2

MANAGEMENT ACCOUNTING

In this January 2010 new edition

- We discuss the **best strategies** for revising and taking your ACCA exams

- We show you how to be well prepared for the **2010 exams**

- We give you **lots of great guidance** on tackling questions

- We provide you with **three** mock exams including the **Pilot paper**

- We provide the **ACCA examiner's answers** as well as our own to the Pilot Paper as an additional revision aid

Our **i-Pass** product also supports this paper.

FOR EXAMS UNTIL 30 NOVEMBER 2011

BPP
LEARNING MEDIA

First edition 2007

Fourth edition January 2010

ISBN 9780 7517 8047 5
(previous ISBN 9780 7517 6653 0)

e-ISBN 9780 7517 8240 0

British Library Cataloguing-in-Publication Data
A catalogue record for this book
is available from the British Library

Published by

BPP Learning Media Ltd
BPP House, Aldine Place
London W12 8AA

www.bpp.com/learningmedia

Printed in the United Kingdom

We are grateful to the Association of Chartered Certified Accountants for permission to reproduce past examination questions. The answers to past examination questions have been prepared by BPP Learning Media Ltd.

Your learning materials, published by BPP Learning Media Ltd, are printed on paper sourced from sustainable, managed forests.

Contents

Question index

The headings in this checklist/index indicate the main topics of questions, but questions often cover several different topics.

Questions set under the old syllabus Paper 1.2 - *Information for management* are included because their style and content are similar to those that appear in the Paper F2 exam. The questions have been amended to reflect the current exam format.

Mixed banks 1 and 2 – 20 questions each (40 marks)

Mock exam 1 – Paper-based exam

Mock exam 2 – Computer-based exam

Mock exam 3 – (Pilot paper)

Using your BPP Learning Media Practice and Revision Kit

Tackling revision and the exam

You can significantly improve your chances of passing by tackling revision and the exam in the right ways. Our advice is based on feedback from ACCA examiners.

- We focus on Paper F2; we discuss revising the syllabus, how to approach different types of question and ways of obtaining easy marks

Selecting questions

We provide a full **question index** to help you plan your revision

Making the most of question practice

At BPP Learning Media we realise that you need more than just questions and simple answers to get the most from your question practice. We include workings and explanations to show you how we arrived at the right answer and why the wrong answers were incorrect.

Attempting mock exams

There are three mock exams that provide practice at coping with the pressures of the exam day. We strongly recommend that you attempt them under exam conditions. **Mock exam 1** reflects the question styles and syllabus coverage of the paper-based exam. **Mock exam 2** reflects what you will see in a computer-based exam. **Mock exam 3** is the Pilot paper. To help you get the most out of doing these exams, we provide help with each answer. The examiner's answers to the Pilot paper are included at the back of the kit.

Using your BPP Learning Media products

This Kit gives you the question practice and guidance you need in the exam. Our other products can also help you pass:

- **Learning to Learn Accountancy** gives further valuable advice on revision
- **Passcards** provide you with clear topic summaries and exam tips
- **Success CDs** help you revise on the move
- **i-Pass CDs** offer tests of knowledge against the clock

You can purchase these products by visiting www.bpp.com/mybpp.

Passing F2

General exam support from BPP Learning Media

BPP Learning Media is committed to giving you the best possible support in your quest for exam success. With this in mind, we have produced **guidance** on how to revise and techniques you can apply to **improve your chances of passing** the exam. This guidance can be found on the BPP Learning Media web site at the following link:

www.bpp.com/acca/examtips/Revising-for-ACCA-exams.doc

A paper copy of this guidance is available by e-mailing learningmedia@bpp.com

Topics to revise

The examiner will test **every area of the syllabus** so you must revise **all topics**. Selective revision will limit the number of questions that you can answer and reduce your chance of passing.

Although the Paper F2 exam does not require you to submit written workings, it is still essential that you **practise the steps** involved in different techniques. If you are familiar with these steps, you will be more confident about tackling any question on the topic.

But do not spend too long on any one topic – it will probably only feature in a few questions.

Question practice - paper based or computer based?

You may take Paper F2 as a **paper based** exam or a **computer based** exam. It is very much a personal choice which one you choose – however your final revision should be tailored towards your choice of exam. You can find general details about computer based exams on page x.

The **computer based** exam contains a **mixture of multiple choice and objective test questions**, whilst the **paper based** exam contains **only multiple choice questions**. Before you decide on the mode of exam you might prefer, it is a good idea to have a look at multiple choice and objective test question banks in this kit to get a feel for the different styles of questions you might be faced with.

Mock Exam 1 and **Mock Exam 3** (pilot paper) are paper based (multiple choice questions only), **Mock Exam 2** contains the style of questions you might face in a computer based exam (even though it is on paper!)

(i)   **Paper based exams**

If you choose the paper based route, your revision must include the following:

- Read 'Tackling multiple choice questions' on page viii

- Attempt all the multiple choice and objective test questions in this kit (you can never get enough question practice!)

- Do Mock Exam 1 and Mock Exam 3 (the pilot paper) under exam conditions

- If time allows, do Mock Exam 2 for additional question practice.

(ii)   **Computer based exams**

If you decide to take the exam on computer, you must include the following in your revision plan:

- Read 'Tackling multiple choice questions' on page ix and 'Tackling objective test questions' on page x
- Attempt all the multiple choice and objective test questions in this kit
- Do **Mock Exam 2** in this kit **under exam conditions**
- **If time allows**, do Mock Exam 1 for additional question practice.

Tackling multiple choice questions

The MCQs in your exam will contain four or five possible answers. You have to **choose the option that best answers the question**. The three or four incorrect options are called distracters. There is a skill in answering MCQs quickly and correctly. By practising MCQs you can develop this skill, giving yourself a better chance of passing the exam.

You may wish to follow the approach outlined below, or you may prefer to adapt it.

Step 1   Skim read all the MCQs and identify which appear to be the easier questions.

Step 2   Work out **how long** you should allocate to each MCQ bearing in mind the number of marks available. Remember that the examiner will not expect you to spend an equal amount of time on each MCQ; some can be answered instantly but others will take time to work out.

Step 3   Attempt each question – **starting with the easier questions** identified in Step 1. Read the question thoroughly. You may prefer to work out the answer before looking at the options, or you may prefer to look at the options at the beginning. Adopt the method that works best for you.

You may find that you recognise a question when you sit the exam. Be aware that the detail and/or requirement may be different. If the question seems familiar, read the requirement and options carefully – do not assume that it is identical.

Step 4   Read the five options and see if one matches your own answer. Be careful with numerical questions, as the distracters are designed to match answers that incorporate **common errors**. Check that your calculation is correct. Have you followed the requirement exactly? Have you included every stage of the calculation?

Step 5   You may find that none of the options matches your answer.

- **Re-read the question** to ensure that you understand it and are answering the requirement
- **Eliminate any obviously wrong answers**
- **Consider which of the remaining answers** is the most likely to be correct and select that option

Step 6   If you are still unsure, **continue to the next question**. Likewise if you are nowhere near working out which option is correct after a couple of minutes, leave the question and come back to it later. Make a note of any questions for which you have submitted answers, but you need to return to later. The computer will list any questions for which you have not submitted answers.

Step 7   Revisit unanswered questions and other questions you're uncertain about. When you come back to a question after a break, you often find you can answer it correctly straightaway. If you are still unsure, have a guess. You are not penalised for incorrect answers, so **never leave a question unanswered!**

Tackling objective test questions

What is an objective test question?

An objective test (**OT**) question is made up of some form of **stimulus**, usually a question, and a **requirement** to do something.

- **MCQs**. Read through the information on page ix about MCQs and how to tackle them.

- **True or false**. You will be asked if a statement is true or false.

- **Data entry**. This type of OT requires you to provide figures such as the answer to a calculation, words to fill in a blank, single word answers to questions, or to identify numbers and words to complete a format.

- **Interpretation**. You may be asked to interpret or analyse graphical data.

- **Multiple response**. These questions provide you with a number of options and you have to identify those that fulfil certain criteria.

- **Listing**. You may be asked to list items in rank order.

- **Matching**. This OT question format could ask you to classify particular costs into one of a range of cost classifications provided, to match descriptions of variances with one of a number of variances listed, and so on.

OT questions in your exam

If you are sitting your exam on computer your exam will contain different types of OT questions. It is not certain how many questions in your exam will be MCQs and how many will be other types of OT, nor what types of OT you will encounter in your exam. For maximum preparation, attempt all the different types of OT questions in this kit.

Dealing with OT questions

Again you may wish to follow the approach we suggest, or you may be prepared to adapt it.

Step 1   Work out **how long** you should allocate to each OT, taking into account the marks allocated to it. Remember that you will not be expected to spend an equal amount of time on each one; some can be answered instantly but others will take time to work out.

Step 2   **Attempt each question**. Read the question thoroughly, and note in particular what the question says about the **format** of your answer and whether there are any **restrictions** placed on it.

Step 3   Read any options you are given and select which ones are appropriate. Check that your calculations are correct. Have you followed the requirement exactly? Have you included every stage of the calculation?

Step 4   You may find that you are unsure of the answer.

- Re-read the question to ensure that you understand it and are answering the requirement

- Eliminate any obviously wrong options if you are given a number of options from which to choose

Step 5   If you are still unsure, **continue to the next question**. The computer will list any questions for which you have not submitted answers.

Step 6   Revisit unanswered questions and other questions you are uncertain about. When you come back to a question after a break you often find you are able to answer it correctly straight away. If you are still unsure have a guess. You are not penalised for incorrect answers, so **never leave a question unanswered!**

Exam information

Format of the exam

Paper-based exam (2 hours)

Number of marks

40 2-mark MCQs 80
10 1-mark MCQs 10
..... 90

Computer based exam (2 hours)

50 MCQs/OTQs (40 2-mark questions and 10 1-mark questions)

The pass mark for both papers is 50%.

FORMULA SHEET GIVEN IN THE EXAM

Regression analysis

$$a = \frac{\Sigma Y}{n} - \frac{b\Sigma x}{n}$$

$$b = \frac{n\Sigma xy - \Sigma x\Sigma y}{n\Sigma x^2 - (\Sigma x)^2}$$

$$r = \frac{x\Sigma xy - \Sigma x\Sigma y}{\sqrt{(n\Sigma x^2 - (\Sigma x^2)(n\Sigma y^2 - (\Sigma y)^2)}}$$

Economic order quantity

$$\sqrt{\frac{2C_0 D}{C_h}}$$

Economic batch quantity

$$\sqrt{\frac{2C_0 D}{C_h \left(1 - \dfrac{D}{R}\right)}}$$

The computer based examination

Computer based examinations must be taken at ACCA Approved Computer Examination Centres. A full list of approved centres can be found on the ACCA web site using the following link:

http://www.accaglobal.com/students/exams/cbes/preparing

How does CBE work?

- Questions are displayed on a monitor and candidates enter their answers directly onto the computer

- When the candidate has completed their examination (two hours are allowed), the computer automatically marks the file containing the candidate's answers

- Candidates are provided with a certificate showing their results before leaving the examination room

- The CBE Licensed Centre uploads the results to ACCA (as proof of the candidate's performance)

Benefits

- **Flexibility** as a CBE and resits can be sat at any time, with no restrictions on number of sittings.

- **Instant feedback** as the computer displays the results at the end of the CBE

- Results are notified to ACCA **within 48 hours**

- **Extended closing date periods** (see ACCA website for further information)

Multiple choice questions

1 Information for management

1   Which of the following is **not** an essential quality of good information?

    A   It should be relevant for its purposes

    B   It should be communicated to the right person

    C   It should be completely accurate

    D   It should be timely   **(2 marks)**

2   Which of the following is/are primary sources of data?

    (i)   Historical records of transport costs to be used to prepare forecasts for budgetary planning

    (ii)   The *Annual Abstract of Statistics*, published by the Office for National Statistics in the United Kingdom

    (iii)   Data collected by a telephone survey to monitor the effectiveness of a bank's customer services

    A   (i) and (ii)

    B   (i) and (iii)

    C   (i) only

    D   (iii) only   **(2 marks)**

3   The sales manager has prepared a manpower plan to ensure that sales quotas for the forthcoming year are achieved. This is an example of:

    A   Strategic planning

    B   Tactical planning

    C   Operational planning

    D   Corporate planning   **(2 marks)**

4   Which of the following statements about management accounts is/are true?

    (i)   They must be stated in purely monetary terms

    (ii)   Limited companies must, by law, prepare management accounts

    (iii)   They serve as a future planning tool and are not used as an historical record

    A   (i), (ii) and (iii)

    B   (i) and (ii)

    C   (ii) only

    D   None of the statements are correct   **(2 marks)**

5   Which of the following statements is/are correct?

    (i)   A management control system is a term used to describe the hardware and software used to drive a database system which produces information outputs that are easily assimilated by management.

    (ii)   An objective is a course of action that an organisation might pursue in order to achieve its strategy.

    (iii)   Information is data that has been processed into a form meaningful to the recipient.

    A   (i), (ii) and (iii)

    B   (i) and (iii)

    C   (ii) and (iii)

    D   (iii) only   **(2 marks)**

6   For which of the following is a profit centre manager normally responsible?

    A   Cost only

    B   Costs and revenues

    C   Costs, revenues and investment.

                                                                (1 mark)

7   Monthly variance reports are an example of which one of the following types of management information?

    A   Tactical

    B   Strategic

    C   Operational

                                                                (1 mark)

                                                                (Total = 12 marks)

2 Cost classification   **27 mins**

1   A firm has to pay a 20c per unit royalty to the inventor of a device which it manufactures and sells.

    The royalty charge would be classified in the firm's accounts as a:

    A   Selling expense

    B   Direct expense

    C   Production overhead

    D   Administrative overhead

                                                                (2 marks)

2   Which of the following would be classed as indirect labour?

    A   Assembly workers in a company manufacturing televisions

    B   A stores assistant in a factory store

    C   Plasterers in a construction company

                                                                (1 mark)

3   A manufacturing firm is very busy and overtime is being worked.

    The amount of overtime premium contained in direct wages would normally be classed as:

    A   Part of prime cost

    B   Factory overheads

    C   Direct labour costs

    D   Administrative overheads

                                                                 (2 marks)

4   Which of the following items would be treated as an indirect cost?

    A   Wood used to make a chair

    B   Metal used for the legs of a chair

    C   Fabric to cover the seat of a chair

    D   Staples to fix the fabric to the seat of a chair

                                                                 (2 marks)

5   Prime cost is:

    A   All costs incurred in manufacturing a product

    B   The total of direct costs

    C   The material cost of a product

                                                                 (1 mark)

6   Over which of the following is the manager of a profit centre likely to have control?

    (i)   Selling prices ✓
    (ii)   Controllable costs ✓
    (iii)   Apportioned head office costs
    (iv)   Capital investment in the centre

    A   All of the above
    B   (i), (ii) and (iii)
    C   (i), (ii) and (iv)
    D ✓ (i) and (ii)   **(2 marks)**

7   Which of the following best describes a controllable cost?

    A   A cost which arises from a decision already taken, which cannot, in the short run, be changed.

    B   A cost for which the behaviour pattern can be easily analysed to facilitate valid budgetary control comparisons.

    C ✓ A cost which can be influenced by its budget holder.

    D   A specific cost of an activity or business which would be avoided if the activity or business did not exist.   **(2 marks)**

8   Which of the following items might be a suitable cost unit within the credit control department of a company?

    (i)   Stationery cost
    (ii)   Customer account
    (iii)   Cheque received and processed

    A   Item (i) only
    B   Item (ii) only
    C   Item (iii) only
    D   Items (ii) and (iii) only ✓   **(2 marks)**

9   Which of the following best describes a period cost?

    A   A cost that relates to a time period which is deducted as expenses for the period and is not included in the inventory valuation.

    B   A cost that can be easily allocated to a particular period, without the need for arbitrary apportionment between periods.

    C ✓ A cost that is identified with a unit produced during the period, and is included in the value of inventory. The cost is treated as an expense for the period when the inventory is actually sold.

    D   A cost that is incurred regularly every period, eg every month or quarter.   **(2 marks)**

10   A company employs four supervisors to oversee the factory production of all its products. The salaries paid to these supervisors are:

    A   A direct labour cost
    B   A direct production expense
    C ✓ A production overhead
    D   An administration overhead ✗   **(2 marks)**

11   **The following question is taken from the June 2009 exam.**

A company manufactures and sells toys and incurs the following three costs:

(i)   Rental of the finished goods warehouse ✗

(ii)   Depreciation of its own fleet of delivery vehicles ✓

(iii)   Commission paid to sales staff ✓

Which of these are classified as distribution costs?

A   (i) and (ii) only

B ✓   (i) and (iii) only

C   (ii) and (iii) only

D   (i), (ii) and (iii)   (2 marks)

                                                             (Total = 20 marks)

---

3 Cost behaviour   **47 mins**

1   Fixed costs are conventionally deemed to be:

A ✓   Constant per unit of output

Ⓑ   Constant in total when production volume changes

C ✗   Outside the control of management   (1 mark)

---

2   The following data relate to the overhead expenditure of a contract cleaners at two activity levels.

| Square metres cleaned | 13,500 | 15,950 | 2450 | |
| Overheads | $84,865 | $97,850 | 12,985. | 5.3 |

What is the estimate of the overheads if 18,300 square metres are to be cleaned?

A ✓ $96,990

Ⓑ $110,305

C $112,267

D $115,039   (2 marks)

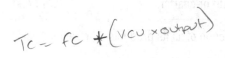

$Tc = Fc + (vcu \times output)$

97,850 = 13,315   15,950 × 5.3
                           = 84,535

~~189300~~ = ~~13,315~~   18,300 × 5.3
110,305 = 13,315 + 96,990

~~15,950~~/ 2450 / 12,985

The following information relates to questions 3 to 7

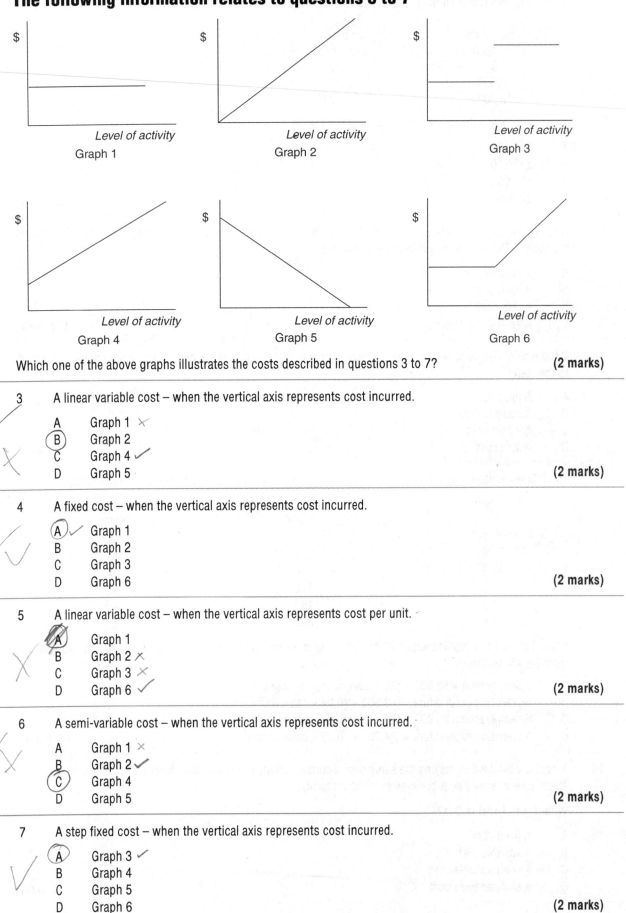

Level of activity
Graph 1

Level of activity
Graph 2

Level of activity
Graph 3

Level of activity
Graph 4

Level of activity
Graph 5

Level of activity
Graph 6

Which one of the above graphs illustrates the costs described in questions 3 to 7?   **(2 marks)**

3   A linear variable cost – when the vertical axis represents cost incurred.

    A   Graph 1
    B   Graph 2
    C   Graph 4
    D   Graph 5   **(2 marks)**

4   A fixed cost – when the vertical axis represents cost incurred.

    A   Graph 1
    B   Graph 2
    C   Graph 3
    D   Graph 6   **(2 marks)**

5   A linear variable cost – when the vertical axis represents cost per unit.

    A   Graph 1
    B   Graph 2
    C   Graph 3
    D   Graph 6   **(2 marks)**

6   A semi-variable cost – when the vertical axis represents cost incurred.

    A   Graph 1
    B   Graph 2
    C   Graph 4
    D   Graph 5   **(2 marks)**

7   A step fixed cost – when the vertical axis represents cost incurred.

    A   Graph 3
    B   Graph 4
    C   Graph 5
    D   Graph 6   **(2 marks)**

8   A company has recorded the following data in the two most recent periods.

Total costs of production $	Volume of production Units
13,500	700
18,300	1,100

What is the best estimate of the company's fixed costs per period?

A $13,500
B $13,200
C ✓ $5,100
D $4,800

(2 marks)

9   A production worker is paid a salary of $650 per month, plus an extra 5 pence for each unit produced during the month. This labour cost is best described as:

A   A variable cost ✓
B   A fixed cost ✗
C   A step cost ✗
(D)   A semi-variable cost

(2 marks)

10   What type of cost is supervisor salary costs, where one supervisor is needed for every ten employees added to the staff?

A   A fixed cost
B   A variable cost
C   A mixed cost
D   A step cost ✓

(2 marks)

11   The following information for advertising and sales has been established over the past six months:

Month	Sales revenue $'000	Advertising expenditure $'000
1	155	3
2	(125)	(2.5)
3	200	6
4	175 100	5.5 4 = 20
5	150	4.5
6	(225)	(6.5)

Using the high-low method which of the following is the correct equation for linking advertising and sales from the above data?

A   Sales revenue = 62,500 + (25 × advertising expenditure)
B   Advertising expenditure = – 2,500 + (0.04 × sales revenue) ✓   225 = 95 + 6.5× 20
(C)   Sales revenue = 95,000 + (20 × advertising expenditure)   130
D   Advertising expenditure = – 4,750 + (0.05 × sales revenue)

(2 marks)

12   A cost is described as staying the same over a certain activity range and then increasing but remaining stable over a revised activity range in the short term.

What type of cost is this?

A   A fixed cost
B   A variable cost
C   A semi-variable cost
D   A stepped fixed cost ✓

(2 marks)

13 A company incurs the following costs at various activity levels:

Total cost $	Activity level units
250,000	5,000
312,500	7,500
400,000	10,000

Using the high-low method what is the variable cost per unit?

A $25

B $30 ✓

C $35

D $40   **(2 marks)**

14 The following diagram represents the behaviour of one element of cost:

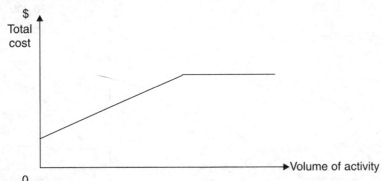

Which ONE of the following statements is consistent with the above diagram?

A   Annual factory power cost where the electricity supplier sets a tariff based on a fixed charge plus a constant unit cost for consumption but subject to a maximum annual charge. ✗

B   Weekly total labour cost when there is a fixed wage for a standard 40 hour week but overtime is paid at a premium rate. ✗

C   Total direct material cost for a period if the supplier charges a lower unit cost on all units once a certain quantity has been purchased in that period. ✗

D ✓ Total direct material cost for a period where the supplier charges a constant amount per unit for all units supplied up to a maximum charge for the period.   **(2 marks)**

15 An organisation manufactures a single product. The total cost of making 4,000 units is $20,000 and the total cost of making 20,000 units is $40,000. Within this range of activity the total fixed costs remain unchanged.
What is the variable cost per unit of the product?

A $0.80

B $1.20

C ✓ $1.25

D $2.00   **(2 marks)**

16,000   20,000

TC = FC + output × vc/unit

16   When total purchases of raw material exceed 30,000 units in any one period then all units purchased, including the initial 30,000, are invoiced at a lower cost per unit.

Which of the following graphs is consistent with the behaviour of the total materials cost in a period?

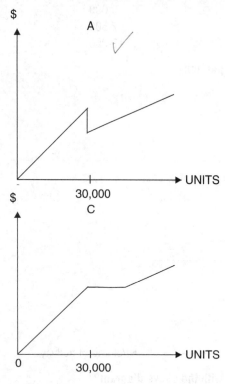

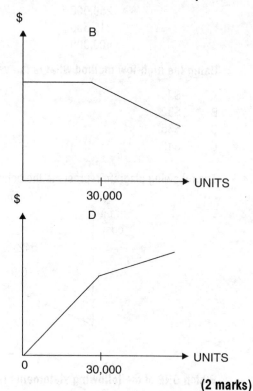

(2 marks)

17   The total cost of production for two levels of activity is as follows:

	Level 1	Level 2
Production (units)	3,000	5,000
Total cost ($)	6,750	9,250

The variable production cost per unit and the total fixed production cost both remain constant in the range of activity shown.

What is the level of fixed costs?

A $2,000   C ✓ $3,000
B $2,500   D $3,500

(2 marks)

(Total = 35 marks)

4 Correlation and regression   42 mins

1   The following four data pairs have been obtained: (1, 5), (2, 6), (4, 9), (5, 11). Without carrying out any calculations, which of the following correlation coefficients best describes the relationship between x and y?

A −0.98   B −0.25   C 0.98 ✓   D 0.25

(2 marks)

2   A company's management accountant is analysing the reject rates achieved by 100 factory operatives working in identical conditions. Reject rates, Y%, are found to be related to months of experience, X, by this regression equation: $Y = 20 - 0.25X$. (The correlation coefficient was $r = -0.9$.)

Using the equation, the predicted reject rate for an operative with 12 months' experience is closest to

    A   17%   B   19%   C   20%   D   23%

$12 = 20 - 0.25x$ $0 = 8 - 0.25x$ **(2 marks)**

---

3   A regression equation $Y = a + bX$ is used to forecast the value of Y for a given value of X. Which of the following increase the reliability of the forecast?

    (i)   A correlation coefficient numerically close to 1

    (ii)   Working to a higher number of decimal places of accuracy

    (iii)   Forecasting for values of X outside the range of those used in the sample

    (iv)   A large sample is used to calculate the regression equation

    A   (i) only   B   (i) and (ii) only   C   (i) and (iii) only   D   (i) and (iv) only

                                                            (2 marks)

---

4   If $\Sigma x = 12$, $\Sigma y = 42$, $\Sigma x^2 = 46$, $\Sigma y^2 = 542$, $\Sigma xy = 157$ and $n = 4$, find the correlation coefficient.

    A   0.98   B   −0.98   C   0.26   D   0.008

                                                             (2 marks)

---

5   Using data from twelve European countries, it has been calculated that the correlation between the level of car ownership and the number of road deaths is 0.73. Which of the statements shown follow from this?

    (i)   High levels of car ownership cause high levels of road deaths

    (ii)   There is a strong relationship between the level of car ownership and the number of road deaths

    (iii)   53% of the variation in the level of road deaths from one country to the next can be explained by the corresponding variation in the level of car ownership

    (iv)   73% of the variation in the level of road deaths from one country to the next can be explained by the corresponding variation in the level of car ownership

    A   (i) and (ii) only   B   (i) and (iii) only   C   (ii) and (iii) only   D   (ii) and (iv) only

                                                             (2 marks)

---

6   20 pairs of values of (X, Y) with X ranging from 15 to 45 were used to obtain the regression equation $Y = 480 - 5X$. The correlation coefficient is −0.95. It has been estimated that when X = 10, Y = 430. Which of the following reduces the reliability of the estimate?

    A   Sample size

    B   The magnitude of the correlation coefficient

    C   X = 10 being outside the range of the sample data

    D   The correlation being negative   **(2 marks)**

---

7   The regression equation $Y = 3 + 2X$ has been calculated from 6 pairs of values, with X ranging from 1 to 10. The correlation coefficient is 0.8. It is estimated that Y = 43 when X = 20. Which of the following are true?

    (i)   The estimate is not reliable because X is outside the range of the data

    (ii)   The estimate is not reliable because the correlation is low

    (iii)   The estimate is reliable

    (iv)   The estimate is not reliable because the sample is small

    A   (i) and (ii) only   B   (i) and (iii) only   C   (ii) and (iv) only   D   (i) and (iv) only

                                                             (2 marks)

8   If $\Sigma X = 100$, $\Sigma Y = 400$, $\Sigma X^2 = 2{,}040$, $\Sigma Y^2 = 32{,}278$, $\Sigma XY = 8{,}104$ and $n = 5$ which of the following values for a and b are correct in the formula $Y = a + bX$?

	a	b
A	28	−2.6
B	28	+2.6
C	−28	−2.6
D	−28	+2.6

                                                 (2 marks)

9   In calculating the regression equation linking two variables, the standard formulae for the regression coefficients are given in terms of X and Y. Which of the following is true?

A   X must be the variable which will be forecast
B   It does not matter which variable is which
C   Y must be the dependent variable
D   Y must be the variable shown on the vertical axis of a scatter diagram   **(2 marks)**

10   A company uses regression analysis to establish a total cost equation for budgeting purposes.

Data for the past four months is as follows:

Month	Total cost $'000	Quantity produced $'000
1	57.5	1.25
2	37.5	1.00
3	45.0	1.50
4	60.0	2.00
	200.0	5.75

The gradient of the regression line is 17.14.

What is the value of a?

A   25.36
B   48.56
C   74.64
D   101.45   **(2 marks)**

11   Which of the following are correct with regard to regression analysis?

(i)   In regression analysis the n stands for the number of pairs of data ✓
(ii) Σx^2 is not the same calculation as $(\Sigma x)^2$ ✓
(iii) Σxy is calculated by multiplying the total value of x and the total value of y ✓

A   (i) and (ii) only
B   (i) and (iii) only
C   (ii) and (iii) only
D   (i), (ii) and (iii) ✓   **(2 marks)**

12   Regression analysis is being used to fine the line of best fit $(y = a + bx)$ from eleven pairs of data. The calculations have produced the following information:

$\Sigma x = 440$, $\Sigma y = 330$, $\Sigma x^2 = 17{,}986$, $\Sigma y^2 = 10{,}366$ and $\Sigma xy = 13{,}467$

What is the value of 'a' in the equation for the line of best fit (to 2 decimal places)?

A   0.63
B   0.69
C   2.33
D   5.33   **(2 marks)**

13 Which of the following is a feasible value for the correlation coefficient?

A   - 2.0
B   - 1.2
C   0
D   + 1.2   (2 marks)

14 A company has recorded its total cost for different levels of activity over the last five months as follows:

Month	Activity level (units)	Total cost ($)
7	300	17,500
8	360	19,500
9	400	20,500
10	320	18,500
11	280	17,000

The equation for total cost is being calculated using regression analysis on the above data. The equation for total cost is of the general form 'y = a + bx' and the value of 'b' has been calculated correctly as 29.53.

What is the value of 'a' (to the nearest $) in the total cost equation?

A   7,338
B   8,796
C   10,430
D   10,995   (2 marks)

15 **The following question is taken from the December 2007 exam paper**

The probability of an organisation making a profit of $180,000 next month is half the probability of it making a profit of $75,000.

What is the expected profit for next month?

A $110,000
B $127,500
C $145,000
D $165,000   (2 marks)

16 **The following question is taken from the June 2008 exam paper**

The management of a company is making a decision which could lead to just three possible outcomes – 'high', 'medium' and 'low' levels of demand. Profit and expected value information are as follows:

Outcome	Profit	Profit x probability of outcome
	$	$
High	25,000	10,000
Medium	16,000	8,000
Low	10,000	1,000

What is the most likely level of profit from making the decision?

A $16,000
B $17,000
C $19,000
D $25,000   (2 marks)

(Total = 32 marks)

5 Spreadsheets

14 mins

1   On a spreadsheet, data is entered into:

    A   A column
    B ✓ A cell
    C   A row

(1 mark)

2   Which of these statements is untrue?

    A   Spreadsheets make the calculation and manipulation of data easier and quicker.
    B   Spreadsheets are very useful for word-processing
    C   Budgeting can be done very easily using spreadsheets

(1 mark)

The following data applies to questions 3 to 5:

	A	B	C	D	F	G
1		Jan	Feb	Mar	Apr	May
2	Sales	15,000	13,400	16,100	17,200	15,300
3	Cost of sales	11,090	10,060	12,040	13,000	11,100
4	Gross profit	3,910	3,340	4,060	4,200	4,200
5	Expenses	1,500	1,500	1,500	1,500	1,500
6	Net profit	2,410	1,840	2,560	2,700	2,700
7						
8	Net profit %					

3   The formula =C2-C3 will give the contents of which cell?

    A   C6
    B ✓ C4
    C   C5
    D   C1

(2 marks)

4   What would be the formula for March net profit?

    A   =D2-D3
    B   =B6+C6
    C ✓ =D4-D5
    D   =D3*D8

(2 marks)

5   What will be the formula to go in G8?

    A ✓ =G6/G2*100
    B   =G4/100*G6
    C   =G2/G6*100
    D   =G6/G4*100

(2 marks)

6   **The following question is taken from the June 2009 exam.**

A company manufactures a single product. In a computer spreadsheet the cells F1 to F12 contain the budgeted monthly sales units for the twelve months of next year in sequence, with January sales in cell F1 and finishing with December sales in F12. The company policy is for the closing inventory of finished goods each month to be 10% of the budgeted sales units for the following month.

Which of the following formulae will generate the budgeted production (in units) for March next year?

A $=[F3 + (0.1*F4)]$

B $=[F3 - (0.1*F4)]$

C $=[(1.1*F3) - (0.1*F4)]$

D $=[(0.9*F3) + (0.1*F4)]$ (2 marks)

(Total = 10 marks)

6 Material costs   30 mins

1   Which of the following functions are fulfilled by a goods received note (GRN)?

(i)   Provides information to update the inventory records on receipt of goods
(ii)   Provides information to check the quantity on the supplier's invoice
(iii)   Provides information to check the price on the supplier's invoice

A   (i) and (ii) only
B   (i) and (iii) only
C   (ii) and (iii) only   (1 mark)

2   There are 27,500 units of Part Number X35 on order with the suppliers and 16,250 units outstanding on existing customers' orders.

If the free inventory is 13,000 units, what is the physical inventory?

A   1,750
B   3,250
C   24,250
D   29,250   (2 marks)

The following information relates to questions 3 and 4

A domestic appliance retailer with multiple outlets sells a popular toaster known as the Autocrisp 2000, for which the following information is available:

Average sales	75 per day
Maximum sales	95 per day
Minimum sales	50 per day
Lead time	12-18 days
Reorder quantity	1,750

3   Based on the data above, at what level of inventory would a replenishment order be issued?

A   600 units
B   1,125 units
C   1,710 units
D   1,750 units   (2 marks)

4   Based on the data above, what is the maximum inventory level?

   A   1,750 units
   B ✓ 2,275 units
   C   2,860 units
   D   2,900 units

(2 marks)

5   The annual demand for a stock item is 2,500 units. The cost of placing an order is $80 and the cost of holding an item in stock for one year is $15. What is the economic order quantity, to the nearest unit?

   A   31 units
   B   115 units
   C ✓ 163 units
   D   26,667 units

$$\sqrt{\frac{2C_0D}{C_h}} \qquad \sqrt{\frac{2 \times 80 \times 2,500}{15}}$$

(2 marks)

6   Which of the following is correct with regard to inventories?

   (i) ✓ Stock-outs arise when too little inventory is held
   (ii) ✓ Safety inventories are the level of units maintained in case there is unexpected demand
   (iii) ✓ A re-order level can be established by looking at the maximum usage and the maximum lead-time

   A   (i) and (ii) only
   B   (i) and (iii) only
   C   (ii) and (iii) only
   D ✓ (i), (ii) and (iii)

(2 marks)

7   What is the economic batch quantity used to establish?

   Optimal

   A ✗ reorder quantity
   B ✗ recorder level
   C ✓ cumulative production quantity
   D   inventory level for production

(2 marks)

8   The demand for a product is 12,500 units for a three month period. Each unit of product has a purchase price of $15 and ordering costs are $20 per order placed.

   $\times 4 = 50,000$ ✓

   The annual holding cost of one unit of product is 10% of its purchase price.

   What is the Economic Order Quantity (to the nearest unit)?

   A   577
   B   816
   C   866
   D ✓ 1,155

$$\sqrt{\frac{2 \times 20 \times 50,000}{1.5}}$$

(2 marks)

9   A company determines its order quantity for a raw material by using the Economic Order Quantity (EOQ) model.

   What would be the effects on the EOQ and the total annual holding cost of a decrease in the cost of ordering a batch of raw material?

	EOQ	Total annual holding cost
A ✓	Higher	Lower
B	Higher	Higher
C	Lower	Higher
D	Lower	Lower

(2 marks)

10   Data relating to a particular stores item are as follows:

Average daily usage	400 units
Maximum daily usage	520 units
Minimum daily usage	180 units
Lead time for replenishment of inventory	10 to 15 days
Reorder quantity	8,000 units

What is the reorder level (in units) which avoids stockouts (running out of inventory)?

A   5,000
B   6,000
C ✓ 7,800
D   8,000   **(2 marks)**

---

11   The material stores control account for a company for March looks like this:

MATERIAL STORES CONTROL ACCOUNT

	$		$
Balance b/d	12,000	Work in progress	40,000
Suppliers	49,000	Overhead control	12,000
Work in progress	18,000	Balance c/d	27,000
	79,000		79,000
Balance b/d	27,000		

Which of the following statements are correct?

(i)   Issues of direct materials during March were $18,000
(ii) ✓ Issues of direct materials during March were $40,000
(iii) ✓ Issues of indirect materials during March were $12,000
(iv) ✓ Purchases of materials during March were $49,000

A   (i) and (iv) only
B   (ii) and (iv) only
C ✓ (ii), (iii) and (iv) only
D   All of them   **(2 marks)**

---

12   **The following question is taken from the June 2008 exam paper**

A manufacturing company uses 25,000 components at an even rate during a year. Each order placed with the supplier of the components is for 2,000 components, which is the economic order quantity. The company holds a buffer inventory of 500 components. The annual cost of holding one component in inventory is $2.

What is the total annual cost of holding inventory of the component?

A $2,000
B $2,500
C $3,000
D $4,000   **(2 marks)**

                                                       (Total = 23 marks)

7 Labour costs

The following information relates to questions 1 and 2

Budgeted and actual production data for the year that has just ended are as follows.

Product	Budgeted production		Actual production
	Units	Standard machine hours	Units
W	15,000	3,000	12,000
X	20,000	8,000	25,000
Y	14,000	7,000	16,000
Z	6,000	9,000	5,000

27,000

58,000

Total machine hours worked in the period amounted to 29,000 hours.

1   What was the capacity ratio in the year, as a percentage to one decimal place?

   A   93.1%
   B   103.3%
   C   105.5%
   D ✓ 107.4%   **(2 marks)**

2   What was the efficiency ratio in the year, as a percentage to one decimal place?

ASK

   A   96.2%
   B   103.3%
   C   103.9%
   D   107.4%   **(2 marks)**

3   The labour cost graph below depicts:

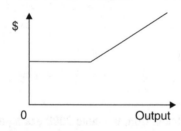

   A ✓ A piece rate scheme with a minimum guaranteed wage
   B   A straight piece rate scheme
   C   A straight time rate scheme
   D   A differential piece rate scheme   **(2 marks)**

4   The following data relate to work in the finishing department of a certain factory.

Normal working day	7 hours (420)
Basic rate of pay per hour	$5
Standard time allowed to produce 1 unit	4 minutes
Premium bonus payable at the basic rate	60% of time saved

EYP 105 day   *7×5=35*

On a particular day one employee finishes 180 units. His gross pay for the day will be

   A $35
   B ✓ $50
   C $56
   D $60   **(2 marks)**

105 × 4 = 420
180 × 4 = 720
300 mins

3hrs @ 5
35
180 mins

5   An employee is paid on a piecework basis. The basis of the piecework scheme is as follows:

     1 to 100 units   – $0.20 per unit   100 x 0.2   20
     101 to 200 units – $0.30 per unit   93 x 0.3   27.90
     201 to 299 units – $0.40 per unit
                                             ‾‾‾‾‾‾‾‾
                                              47.90

     with only the additional units qualifying for the higher rates. Rejected units do not qualify for payment.

     During a particular day the employee produced 210 units of which 17 were rejected as faulty.

     What did the employee earn for their day's work?

     A   ✓ $47.90
     B $54.00
     C $57.90
     D $63.00   **(2 marks)**

6   Employee A is a carpenter and normally works 36 hours per week. The standard rate of pay is $3.60 per
     hour. A premium of 50% of the basic hourly rate is paid for all overtime hours worked. During the last week
     of October, Employee A worked for 42 hours. The overtime hours worked were for the following reasons:

     Machine breakdown: 4 hours IN   36 x 3.60   129.60
     To complete a special job at the request of a customer: 2 hours DIR   2 x 5.40   10.80
                                                                                          ‾‾‾‾‾‾
     How much of Employee A's earnings for the last week of October would have been treated as direct wages?

     A $162.00
     B $129.60
     C   ✓ $140.40
     D $151.20   **(2 marks)**

7   Which of the following statements is/are true about group bonus schemes?

     (i)   ✓ Group bonus schemes are appropriate when increased output depends on a number of people all
            making extra effort

     (ii)   ✗ With a group bonus scheme, it is easier to award each individual's performance

     (iii) ✓ Non-production employees can be rewarded as part of a group incentive scheme

     A   (i) only
     B   (i) and (ii) only
     C   ✓   (i) and (iii) only   **(1 mark)**

8   X Co has recorded the following wages costs for direct production workers for November.

                                         $
     Basic pay   70,800   DIR
     Overtime premium   2,000   IN
     Holiday pay   500   IN
                                        ‾‾‾‾‾‾
     Gross wages incurred   73,300
                                        ‾‾‾‾‾‾

     The overtime was not worked for any specific job.

The accounting entries for these wages costs would be:

		Debit $	Credit $
A	Work in progress account	72,800	
	Overhead control account	500	
	Wages control account		73,300
B	Work in progress account	70,800	
	Overhead control account	2,500	
	Wages control account		73,300
C	Wages control account	73,300	
	Work in progress account		70,800
	Overhead control account		2,500
D	Wages control account	73,300	
	Work in progress account		72,800
	Overhead control account		500

(2 marks)

9   A company had 30 direct production employees at the beginning of last year and 20 direct production employees at the end of the year. During the year, a total of 15 direct production employees had left the company to work for a local competitor. The labour turnover rate for last year was:

A   16.7%
B   20.0%
C   25.0%
D   60.0%

$30 + 20/2 = 25$ $\frac{15}{}$

(2 marks)

10   Jane works as a member of a three-person team in the assembly department of a factory. The team is rewarded by a group bonus scheme whereby the team leader receives 40 per cent of any bonus earned by the team, and the remaining bonus is shared evenly between Jane and the other team member. Details of output for one day are given below.

Hours worked by team	8 hours
Team production achieved	80 units
Standard time allowed to produce one unit	9 minutes
Group bonus payable at $6 per hour	70% of time saved

The bonus element of Jane's pay for this particular day will be

A $5.04
B $7.20
C $10.08
D $16.80

(2 marks)

11   Which one of the following groups of workers would be classified as indirect labour?

A   Machinists in an organisation manufacturing clothes
B   Bricklayers in a house building company
C   Maintenance workers in a shoe factory

(1 mark)

(Total = 20 marks)

8 Overheads and absorption costing

41 mins

1   The following extract of information is available concerning the four cost centres of EG Limited.

	Production cost centres			Service cost centre
	Machinery	Finishing	Packing	Canteen
Number of direct employees	7	6	2	–
Number of indirect employees	3	2	1	4
Overhead allocated and apportioned	$28,500	$18,300	$8,960	$8,400

The overhead cost of the canteen is to be re-apportioned to the production cost centres on the basis of the number of employees in each production cost centre. After the re-apportionment, the total overhead cost of the packing department, to the nearest $, will be

A $1,200
B $9,968
C $10,080
D ✓ $10,160   **(2 marks)**

The following information relates to questions 2 and 3

Budgeted information relating to two departments in a company for the next period is as follows.

Department	Production overhead $	Direct material cost $	Direct labour cost $	Direct labour hours	Machine hours
1	27,000	67,500	13,500	2,700	45,000
2	18,000	36,000	100,000	25,000	300

Individual direct labour employees within each department earn differing rates of pay, according to their skills, grade and experience.

2   What is the most appropriate production overhead absorption rate for department 1?

A ✓ 40% of direct material cost
B   200% of direct labour cost
C $10 per direct labour hour
D $0.60 per machine hour   **(2 marks)**

3   What is the most appropriate production overhead absorption rate for department 2?

A ✓ 50% of direct material cost
B   18% of direct labour cost
C $0.72 per direct labour hour
D $60 per machine hour   **(2 marks)**

4   Which of the following statements about predetermined overhead absorption rates are true?

(i)   Using a predetermined absorption rate avoids fluctuations in unit costs caused by abnormally high or low overhead expenditure or activity levels

(ii)   Using a predetermined absorption rate offers the administrative convenience of being able to record full production costs sooner

(iii) Using a predetermined absorption rate avoids problems of under/over absorption of overheads because a constant overhead rate is available.

A ✓ (i) and (ii) only
B   (i) and (iii) only
C   (ii) and (iii) only
D   All of them   **(2 marks)**

5   Over-absorbed overheads occur when

A   ✓ Absorbed overheads exceed actual overheads
B   Absorbed overheads exceed budgeted overheads
C   Actual overheads exceed budgeted overheads   (1 mark)

The following information relates to questions 6 and 7

A company has the following actual and budgeted data for year 4.

	Budget	Actual
Production	8,000 units	9,000 units
Variable production overhead per unit	$3	$3
Fixed production overheads	$360,000	$432,000
Sales	6,000 units	8,000 units

Overheads are absorbed using a rate per unit, based on budgeted output and expenditure.

6   The fixed production overhead absorbed during year 4 was:

A $384,000
B   ✓ $405,000
C $432,000
D $459,000   (2 marks)

7   Fixed production overhead was:

A   ✓ under absorbed by $27,000
B   under absorbed by $72,000
C   under absorbed by $75,000
D   over absorbed by $27,000   (2 marks)

8   Which of the following would be the most appropriate basis for apportioning machinery insurance costs to cost centres within a factory?

A   The number of machines in each cost centre
B   The floor area occupied by the machinery in each cost centre
C   ✓ The value of the machinery in each cost centre
D   The operating hours of the machinery in each cost centre   (2 marks)

9   Factory overheads can be absorbed by which of the following methods?

(i)   ✓ Direct labour hours
(ii) ✓ Machine hours
(iii) ✓ As a percentage of prime cost
(iv) $x per unit

A   (i), (ii), (iii) and (iv)
B   (i) and (ii) only
C   ✓ (i), (ii) and (iii) only
D   (ii), (iii) and (iv) only   (2 marks)

10   The production overhead control account for R Limited at the end of the period looks like this.

PRODUCTION OVERHEAD CONTROL ACCOUNT

	$		$
Stores control	22,800	Work in progress	404,800
Wages control	180,400	Profit and loss	8,400
Expense creditors	210,000		
	413,200		413,200

Which of the following statements are correct?

(i) ✓ Indirect material issued from inventory was $22,800
(ii) ✗ Overhead absorbed during the period was $210,000
(iii) ✓ Overhead for the period was over absorbed by $8,400
(iv) ✓ Indirect wages costs incurred were $180,400

X

A   (i), (ii) and (iii)
B ✓ (i), (iii) and (iv)
C   (i) and (iv)
D   All of them   (2 marks)

---

11   Which of the following is correct when considering the allocation, apportionment and reapportionment of overheads in an absorption costing situation?

✓

A ✓ Only production related costs should be considered
B ✗ Allocation is the situation where part of an overhead is assigned to a cost centre
C ✗ Costs may only be reapportioned from production centres to service centres
D ✗ Any overheads assigned to a single department should be ignored   (2 marks)

---

12   A company has over-absorbed fixed production overheads for the period by $6,000. The fixed production overhead absorption rate was $8 per unit and is based on the normal level of activity of 5,000 units. Actual production was 4,500 units.

What was the actual fixed production overheads incurred for the period?

Budget Absorbed 36,000
S/h absorbed 30,000

✓

A ✓ $30,000
B $36,000
C $40,000   6000
D $42,000   (2 marks)

---

13   A company manufacturers two products, X and Y, in a factory divided into two production cost centres, Primary and Finishing. The following budgeted data are available:

Cost centre	Primary	Finishing
Allocated and apportioned fixed overhead costs	$96,000	$82,500
Direct labour minutes per unit:		
6000 – product X	36	25
7500 – product Y	48	35

ASK

Budgeted production is 6,000 units of product X and 7,500 units of product Y. Fixed overhead costs are to be absorbed on a direct labour hour basis.

What is the budgeted fixed overhead cost per unit for product Y?

A $11
B $12
C $14
D $15   (2 marks)

---

14   A company uses an overhead absorption rate of $3.50 per machine our, based on 32,000 budgeted machine hours for the period. During the same period the actual total overhead expenditure amounted to $108,875 and 30,000 machine hours were recorded on actual production.

By how much was the total overhead under or over absorbed for the period?

A   Under absorbed by $3,875
B ✓ Under absorbed by $7,000
C   Over absorbed by $3,875
D   Over absorbed by $7,000

(2 marks)

15   A factory consists of two production cost centres (P and Q) and two service cost centres (X and Y). The total allocated and apportioned overhead for each is as follows:

P	Q	X	Y
$95,000	$82,000	$46,000	$30,000

It has been estimated that each service cost centre does work for the other cost centres in the following proportions:

	P	Q	X	Y
Percentage of service cost centre X to	40	40	–	20
Percentage of service cost centre Y to	30	60	10	–

After the reapportionment of service cost centre costs has been carried out using a method that fully recognises the reciprocal service arrangements in the factory, what is the total overhead for production cost centre P?

A $122,400
B $124,716
C $126,000
D ✓ $127,000

(2 marks)

16   The following data is available for a paint department for the latest period.

Budgeted production overhead	$150,000
Actual production overhead	$150,000
Budgeted machine hours	60,000
Actual machine hours	55,000

Which of the following statements is correct?

A   There was no under or over absorption of overhead
B   Overhead was $13,636 over absorbed
C ✓ Overhead was $12,500 over absorbed
D   Overhead was $12,500 under absorbed

(2 marks)

(Total = 31 marks)

9 Marginal and absorption costing   **45 mins**

1   The following data is available for period 9.

Opening inventory	10,000 units
Closing inventory	8,000 units
Absorption costing profit	$280,000

The profit for period 9 using marginal costing would be:

A $278,000
B $280,000
C $282,000
D ✓ Impossible to calculate without more information

(2 marks)

2   The overhead absorption rate for product T is $4 per machine hour. Each unit of T requires 3 machine hours. Inventories of product T last period were:

	Units
Opening inventory	2,400
Closing inventory	2,700

Compared with the marginal costing profit for the period, the absorption costing profit for product T will be:

A $1,200 higher
B $3,600 higher
C $1,200 lower
D $3,600 lower   (2 marks)

3   In a period where opening inventories were 15,000 units and closing inventories were 20,000 units, a firm had a profit of $130,000 using absorption costing. If the fixed overhead absorption rate was $8 per unit, the profit using marginal costing would be:

A $90,000
B $130,000
C $170,000
D   Impossible to calculate without more information   (2 marks)

The following information relates to questions 4 and 5

Cost and selling price details for product Z are as follows.

	$ per unit
Direct materials	6.00
Direct labour	7.50
Variable overhead	2.50
Fixed overhead absorption rate	5.00
	21.00
Profit	9.00
Selling price	30.00

Budgeted production for the month was 5,000 units although the company managed to produce 5,800 units, selling 5,200 of them and incurring fixed overhead costs of $27,400.

4   The marginal costing profit for the month is:

A $45,400
B $46,800
C $53,800
D $72,800   (2 marks)

5   The absorption costing profit for the month is:

A $45,200   C $46,800
B $45,400   D $48,400   (2 marks)

6   In a period, a company had opening inventory of 31,000 units and closing inventory of 34,000 units. Profits based on marginal costing were $850,500 and on absorption costing were $955,500.

If the budgeted total fixed costs for the company was $1,837,500, what was the budgeted level of activity in units?

A   32,500   C   65,000
B   52,500   D   105,000   (2 marks)

7   A company had opening inventory of 48,500 units and closing inventory of 45,500 units. Profits based on marginal costing were $315,250 and on absorption costing were $288,250. What is the fixed overhead absorption rate per unit?

    A $5.94   C $6.50

    B $6.34 ✓ D $9.00   **(2 marks)**

8   Which of the following are acceptable bases for absorbing production overheads?

    (i)   Direct labour hours

    (ii)   Machine hours

    (iii)   As a percentage of the prime cost

    (iv)   Per unit

    A   Method (i) and (ii) only

    B   Method (iii) and (iv) only

    C ✓ Method (i), (ii), (iii) and (iv)

    D   Method (i), (ii) or (iii) only   **(2 marks)**

9   Absorption costing is concerned with which of the following?

    A   Direct materials

    B   Direct labour

    C ✓ Fixed costs

    D   Variable and fixed costs   **(2 marks)**

10 A company has established a marginal costing profit of $72,300. Opening inventory was 300 units and closing inventory is 750 units. The fixed production overhead absorption rate has been calculated as $5/unit.

What was the profit under absorption costing?

    A ✕ $67,050

    B ✕ $70,050

    C ✓ $74,550

    D $77,550   **(2 marks)**

11 A company produces and sells a single product whose variable cost is $6 per unit.

Fixed costs have been absorbed over the normal level of activity of 200,000 units and have been calculated as $2 per unit.

The current selling price is $10 per unit.

How much profit is made under marginal costing if the company sells 250,000 units?

    A $500,000

    B $600,000

    C $900,000

    D $1,000,000   **(2 marks)**

12 A company wishes to make a profit of $150,000. It has fixed costs of $75,000 with a C/S ratio of 0.75 and a selling price of $10 per unit.

How many units would the company need to sell in order to achieve the required level of profit?

    A   10,000 units

    B   15,000 units

    C   22,500 units

    D   30,000 units   **(2 marks)**

13 A company which uses marginal costing has a profit of $37,500 for a period. Opening inventory was 100 units and closing inventory was 350 units.

The fixed production overhead absorption rate is $4 per unit.

4 × 250 = 1000

What is the profit under absorption costing?

A $35,700
B $35,500
C   ✓ $38,500
D $39,300

(2 marks)

14 A company manufactures and sells a single product. For this month the budgeted fixed production overheads are $48,000, budgeted production is 12,000 units and budgeted sales are 11,720 units.

The company currently uses absorption costing.

If the company used marginal costing principles instead of absorption costing for this month, what would be the effect on the budgeted profit?

48/12 = $4   × 11720 - 12000

= 280 × 4 = 1120

A $1,120 higher
B   ✓ $1,120 lower
C $3,920 higher
D $3,920 lower

(2 marks)

15 A company operates a standard marginal costing system. Last month its actual fixed overhead expenditure was 10% above budget resulting in a fixed overhead expenditure variance of $36,000.

What was the actual expenditure on fixed overheads last month?

A $324,000
B $360,000

10% 36,000

C   ✓ $396,000
D $400,000

100% 360,000

(2 marks)

16 Last month, when a company had an opening stock of 16,500 units and a closing stock of 18,000 units, the profit using absorption costing was $40,000. The fixed production overhead rate was $10 per unit.

What would the profit for last month have been using marginal costing?

A $15,000
B   ✓ $25,000
C $55,000
D $65,000

1500 × 10 = 15,000

- 40,000

(2 marks)

17 **This question is taken from the December 2008 exam.**

Last month a manufacturing company's profit was $2,000, calculated using absorption costing principles. If marginal costing principles has been used, a loss of $3,000 would have occurred. The company's fixed production cost is $2 per unit. Sales last month were 10,000 units.

What was last month's production (in units)?

A 7,500   B 9,500 ✓   C 10,500   D 12,500

(2 marks)

(Total = 34 marks)

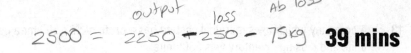
10 Process costing
39 mins

1   A chemical process has a normal wastage of 10% of input. In a period, 2,500 kgs of material were input and there was an abnormal loss of 75 kgs.

What quantity of good production was achieved?

A 2,175 kgs   B 2,250 kgs   C 2,325 kgs   D 2,425 kgs

(2 marks)

The following information relates to questions 2 and 3

A company manufactures Chemical X, in a single process. At the start of the month there was no work-in-progress. During the month 300 litres of raw material were input into the process at a total cost of $6,000. Conversion costs during the month amounted to $4,500. At the end of the month 250 litres of Chemical X were transferred to finished goods inventory. The remaining work-in-progress was 100% complete with respect to materials and 50% complete with respect to conversion costs. There were no losses in the process.

2   The equivalent units for closing work-in-progress at the end of the month would have been:

	Material	Conversion costs
A	25 litres	25 litres
B	25 litres	50 litres
C	50 litres	25 litres
D	50 litres	50 litres

300 L   6,000   Cost
                4,500   Cost
              ⎯⎯⎯⎯⎯
               10,500

250 → fg
50   WIP   50
        CC   25

(2 marks)

3   If there had been a normal process loss of 10% of input during the month the value of this loss would have been:

A   Nil
B $450
C $600
D $1,050

(2 marks)

4   In a particular process, the input for the period was 2,000 units. There were no inventories at the beginning or end of the process. Normal loss is 5 per cent of input. In which of the following circumstances is there an abnormal gain?

Input.   Norm loss   output
2000 =   100   +   1900

(i)   Actual output = 1,800 units
(ii)   Actual output = 1,950 units
(iii) Actual output = 2,000 units

A   (i) only
B   (ii) only
C   (i) and (ii) only
D   (ii) and (iii) only

(2 marks)

5   In a process account, abnormal losses are valued:

A   At their scrap value
B   The same as good production
C   At the cost of raw materials

(1 mark)

6   A company needs to produce 340 litres of Chemical X. There is a normal loss of 10% of the material input into the process. During a given month the company did produce 340 litres of good production, although there was an abnormal loss of 5% of the material input into the process.

How many litres of material were input into the process during the month?

A 357 litres   B 374 litres   C 391 litres   D 400 litres

(2 marks)

391 =   output   Norm   Ab
         340L - loss - loss
                  34L   17

The following information relates to questions 7 and 8

A company produces a certain food item in a manufacturing process. On 1 November, there was no opening inventory of work in process. During November, 500 units of material were input to the process, with a cost of $9,000. Direct labour costs in November were $3,840. Production overhead is absorbed at the rate of 200% of direct labour costs. Closing inventory on 30 November consisted of 100 units which were 100% complete as to materials and 80% complete as to labour and overhead. There was no loss in process.

7   The full production cost of completed units during November was

 A $10,400

 B $16,416

 C $16,800

 D $20,520 (2 marks)

(handwritten: 9,000 + 3840×2 = 16,680 ✗ ask)

8   The value of the closing work in progress on 30 November is

 A $2,440

 B $3,720

 C $4,104

 D $20,520 (2 marks)

The following information relates to questions 9 and 10

A company makes a product in two processes. The following data is available for the latest period, for process 1.

Opening work in progress of 200 units was valued as follows.

Material	$2,400
Labour	$1,200
Overhead	$400

No losses occur in the process.

Units added and costs incurred during the period:

Material	$6,000 (500 units)
Labour	$3,350
Overhead	$1,490

Closing work in progress of 100 units had reached the following degrees of completion:

Material	100%
Labour	50%
Overhead	30%

The company uses the weighted average method of inventory valuation.

9   How many equivalent units are used when calculating the cost per unit in relation to overhead?

 A 500   B 600   C 630   D 700

                  (2 marks)

10   The value of the units transferred to process 2 was

 A $7,200   B $13,200   C $14,840   D $15,400

                  (2 marks)

11   A company uses process costing to establish the cost per unit of its output.

The following information was available for the last month:

Input units	10,000
Output units	9,850
Opening inventory	300 units, 100% complete for materials and 70% complete for conversion costs
Closing inventory	450 units, 100% complete for materials and 30% complete for conversion costs

The company uses the weighted average method of valuing inventory.

What were the equivalent units for conversion costs?

A   9,505 units
B   9,715 units
C   9,775 units
D   9,985 units

(2 marks)

---

12   A company uses process costing to value its output. The following was recorded for the period;

Input materials	2,000 units at $4.50 per unit
Conversion costs	13,340
Normal loss	5% of input valued at $3 per unit
Actual loss	150 units

There were no opening or closing inventories.

What was the valuation of one unit of output to one decimal place?

A $11.8
B $11.6
C $11.2
D $11.0

(2 marks)

---

13   A company operates a continuous process into which 3,000 units of material costing $9,000 was input in a period. Conversion costs for this period were $11,970 and losses, which have a scrap value of $1.50, are expected at a rate of 10% of input. There were no opening or closing inventories and output for the period was 2,900 units.

What was the output valuation?

A $20,271
B $20,520
C $20,970
D $22,040

(2 marks)

---

14   The following information relates to a company's polishing process for the previous period.

Output to finished goods	5,408 units valued at $29,744
Normal loss	276 units
Actual loss	112 units

All losses have a scrap value of $2.50 per unit and there was no opening or closing work in progress.

The value of the input during the period was:

A $28,842
B $29,532
C $29,744
D $30,434

(2 marks)

15　Which of the following statements about process losses are correct?

(i)　Units of normal loss should be valued at full cost per unit.
(ii)　Units of abnormal loss should be valued at their scrap value.

A　(i) only
B　(ii) only
C　Both of them
D　Neither of them　　　　　　　　　　　　　　　　　　　　　(2 marks)

(Total = 29 marks)

11 Process costing, joint products and by-products　18 mins

The following data relates to questions 1 and 2

A company manufactures two joint products, P and R, in a common process. Data for June are as follows.

	$
Opening inventory	1,000
Direct materials added	10,000
Conversion costs	12,000
Closing inventory	3,000

22,000

	Production Units	Sales Units	Sales price $ per unit
P	4,000	5,000	5
R	6,000	5,000	10

1　If costs are apportioned between joint products on a sales value basis, what was the cost per unit of product R in June?

A　$1.25
B　$2.22
C　$2.50 ✓
D　$2.75　　　　　　　　　　　　　　　　　　　　　　　　　　(2 marks)

2　If costs are apportioned between joint products on a physical unit basis, what was the total cost of product P production in June?

A　$8,000
B　$8,800
C　$10,000 ✓
D　$12,000　　　　　　　　　　　　　　　　　　　　　　　　　(2 marks)

3　Which of the following statements is/are correct?

(i)　A by-product is a product produced at the same time as other products which has a relatively low volume compared with the other products.

(ii)　Since a by-product is a saleable item it should be separately costed in the process account, and should absorb some of the process costs.

(iii)　Costs incurred prior to the point of separation are known as common or joint costs.

A　(i) and (ii)
B　(i) and (iii)
C　(ii) and (iii)
D　(iii) only　　　　　　　　　　　　　　　　　　　　　　　　　(2 marks)

4   A company manufactures two joint products and one by-product in a single process. Data for November are as follows.

	$
Raw material input	216,000
Conversion costs	72,000

298,000

There were no inventories at the beginning or end of the period.

	Output Units		Sales price $ per unit	
Joint product E	21,000	×	15	*315,000*
✳ Joint product Q	18,000	×	10	*180,000*
By-product X	2,000	×	2	*4000*

499,000

By-product sales revenue is credited to the process account. Joint costs are apportioned on a sales value basis. What were the full production costs of product Q in November (to the nearest $)?

A $102,445
B $103,273
C $104,727
D $180,727

(2 marks)

5   A company manufactures three joint products and one by-product from a single process.

Data for May are as follows.

Opening and closing inventories	Nil
Raw materials input	$180,000
Conversion costs	$50,000

Output

		Units	Sales price $ per unit
Joint product	L	3,000	32
	M	2,000	42
	N	4,000	38
By-product R		1,000	2

By-product sales revenue is credited to the sales account. Joint costs are apportioned on a sales value basis.

What were the full production costs of product M in May (to the nearest $)?

A $57,687
B $57,844
C $58,193
D $66,506

(2 marks)

6   Two products G and H are created from a joint process. G can be sold immediately after split-off. H requires further processing before it is in a saleable condition. There are no opening inventories and no work in progress. The following data are available for last period:

	$
Total joint production costs	384,000
Further processing costs (product H)	159,600

Product	Selling price per unit	Sales Units	Production Units
G	$0.84	400,000	412,000
H	$1.82	200,000	228,000

Using the physical unit method for apportioning joint production costs, what was the cost value of the closing inventory of product H for last period?

A $36,400
B $37,520
C $40,264
D $45,181   (2 marks)

7   **The following question is taken from the December 2007 exam paper**

Two products (W and X) are created from a joint process. Both products can be sold immediately after split-off. There are no opening inventories or work in progress. The following information is available for last period:

Total joint production costs $776,160

Product	Production units	Sales units	Selling price per unit
W	12,000	10,000	$10
X	10,000	8,000	$12

Using the sales value method of apportioning joint production costs, what was the value of the closing inventory of product X for last period?   (2 marks)

(Total = 14 marks)

12 Job, batch and service costing   35 mins

1   Which of the following costing methods is most likely to be used by a company involved in the manufacture of liquid soap?

A ✓ Batch costing
B   Service costing
C   Job costing
D ✓ Process costing   (2 marks)

2   A company calculates the prices of jobs by adding overheads to the prime cost and adding 30% to total costs as a mark up. Job number Y256 was sold for $1,690 and incurred overheads of $694. What was the prime cost of the job?

A $489
B ✓ $606
C $996
D $1,300   (2 marks)

130 %   *1690 / 130*
            x 100

= 1300
694   *606*

3   A company operates a job costing system.

The estimated costs for job 173 are as follows.

Direct materials   5 metres @ $20 per metre
Direct labour   14 hours @ $8 per hour

Variable production overheads are recovered at the rate of $3 per direct labour hour.

Fixed production overheads for the year are budgeted to be $200,000 and are to be recovered on the basis of the total of 40,000 direct labour hours for the year.

Other overheads, in relation to selling, distribution and administration, are recovered at the rate of $80 per job.

The total cost of job 173 is

A $404   B $300   C $254   D $324

                                                                                    (2 marks)

The following information relates to questions 4 and 5

A firm makes special assemblies to customers' orders and uses job costing.

The data for a period are:

	Job number AA10 $	Job number BB15 $	Job number CC20 $
Opening WIP	26,800	42,790	0
Material added in period	17,275	0	18,500
Labour for period	14,500	3,500	24,600

The budgeted overheads for the period were $126,000.

---

4   What overhead should be added to job number CC20 for the period?

    A $65,157

    B $69,290

    C $72,761

    D $126,000

    (2 marks)

---

5   What was the approximate value of closing work-in-progress at the end of the period?

    A $58,575

    B $101,675

    C $217,323

    D $227,675

    (2 marks)

---

6   The following items may be used in costing batches.

    (i)   Actual material cost

    (ii)   Actual manufacturing overheads

    (iii)   Absorbed manufacturing overheads

    (iv)   Actual labour cost

    Which of the above are contained in a typical batch cost?

    A   (i), (ii) and (iv) only

    B   (i) and (iv) only

    C   (i), (iii) and (iv) only

    D   All four of them

    (2 marks)

---

7   What would be the most appropriate cost unit for a cake manufacturer?

    Cost per:

    A   Cake

    B   Batch

    C   Kg

    (1 mark)

---

8   Which of the following would be appropriate cost units for a passenger coach company?

    (i)   Vehicle cost per passenger-kilometre

    (ii)   Fuel cost for each vehicle per kilometre

    (iii)   Fixed cost per kilometre

    A (i) only   B (i) and (ii) only   C (i) and (iii) only

    (1 mark)

---

9   The following information is available for a hotel company for the latest thirty day period.

Number of rooms available per night   40
Percentage occupancy achieved   65%
Room servicing cost incurred $3,900

The room servicing cost per occupied room-night last period, to the nearest penny, was:

A $3.25   B $5.00   C $97.50   D $150.00

(2 marks)

10   Annie is to set up a small hairdressing business at home. She anticipates working a 35-hour week and taking four weeks' holiday per year. Her expenses for materials and overheads are expected to be $3,000 per year, and she has set herself a target profit of $18,000 for the first year.

Assuming that only 90% of her working time will be chargeable to clients, what price should she charge for a 'colour and cut' which would take 3 hours?

A $13.89
B $35.71
C $37.50
D $41.67   (2 marks)

11   Which of the following is **not** a characteristic of service costing?

A   High levels of direct costs as a proportion of total costs
B   Intangibility of output
C   Use of composite cost units
D   Can be used for internal services as well as external services   (2 marks)

12   Which of the following are likely to use service costing?

(i)   A college
(ii)   A hotel
(iii)   A plumber

A   (i), (ii) and (iii)
B   (i) and (ii)
C   (ii) only   (1 mark)

13   Which of the following would be considered a service industry?

(i)   An airline company
(ii)   A railway company
(iii)   A firm of accountants

A   (i) and (ii) only
B   (i) and (iii) only
C   (i), (ii) and (iii)   (1 mark)

14   The following information relates to a management consultancy organisation:

	$
Salary cost per hour for senior consultants	40
Salary cost per hour for junior consultants	25
Overhead absorption rate per hour applied to all hours	20

The organisation adds 40% to total cost to arrive at the final fee to be charged to a client.

Assignment number 789 took 54 hours of a senior consultant's time and 110 hours of junior consultants' time.

What is the final fee to be charged for Assignment 789?

A $6,874   C $11,466
B $10,696   D $12,642   (2 marks)

15   A company operates a job costing system. Job number 1012 requires $45 of direct materials and $30 of direct labour. Direct labour is paid at the rate of $7.50 per hour. Production overheads are absorbed at a rate of $12.50 per direct labour hour and non-production overheads are absorbed at a rate of 60% of prime cost.

What is the total cost of job number 1012?

A $170
B $195
C $200
D $240

(2 marks)

(Total = 26 marks)

13 Budgeting

39 mins

1   Which of the following may be considered to be objectives of budgeting?

(i)   Co-ordination
(ii)   Communication
(iii)   Expansion
(iv)   Resource allocation

A   All of them
B   (i), (ii) and (iv)
C   (ii), (iii) and (iv)

(1 mark)

2   Which of the following would probably **not** be contained in a budget manual?

A   A timetable for budget preparation
B   The production cost budget
C   An organisation chart

(1 mark)

3   A master budget comprises

A   the budgeted income statement
B   the budgeted cash flow, budgeted income statement and budgeted balance sheet
C   the budgeted cash flow
D   the entire set of budgets prepared

(2 marks)

4   What does the statement 'sales is the principal budget factor' mean?

A   The level of sales will determine the level of cash at the end of the period
B   The level of sales will determine the level of profit at the end of the period
C   The company's activities are limited by the level of sales it can achieve

(1 mark)

5   Which of the following is **not** a functional budget?

A   Production budget
B   Distribution cost budget
C   Selling cost budget
D   Cash budget

(2 marks)

6   Which of the following tasks would usually be carried out first in the budgetary planning process?

A   Identify the principal budget factor
B   Establish the level of sales demand
C   Calculate the predetermined overhead absorption rate
D   Establish the organisation's long term objectives

(2 marks)

7   If a company has no production resource limitations, in which order would the following budgets be prepared?

1   Material usage budget   4   Finished goods inventory budget
2   Sales budget   5   Production budget
3   Material purchase budget   6   Material inventory budget

A   5, 4, 1, 6, 3, 2
B   2, 4, 5, 1, 6, 3
C   2, 4, 5, 1, 3, 6
D   2, 5, 4, 1, 6, 3   (2 marks)

8   In a situation where there are no production resource limitations, which of the following items of information must be available for the production budget to be completed?

(i)   Sales volume from the sales budget
(ii)   Material purchases from the purchases budget
(iii) Budgeted change in finished goods inventory
(iv)   Standard direct labour cost per unit

A   (i), (ii) and (iii)
B   (i), (iii) and (iv)
C   (i) and (iii)
D   All of them   (2 marks)

9   When preparing a production budget, the quantity to be produced equals

A   sales quantity + opening inventory of finished goods + closing inventory of finished goods
B   sales quantity – opening inventory of finished goods + closing inventory of finished goods
C   sales quantity – opening inventory of finished goods – closing inventory of finished goods
D   sales quantity + opening inventory of finished goods – closing inventory of finished goods (2 marks)

10   The quantity of material in the material purchases budget is greater than the quantity of material in the material usage budget. Which of the following statements can be inferred from this situation?

A   Wastage of material occurs in the production process
B   Finished goods inventories are budgeted to increase
C   Raw materials inventories are budgeted to increase
D   Raw materials inventories are budgeted to decrease   (2 marks)

11   A company plans to sell 24,000 units of product R next year. Opening inventory of R is expected to be 2,000 units and PQ Co plans to increase inventory by 25 per cent by the end of the year. How many units of product R should be produced next year?

A   23,500 units
B   24,000 units
C   24,500 units
D   30,000 units   (2 marks)

12 Each unit of product Alpha requires 3 kg of raw material. Next month's production budget for product Alpha is as follows.

Opening inventories:

Raw materials	15,000 kg
Finished units of Alpha	2,000 units
Budgeted sales of Alpha	60,000 units

Planned closing inventories:

Raw materials	7,000 kg
Finished units of Alpha	3,000 units

The number of kilograms of raw materials that should be purchased next month is:

A 172,000
B 175,000
C 183,000
D 191,000

(2 marks)

13 Budgeted sales of X for December are 18,000 units. At the end of the production process for X, 10% of production units are scrapped as defective. Opening inventories of X for December are budgeted to be 15,000 units and closing inventories will be 11,400 units. All inventories of finished goods must have successfully passed the quality control check. The production budget for X for December, in units is

A 12,960
B 14,400
C 15,840
D 16,000

(2 marks)

14 A company manufactures a single product, M. Budgeted production output of product M during August is 200 units. Each unit of product M requires 6 labour hours for completion and PR Co anticipates 20 per cent idle time. Labour is paid at a rate of $7 per hour. The direct labour cost budget for August is

A $6,720   C $10,080
B $8,400   D $10,500

(2 marks)

15 Each unit of product Echo takes five direct labour hours to make. Quality standards are high, and 8% of units are rejected after completion as sub-standard. Next month's budgets are as follows.

Opening inventories of finished goods	3,000 units
Planned closing inventories of finished goods	7,600 units
Budgeted sales of Echo	36,800 units

All inventories of finished goods must have successfully passed the quality control check.

What is the direct labour hours budget for the month?

A 190,440 hours
B 207,000 hours
C 223,560 hours
D 225,000 hours

(2 marks)

16 **The following question is taken from the June 2009 exam.**

Budgeted production in a factory for next period is 4,800 units. Each unit requires five labour hours to make. Labour is paid $10 per hour. Idle time represents 20% of the total labour time.

What is the budgeted total labour cost for the next period?

A $192,000   C $288,000
B $240,000   D $300,000

(2 marks)

(Total = 29 marks)

14 Standard costing

20 mins

1 A company is in the process of setting standard unit costs for next period. Product J uses two types of material, P and S. 7 kg of material P and 3 kg of material S are needed, at a standard price of $4 per kg and $9 per kg respectively.

Direct labour will cost $7 per hour and each unit of J requires 5 hours of labour.

Production overheads are to be recovered at the rate of $6 per direct labour hour, and general overhead is to be absorbed at a rate of ten per cent of production cost.

The standard prime cost for one unit of product J will be:

A $55   B $90   C $120   D $132

(2 marks)

2 Information on standard rates of pay would be provided by:

A   A trade union
B   A production manager
C   A personnel manager   (1 mark)

3 What is an attainable standard?

A   A standard which includes no allowance for losses, waste and inefficiencies. It represents the level of performance which is attainable under perfect operating conditions

B   A standard which includes some allowance for losses, waste and inefficiencies. It represents the level of performance which is attainable under efficient operating conditions

C   A standard which is based on currently attainable operating conditions

D   A standard which is kept unchanged, to show the trend in costs   (2 marks)

4 Which of the following statements is correct?

A   The operating standards set for production should be the most ideal possible.
B   The operating standards set for production should be the minimal level.
C   The operating standards set for production should be the attainable level.
D   The operating standards set for production should be the maximum level.   (2 marks)

5 Which of the following would **not** be directly relevant to the determination of standard labour times per unit of output?

A   The type of performance standard to be used
B   The volume of output from the production budget
C   Technical specifications of the proposed production methods   (1 mark)

6 A company manufactures a carbonated drink, which is sold in 1 litre bottles. During the bottling process there is a 20% loss of liquid input due to spillage and evaporation. The standard usage of liquid per bottle is

A   0.80 litres   C   1.20 litres
B   1.00 litres   D   1.25 litres   (2 marks)

7 Which of the following best describes management by exception?

A   Using management reports to highlight exceptionally good performance, so that favourable results can be built upon to improve future outcomes.

B   Sending management reports only to those managers who are able to act on the information contained within the reports.

C   Focusing management reports on areas which require attention and ignoring those which appear to be performing within acceptable limits.   (1 mark)

8   Standard costing provides which of the following?

    (i)   Targets and measures of performance
    (ii)   Information for budgeting
    (iii)   Simplification of inventory control systems
    (iv)   Actual future costs

    A   (i), (ii) and (iii) only
    B   (ii), (iii) and (iv) only
    C   (i), (iii) and (iv) only
    D   (i), (ii) and (iv) only   **(2 marks)**

9   A unit of product L requires 9 active labour hours for completion. The performance standard for product L allows for ten per cent of total labour time to be idle, due to machine downtime. The standard wage rate is $9 per hour. What is the standard labour cost per unit of product L?

    A $72.90
    B $81.00
    C $89.10
    D $90.00   **(2 marks)**

(Total = 15 marks)

15 Basic variance analysis

39 mins

1   A company manufactures a single product L, for which the standard material cost is as follows.

	$ per unit
Material 14 kg × $3	42

During July, 800 units of L were manufactured, 12,000 kg of material were purchased for $33,600, of which 11,500 kg were issued to production.

SM Co values all inventory at standard cost.

The material price and usage variances for July were:

	Price	Usage
A	$2,300 (F)	$900 (A)
B	$2,300 (F)	$300 (A)
C	$2,400 (F)	$900 (A)
D	$2,400 (F)	$840 (A)

          (2 marks)

The following information relates to questions 2 and 3

A company expected to produce 200 units of its product, the Bone, in 20X3. In fact 260 units were produced. The standard labour cost per unit was $70 (10 hours at a rate of $7 per hour). The actual labour cost was $18,600 and the labour force worked 2,200 hours although they were paid for 2,300 hours.

2   What is the direct labour rate variance for the company in 20X3?

    A $400 (A)   C $2,500 (A)
    B $2,500 (F)   D $3,200 (A)   **(2 marks)**

3   What is the direct labour efficiency variance for the company in 20X3?

    A $400 (A)
    B $2,100 (F)
    C $2,800 (A)
    D $2,800 (F)   **(2 marks)**

4 What is the idle time variance?

A $700 (F)   C $809 (A)

B $700 (A)   D $809 (F)   **(2 marks)**

---

5 Extracts from a company's records from last period are as follows.

	Budget	Actual
Production	1,925 units	2,070 units
Variable production overhead cost	$11,550	$14,904
Labour hours worked	5,775	8,280

The variable production overhead variances for last period are:

	Expenditure	Efficiency
A	$1,656 (F)	$2,070 (A)
B	$1,656 (F)	$3,726 (A)
C	$1,656 (F)	$4,140 (A)
D	$3,354 (A)	$4,140 (A)

(2 marks)

---

6 A company has budgeted to make and sell 4,200 units of product X during the period.

The standard fixed overhead cost per unit is $4.

During the period covered by the budget, the actual results were as follows.

Production and sales	5,000 units
Fixed overhead incurred	$17,500

The fixed overhead variances for the period were

	Fixed overhead expenditure variance	Fixed overhead volume variance
A	$700 (F)	$3,200 (F)
B	$700 (F)	$3,200 (A)
C	$700 (A)	$3,200 (F)
D	$700 (A)	$3,200 (A)

(2 marks)

---

7 A company manufactures a single product, and relevant data for December is as follows.

	Budget/standard	Actual
Production units	1,800	1,900
Labour hours	9,000	9,400
Fixed production overhead	$36,000	$39,480

The fixed production overhead capacity and efficiency variances for December are:

	Capacity	Efficiency
A	$1,600 (F)	$400 (F)
B	$1,600 (A)	$400 (A)
C	$1,600 (A)	$400 (F)
D	$1,600 (F)	$400 (A)

(2 marks)

---

8 Which of the following would help to explain a favourable direct labour efficiency variance?

(i)   Employees were of a lower skill level than specified in the standard

(ii)   Better quality material was easier to process

(iii)   Suggestions for improved working methods were implemented during the period

A   (i), (ii) and (iii)

B   (i) and (ii) only

C   (ii) and (iii) only   **(1 mark)**

9   Which of the following statements is correct?

A   An adverse direct material cost variance will always be a combination of an adverse material price
variance and an adverse material usage variance

B   An adverse direct material cost variance will always be a combination of an adverse material price
variance and a favourable material usage variance

C   An adverse direct material cost variance can be a combination of a favourable material price variance
and a favourable material usage variance

D   An adverse direct material cost variance can be a combination of a favourable material price variance
and an adverse material usage variance   (2 marks)

The following information relates to Questions 10 and 11

A company has a budgeted material cost of $125,000 for the production of 25,000 units per month. Each unit is
budgeted to use 2 kg of material. The standard cost of material is $2.50 per kg.

Actual materials in the month cost $136,000 for 27,000 units and 53,000 kg were purchased and used.

10   What was the adverse material price variance?

A $1,000
B $3,500
C $7,500
D $11,000   (2 marks)

11   What was the favourable material usage variance?

A $2,500
B $4,000
C $7,500
D $10,000   (2 marks)

The following information relates to questions 12 and 13

A company operating a standard costing system has the following direct labour standards per unit for one of its
products:

4 hours at $12.50 per hour

Last month when 2,195 units of the product were manufactured, the actual direct labour cost for the 9,200 hours
worked was $110,750.

12   What was the direct labour rate variance for last month?

A $4,250 favourable
B $4,250 adverse
C $5,250 favourable
D $5,250 adverse   (2 marks)

13   What was the direct labour efficiency variance for last month?

A $4,250 favourable
B $4,250 adverse
C $5,250 favourable
D $5,250 adverse   (2 marks)

14 The following information relates to labour costs for the past month:

Budget

	Labour rate	$10 per hour
	Production time	15,000 hours
	Time per unit	3 hours
	Production units	5,000 units

Actual

	Wages paid	$176,000
	Production	5,500 units
	Total hours worked	14,000 hours

There was no idle time

What were the labour rate and efficiency variances?

	Rate variance	Efficiency variance
A	$26,000 adverse	$25,000 favourable
B	$26,000 adverse	$10,000 favourable
C	$36,000 adverse	$2,500 favourable
D	$36,000 adverse	$25,000 favourable

(2 marks)

---

15 **The following question is taken from the December 2008 exam.**

A manufacturing company operates a standard absorption costing system. Last month 25,000 production hours were budgeted and the budgeted fixed production overhead cost was $125,000. Last month the actual hours worked were 24,000 and the standard hours for actual production were 27,000.

What was the fixed production overhead capacity variance for last month?

A $5,000 Adverse
B $5,000 Favourable
C $10,000 Adverse
D $10,000 Favourable

(2 marks)

(Total = 29 marks)

---

16 Further variance analysis   45 mins

1   A company currently uses a standard absorption costing system. The fixed overhead variances extracted from the operating statement for November are:

	$
Fixed production overhead expenditure variance	5,800 adverse
Fixed production overhead capacity variance	4,200 favourable
Fixed production overhead efficiency variance	1,400 adverse

PQ Limited is considering using standard marginal costing as the basis for variance reporting in future. What variance for fixed production overhead would be shown in a marginal costing operating statement for November?

A   No variance would be shown for fixed production overhead
B   Expenditure variance: $5,800 adverse
C   Volume variance: $2,800 favourable
D   Total variance: $3,000 adverse

(2 marks)

2   Which of the following situations is most likely to result in a favourable selling price variance?

A   The sales director decided to change from the planned policy of market skimming pricing to one of market penetration pricing.

B   Fewer customers than expected took advantage of the early payment discounts offered.

C   Competitors charged lower prices than expected, therefore selling prices had to be reduced in order to compete effectively.

D   Demand for the product was higher than expected and prices could be raised without adverse effects on sales volumes.

(2 marks)

The following information relates to questions 3 to 6

A company manufactures a single product. An extract from a variance control report together with relevant standard cost data is shown below.

Standard selling price per unit	$70
Standard direct material cost (5kg × $2 per kg)	$10 per unit
Budgeted total material cost of sales	$2,300 per month
Budgeted profit margin	$6,900 per month

Actual results for February

Sales revenue	$15,200
Total direct material cost	$2,400
Direct material price variance	$800 adverse
Direct material usage variance	$400 favourable

There was no change in inventory levels during the month.

3   What was the actual production in February?

A	200 units	C	240 units
B	217 units	D	280 units

(2 marks)

4   What was the actual usage of direct material during February?

A	800 kg	C	1,200 kg
B	1,000 kg	D	None of these

(2 marks)

5   What was the selling price variance for February?

A	$120 (F)	C	$1,200 (A)
B	$900 (A)	D	$1,200 (F)

(2 marks)

6   What was the sales volume profit variance for February?

A	$900 (F)	C	$900 (A)
B	$1,200 (F)	D	$2,100 (A)

(2 marks)

7   A company uses a standard absorption costing system. The following details have been extracted from its budget for April.

Fixed production overhead cost	$48,000
Production (units)	4,800

In April the fixed production overhead cost was under absorbed by $8,000 and the fixed production overhead expenditure variance was $2,000 adverse.

The actual number of units produced was

A	3,800	C	4,800
B	4,200	D	5,800

(2 marks)

8   A company purchased 6,850 kgs of material at a total cost of $21,920. The material price variance was $1,370 favourable. The standard price per kg was:

   A $0.20
   B $3.00
   C $3.20
   D $3.40   **(2 marks)**

9   The following data relates to one of a company's products.

	$ per unit	$ per unit
Selling price		27.00
Variable costs	12.00	
Fixed costs	9.00	
		21.00
Profit		6.00

   Budgeted sales for control period 7 were 2,400 units, but actual sales were 2,550 units. The revenue earned from these sales was $67,320.

   Profit reconciliation statements are drawn up using marginal costing principles. What sales variances would be included in such a statement for period 7?

	Price	Volume
A	$1,530 (A)	$900 (F)
B	$1,530 (A)	$2,250 (F)
C	$1,530 (A)	$2,250 (A)
D	$1,530 (F)	$2,250 (F)

                                                                                          (2 marks)

10   A company uses variance analysis to control costs and revenues.

   Information concerning sales is as follows:

Budgeted selling price	$15 per unit
Budgeted sales units	10,000 units
Budgeted profit per unit	$5 per unit
Actual sales revenue	$151,500
Actual units sold	9,800 units

   What is the sales volume profit variance?

   A $500 favourable
   B $1,000 favourable
   C $1,000 adverse
   D $3,000 adverse   **(2 marks)**

The following information relates to questions 11 and 12

The standard direct material cost per unit for a product is calculated as follows:

10.5 litres at $2.50 per litre

Last month the actual price paid for 12,000 litres of material used was 4% above standard and the direct material usage variance was $1,815 favourable. No stocks of material are held.

11   What was the adverse direct material price variance for last month?

   A $1,000
   B $1,200
   C $1,212
   D $1,260   **(2 marks)**

12   What was the actual production last month (in units)?

    A   1,074
    B   1,119
    C   1,212
    D   1,258   (2 marks)

13   Last month a company budgeted to sell 8,000 units at a price of $12.50 per unit. Actual sales last month
      were 9,000 units giving a total sales revenue of $117,000.

      What was the sales price variance for last month?

      A $4,000 favourable
      B $4,000 adverse
      C $4,500 favourable
      D $4,500 adverse   (2 marks)

14   A company uses a standard absorption costing system. Last month budgeted production was 8,000 units
      and the standard fixed production overhead cost was $15 per unit. Actual production last month was 8,500
      units and the actual fixed production overhead cost was $17 per unit.

      What was the total adverse fixed production overhead variance for last month?

      A $7,500
      B $16,000
      C $17,000
      D $24.500   (2 marks)

15   A cost centre had an overhead absorption rate of $4.25 per machine hour, based on a budgeted activity level
      of 12,400 machine hours.

      In the period covered by the budget, actual machine hours worked were 2% more than the budgeted hours
      and the actual overhead expenditure incurred in the cost centre was $56,389.

      What was the total over or under absorption of overheads in the cost centre for the period?

      A $1,054 over absorbed
      B $2,635 under absorbed
      C $3,689 over absorbed
      D $3,689 under absorbed   (2 marks)

16   **The following question is taken from the December 2007 exam paper**

      A company uses standard marginal costing. Last month the standard contribution on actual sales was
      $10,000 and the following variances arose:

                                                    $
      Total variable costs variance   2,000 Adverse
      Sales price variance   500 Favourable
      Sales volume contribution variance   1,000 Adverse

      What was the actual contribution for last month?

      A $7,000
      B $7,500
      C $8,000
      D $8,500   (2 marks)

17   **The following question is taken from the June 2008 exam paper**

A company uses standard marginal costing. Last month, when all sales were at the standard selling price, the standard contribution from actual sales was $50,000 and the following variances arose:

	$
Total variable costs variance	3,500 Adverse
Total fixed costs variance	1,000 Favourable
Sales volume contribution variance	2,000 Favourable

What was the actual contribution for last month?

A	$46,500	B	$47,500	
C	$48,500	D	$49,500	(2 marks)

(Total = 34 marks)

17 Cost-volume-profit (CVP) analysis   48 mins

The following data relates to questions 1 and 2

Data concerning a company's single product is as follows.

	$ per unit
Selling price	6.00
Variable production cost	1.20
Variable selling cost	0.40
Fixed production cost	4.00
Fixed selling cost	0.80

Budgeted production and sales for the year are 10,000 units.

1   What is the company's breakeven point, to the nearest whole unit?

A	8,000 units	C	10,000 units	
B	8,333 units	D	10,909 units	(2 marks)

2   It is now expected that the variable production cost per unit and the selling price per unit will each increase by 10%, and fixed production costs will rise by 25%.

What will be the new breakeven point, to the nearest whole unit?

A	8,788 units	C	11,885 units	
B	11,600 units	D	12,397 units	(2 marks)

3   A company manufactures a single product, P. Data for the product are as follows.

	$ per unit
Selling price	20
Direct material cost	4
Direct labour cost	3
Variable production overhead cost	2
Variable selling overhead cost	1
Fixed overhead cost	5
Profit per unit	5

The profit/volume ratio for product P is

A	25%	C	55%	
B	50%	D	60%	(2 marks)

4   A company's breakeven point is 6,000 units per annum. The selling price is $90 per unit and the variable cost is $40 per unit. What are the company's annual fixed costs?

A $120
B $240,000
C $300,000 ✓
D $540,000

90 - 40 = 50 × 6,000

(2 marks)

5   A company makes a single product which it sells for $16 per unit. Fixed costs are $76,800 per month and the product has a profit/volume ratio of 40%. In a period when actual sales were $224,000, Z plc's margin of safety, in units, was:

A   2,000
B   12,000
C   14,000
D   32,000

(2 marks)

6   A company generates a 12 per cent contribution on its weekly sales of $280,000. A new product, Z, is to be introduced at a special offer price in order to stimulate interest in all the company's products, resulting in a 5 per cent increase in weekly sales of the company's other products. Product Z will incur a variable unit cost of $2.20 to make and $0.15 to distribute. Weekly sales of Z, at a special offer price of $1.90 per unit, are expected to be 3,000 units.

The effect of the special offer will be to increase the company's weekly profit by:

A $330
B $780
C $12,650
D $19,700

(2 marks)

7

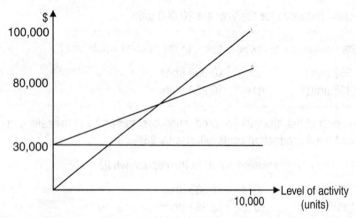

The above breakeven chart has been drawn for a company's single product. Which of the following statements about the product is/are correct?

(i)   The product's selling price is $10 per unit ✓
(ii)   The product's variable cost is $8 per unit ✗
(iii)   The product incurs fixed costs of $30,000 per period ✓
(iv)   The product earns a profit of $70,000 at a level of activity of 10,000 units

A   (i), (ii) and (iii) only
B   (i) and (iii) only ✓
C   (i), (iii) and (iv) only
D   (iii) and (iv) only

(2 marks)

The following graph relates to questions 8 and 9

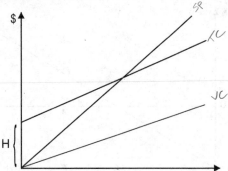

8 H on the graph indicates the value of

A   Contribution
B   Fixed cost
C   Sales value
D   Variable cost   **(2 marks)**

9 This graph is known as a

A   Contribution breakeven chart
B   Conventional breakeven chart
C   Profit-volume chart
D   Semi-variable cost chart   **(2 marks)**

10 Which of the following statements about profit-volume graphs is/are correct?

(i)   The profit-volume line crosses the x axis at the breakeven point.

(ii)   Any point on the profit-volume line above the x axis indicates the profit (as measured on the vertical axis) at that level of activity.

(iii)   The profit-volume line starts at the origin.

A   (i) and (ii) only
B   (ii) and (iii) only
C   (i) and (iii) only
D   (i), (ii) and (iii)   **(2 marks)**

11 The following graph has been established for a given set of constraints:

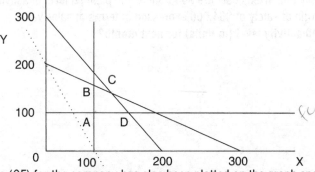

The objective function (OF) for the company has also been plotted on the graph and the feasible region is bounded by the area ABCD.

At which point on the graph will profits be maximised?

A
B
C
D   **(2 marks)**

12   The following represents a profit/volume graph for an organisation:

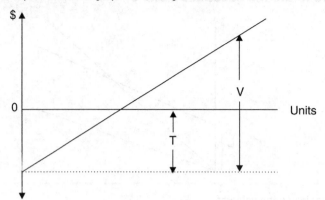

At the specific levels of activity indicated, what do the lines depicted as 'T' and 'V' represent?

	Line 'T'	Line 'V'
A	Loss	Profit
B	Loss	Contribution
C	Total fixed costs	Profit
D	Total fixed costs	Contribution

(2 marks)

13   An organisation manufacturers and sells a single product. At the budgeted level of output of 2,400 units per week, the unit cost and selling price structure is as follows:

	$ per unit	$ per unit
Selling price		60
Less – variable production cost	15	
other variable cost	5	
fixed cost	30	
		(50)
Profit		10

What is the breakeven point (in units per week)?

A   1,200
B   1,600
C   1,800
D   2,400

(2 marks)

14   A company manufactures one product which it sells for $40 per unit. The product has a contribution to sales ratio of 40%. Monthly total fixed costs are $60,000. At the planned level of activity for next month, the company has a margin of safety of $64,000 expressed in terms of sales value.

What is the planned activity level (in units) for next month?

A   3,100
B   4,100
C   5,350
D   7,750

(2 marks)

15 A break-even chart for a company is depicted as follows:

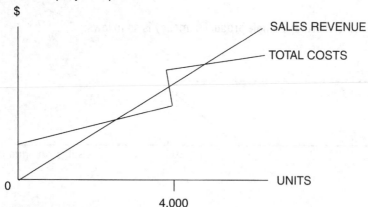

Which one of the following statements is consistent with the above chart?

A   Both selling price per unit and variable cost per unit are constant.

B   Selling price per unit is constant but variable cost per unit increases for sales over 4,000 units.

C   Variable cost per unit is constant but the selling price per unit increases for sales over 4,000 units.

D   Selling price per unit increases for sales over 4,000 units and there is an increase in the total fixed costs at 4,000 units.

(2 marks)

16 A company sells a single product which has a contribution of $27 per unit and a contribution to sales ratio of 45%. This period it is forecast to sell 1,000 units giving it a margin of safety of $13,500 in sales revenue terms.

What are the company's total fixed costs per period?

A $6,075
B $7,425
C $13,500
D $20,925

(2 marks)

17 A company has the following budgeted information for the coming month:

Budgeted sales revenue $500,000
Budgeted contribution $200,000
Budgeted profit $50,000

What is the budgeted break-even sales revenue?

A $125,000
B $350,000
C $375,000
D $450,000

(2 marks)

18 The following question was taken from the December 2008 exam.

The profit/volume chart for a single product company is as follows:

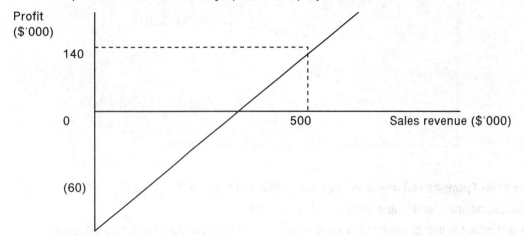

What is the product's contribution to sales ratio (expressed as a %)?

A	16%	C	40%
B	28%	D	72%

(2 marks)

(Total = 36 marks)

18 Relevant costing and decision-making   25 mins

1   You are currently employed as a Management Accountant in an insurance company. You are contemplating starting your own business. In considering whether or not to start your own business, your current salary level would be:

A	A sunk cost	C	An irrelevant cost
B	An incremental cost	D	An opportunity cost

(2 marks)

2   Your company regularly uses material X and currently has in inventory 500 kgs for which it paid $1,500 two weeks ago. If this were to be sold as raw material, it could be sold today for $2.00 per kg. You are aware that the material can be bought on the open market for $3.25 per kg, but it must be purchased in quantities of 1,000 kgs.

You have been asked to determine the relevant cost of 600 kgs of material X to be used in a job for a customer. The relevant cost of the 600 kgs is:

A	$1,325	C	$1,950
B	$1,825	D	$3,250

(2 marks)

3   A company is considering its option with regard to a machine which cost $60,000 four years ago.

If sold the machine would generate scrap proceeds of $75,000. If kept, this machine would generate net income of $90,000.

The current replacement cost for this machine is $105,000.

What is the relevant cost of the machine?

A	$105,000	C	$75,000
B	$90,000	D	$60,000

(2 marks)

4   A company manufactures and sells two products (X and Y) both of which utilise the same skilled labour. For the coming period, the supply of skilled labour is limited to 2,000 hours. Data relating to each product are as follows:

Product	X	Y
Selling price per unit	$20	$40
Variable cost per unit	$12	$30
Skilled labour hours per unit	2	4
Maximum demand (units) per period	800	400

In order to maximise profit in the coming period, how many units of each product should the company manufacture and sell?

A   200 units of X and 400 units of Y
B   400 units of X and 300 units of Y
C   600 units of X and 200 units of Y
D   800 units of X and 100 units of Y   (2 marks)

---

5   In the short-term decision-making context, which ONE of the following would be a relevant cost?

A   Specific development costs already incurred
B   The cost of special material which will be purchased
C   The original cost of raw materials currently in inventory which will be used on the project   (1 mark)

---

6   A company manufactures and sells a single product. The variable cost of the product is $2.50 per unit and all production each month is sold at a price of $3.70 per unit. A potential new customer has offered to buy 6,000 units per month at a price of $2.95 per unit. The company has sufficient spare capacity to produce this quantity. If the new business is accepted, sales to existing customers are expected to fall by two units for every 15 units sold to the new customer.

What would be the overall increase in monthly profit which would result from accepting the new business?

A $1,740   C $2,340
B $2,220   D $2,700   (2 marks)

---

7   A company is evaluating a project that requires two types of material (T and V). Data relating to the material requirements are as follows:

Material type	Quantity needed for project	Quantity currently in inventory	Original cost of quantity in inventory	Current purchase price	Current resale price
	kg	kg	$/kg	$/kg	$/kg
T	500	100	40	45	44
V	400	200	55	52	40

Material T is regularly used by the company in normal production. Material V is no longer in use by the company and has no alternative use within the business.

What is the total relevant cost of materials for the project?

A $40,400   C $43,400
B $40,900   D $43,900   (2 marks)

---

8   A machine owned by a company has been idle for some months but could now be used on a one year contract which is under consideration. The net book value of the machine is $1,000. If not used on this contract, the machine could be sold now for a net amount of $1,200. After use on the contract, the machine would have no saleable value and the cost of disposing of it in one year's time would be $800.

What is the total relevant cost of the machine to the contract?

A $400   C $1,200
B $800   D $2,000   (2 marks)

9 A company has just secured a new contract which requires 500 hours of labour.

There are 400 hours of spare labour capacity. The remaining hours could be worked as overtime at time and a half or labour could be diverted from the production of product x. Product X currently earns a contribution of $4 in two labour hours and direct labour is currently paid at a rate of $12 per normal hour.

What is the relevant cost of labour for the contract?

A	$200	B	$1,200
C	$1,400	D	$1,800

(2 marks)

10 A company uses limiting factor analysis to calculate an optimal production plan given a scarce resource.

The following applies to the three products of the company:

Product	I	II	III
	$	$	$
Direct materials (at $6/kg)	36	24	15
Direct labour (at $10/hour)	40	25	10
Variable overheads ($2/hour)	8	5	2
	84	54	27
Maximum demand (units)	2,000	4,000	4,000
Optimal production plan	2,000	1,500	4,000

How many kg of material were available for use in production?

A	15,750 kg	B	28,000 kg
C	30,000 kg	D	38,000 kg

(2 marks)

(Total = 19 marks)

19 Linear programming   23 mins

1 A company is using linear programming to decide how many units of each of its two products to make each week. Weekly production will be x units of product X and y units of product Y. At least 50 units of X must be produced each week, and at least twice as many units of Y as of X must be produced each week. Each unit of X requires 30 minutes of labour, and each unit of Y requires 2 hours of labour. There are 5,000 hours of labour available each week. Which of the following is the correct set of constraints?

A $0.5x + 2y \le 5,000$
    $x \ge 50$
    $y \ge 2x$

B $x + 4y \le 5,000$
    $x \ge 50$
    $y \ge 2x$

C $0.5x + 2y \le 5,000$
    $x \ge 50$
    $y \ge 100$

D $0.5x + 2y \le 10,000$
    $x \ge 0.5y$
    $y \ge 100$

(2 marks)

2　In a linear programming problem, the constraints are as follows:

$$x \geq 0$$
$$y \geq 150$$
$$x + y \leq 450$$
$$4x + y \leq 600$$

What is the maximum possible value of the objective function, $3x + y$, given these constraints?

A　450.0
B　487.5
C　537.5
D　550.0　　　　　　　　　　　　　　　　　　　　　　　　　　　　　　　　**(2 marks)**

3　A confectionery company manufactures two chocolate products – golf balls and teddy bears. Each product is manufactured in batches of one thousand. Relevant information is as follows.

	Golf balls (per batch)	Teddy bears (per batch)	Minutes available each day
Labour (minutes)	5	10	20,000
Machine time (minutes)	10	2	25,000

If the optimal production mix occurs at the intersection of the above constraints, how many batches of golf balls and teddy bears should be produced at this point?

A　2,334 golf balls and 833 teddy bears
B　833 golf balls and 2,334 teddy bears
C　2,334,000 golf balls and 833,000 teddy bears
D　833,000 golf balls and 2,334,000 teddy bears　　　　　　　　　　　　**(2 marks)**

4　A marketing manager may use large posters and/or small posters to advertise a new product. There must be at least half as many large posters as small posters and at least 50 large posters. There must be at least 100 posters in total, and not more than 150 small posters. Each large poster costs $4 and each small poster costs $2. What is the minimum total cost?

A　$300
B　$400
C　$500
D　$600　　　　　　　　　　　　　　　　　　　　　　　　　　　　　　　　**(2 marks)**

5　An office manager wishes to minimise the cost of telephone calls made. 40% of calls in peak hours cost $1 each and the remainder of such calls cost $1.50 each. 30% of calls at other times cost $0.80 each, 50% of them cost $0.90 each, and 20% of them cost $1 each. These proportions cannot be varied, though the total number of calls made in peak hours and of calls made at other times can be. If x = the number of calls made each day in peak hours, and y = the number of calls made each day at other times, the office manager's objective is to:

A　Minimise $120x + 89y$
B　Minimise $120x + 90y$
C　Minimise $130x + 89y$
D　Minimise $130x + 90y$　　　　　　　　　　　　　　　　　　　　　　　　**(2 marks)**

6　If X is the number of managers and Y is the number of non-managerial staff, which of the following inequalities expresses the constraint that the number of managers must be no more than 25% of the total number of staff?

A　$4X \leq Y$
B　$X \leq 4Y$
C　$3X \leq Y$
D　$X/4 \leq X + Y$　　　　　　　　　　　　　　　　　　　　　　　　　　　**(2 marks)**

7   A farmer wants to find the possible amounts of two different chemicals, P and Q, to use on arable land, and is using linear programming. He must use at least 50 kg of P per hectare. The weight of Q per hectare may be between two and five times the weight of P per hectare. The total weight of chemicals per hectare must not exceed 500 kg. If p = kg per hectare of chemical P, and q = kg per hectare of chemical Q, which of the following is the correct set of constraints?

A	B	C	D
$p \geq 50$	$p \geq 50$	$p \geq 50$	$p \geq 50$
$q \geq 2p$	$p \geq 2p$	$q \geq 100$	$q \geq 2p$
$q \leq 5p$	$p \leq 5p$	$q \leq 250$	$q \leq 5p$
$p + q \leq 1,000$	$p + q \leq 500$	$p + q \leq 500$	$p + q \leq 500$

(2 marks)

8   Which of the following is correct?

A   When considering limiting factors the products should always be ranked according to contribution per unit sold

B   If there is only one scarce resource linear programming should be used

C   In linear programming the point furthest from the origin will always be the point of profit maximisation

D   The slope of the objective function depends on the contributions of the products.   **(2 marks)**

9   The following graph relates to a linear programming problem:

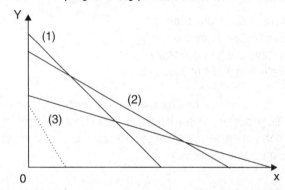

The objective is to maximise contribution and the dotted line on the graph depicts this function. There are three constraints which are all of the 'less that or equal to' type which are depicted on the graph by the three solid lines labelled (1), (2) and (3).

At which of the following intersections is contribution maximised?

A   Constraints (1) and (2)
B   Constraints (2) and (3)
C   Constraints (1) and (3)
D   Constraints (1) and the x-axis   **(2 marks)**

(Total = 18 marks)

Objective test questions

20 Information for management   10 mins

1   **Data** which has been processed in such a way as to be meaningful is referred to as ☐   **(1 mark)**

2   Good information should be: (Tick all those which apply)

☐ Complete
☐ Extensive
☐ Relevant
☐ Accurate   **(2 marks)**

3   Management information is used for **planning**, **control** and ☐   **(1 mark)**

4   **Strategic planning** is carried out by front-line managers.

☐ True
☐ False   **(1 mark)**

5   Information is provided for the use of managers within an organisation by: (tick one)

☐ **Financial accounting systems**
☐ **Management accounting systems**   **(1 mark)**

6   Non-financial information is relevant to management accounting

☐ True
☐ False   **(1 mark)**

(Total = 7 marks)

21 Cost classification   8 mins

1   A company has to pay a $1 per unit royalty to the designer of a product which it manufactures and sells.

The royalty charge would be classified in the company's accounts as a (tick the correct answer):

☐ Direct expense
☐ Production overhead
☐ Administrative overhead
☐ Selling overhead   **(1 mark)**

2   Fixed costs are conventionally deemed to be (tick the correct answer):

☐ Constant per unit of activity
☐ Constant in total when activity changes
☐ Outside the control of management
☐ Unaffected by inflation   **(1 mark)**

3   A cost centre is (tick the correct answer):

☐   a unit of output or service for which costs are ascertained

☐   a function or location for which costs are ascertained

☐   a segment of the organisation for which budgets are prepared

☐   an amount of expenditure attributable to a particular activity   **(1 mark)**

---

4   Depreciation on production equipment is (tick all answers that are correct):

☐   Not a cash cost

☐   Part of production overheads

☐   Part of prime cost

☐   Always calculated using a machine-hour rate   **(2 marks)**

---

5   Which one of the following would be classed as indirect labour?

☐   Machine operators in a company manufacturing washing machines

☐   A stores assistant in a factory store

☐   Plumbers in a construction company

☐   A committee in a firm of management consultants   **(1 mark)**

(Total = 6 marks)

---

22 Cost behaviour   18 mins

1   The following data relate to two activity levels of an X-ray department in a hospital:

Number of X-rays taken	4,500	4,750
Overheads	$269,750	$273,625

Fixed overheads are $200,000 per period.

The variable cost per X-ray is $ ☐   **(2 marks)**

---

2   An organisation has found that there is a linear relationship between sales volume and delivery costs.

It has found that a sales volume of 400 units corresponds to delivery costs of $10,000 and that a sales volume of 800 units corresponds to delivery costs of $12,000.

The delivery costs for a sales volume of 700 units will be $ ☐   **(2 marks)**

3   Which of these graphs represents a fixed cost – when the vertical axis represents cost incurred?

☐ Graph 1
☐ Graph 2
☐ Graph 3

$ |
_____
|_____
Level of activity
Graph 1

$ |
          /
        /
      /
| /
|/_____
Level of activity
Graph 2

$ |
          _____
|
|___
|_____
Level of activity
Graph 3

(1 mark)

4   Which of these graphs represents a variable cost – when the vertical axis represents total cost incurred?

☐ Graph 1
☐ Graph 2
☐ Graph 3

$ |
_____
|_____
Level of activity
Graph 1

$ |
          /
        /
      /
| /
|/_____
Level of activity
Graph 2

$ |
          _____
|
|___
|_____
Level of activity
Graph 3

(1 mark)

5   Which of these graphs represents a semi-variable or mixed cost – when the vertical axis represents total cost incurred (tick all that are correct)?

☐ Graph 1
☐ Graph 2
☐ Graph 3
☐ Graph 4

$ |
           /
          /
|_____ /
| \/
|_____
Level of activity
Graph 1

$ |
          /
        /
      /
| /
|/_____
Level of activity
Graph 2

$ |
         /
       /
     /
| /
|/_____
Level of activity
Graph 3

$ |
       _____
     /
   /
|/_____
Level of activity
Graph 4

(2 marks)

6   A company operates a single outlet selling direct to the public. Profit statements for August and September 20X6 are as follows.

	August $	September $
Sales	80,000	90,000
Cost of sales	50,000	55,000
Gross profit	30,000	35,000
Less:		
Selling and distribution	8,000	9,000
Administration	15,000	15,000
Net profit	7,000	11,000

(a)   The cost of sales consists of a fixed cost of $ [   ] and a variable cost of $ [   ] per $ of sale.   **(2 marks)**

(b)   The selling and distribution cost is a [   ] cost of $ [   ] per $ of sale.   **(2 marks)**

(c)   The administration cost is a [   ] cost.   **(1 mark)**

(Total = 13 marks)

23 Correlation and regression   **27 mins**

1   The coefficient of determination (r^2) explains the percentage variation in the independent variable which is explained by the dependent variable.

[ ]   True
[ ]   False   **(1 mark)**

2   The coefficient of determination, r^2, must always fall within the range

Lowest value = [   ]

Highest value = [   ]   **(2 marks)**

3   A company is building a model in order to forecast total costs based on the level of output. The following data is available for last year.

20X2 Month	Output '000 units (X)	Costs $'000 (Y)
January	16	170
February	20	240
March	23	260
April	25	300
May	25	280
June	19	230
July	16	200
August	12	160
September	19	240
October	25	290
November	28	350
December	12	200

The relationship between output and costs can be expressed as

$Y = a + bX$

where $X =$ output ('000 units)

              $Y =$ costs ($'000)

Using the data above and the formulae given below, calculate the following values for the formula $Y = a + bX$.

$$b = \frac{n\Sigma XY - \Sigma X \Sigma Y}{n\Sigma X^2 - (\Sigma X)^2}$$

$$a = \frac{\Sigma Y}{n} - \frac{b\Sigma X}{n}$$

a = [   ]   **(2 marks)**

b = [   ]   **(2 marks)**

---

4   In a forecasting model based on $Y = a + bX$, the intercept is $248. If the value of Y is $523 and X is 25, then the value of the slope, to two decimal places, is [   ]   **(2 marks)**

---

5   What is the equation of the least-squares regression line of y on x for the following four data pairs?

x	y
1	4
2	6
3	10
4	10

y = [   ]   **(2 marks)**

---

6   What is the equation of the least-squares regression line of x on y for the following five data pairs?

x	y
9	2
10	3
9	1
8	1
9	2

x = [   ]   **(2 marks)**

---

7   The correlation coefficient between two variables, x and y, is +0.68. The proportion of variation in x that is explained by variation in y is [   ] (to 4 decimal places)   **(2 marks)**

---

8   A scatter diagram shows the weekly total costs of production ($) in a certain factory plotted against the weekly outputs (units). A broadly linear pattern is evident, with r = 0.9. The regression equation is

Costs = 1,500 + (15 × output)

Fifty data points have been included in the analysis, with output ranging from 100 units to 1,000 units. Output next week is planned to be 500 units.

(a)   Weekly fixed costs are approximately $ [   ] (to the nearest $)   **(1 mark)**

(b)   Variable costs per unit are on average $ [   ] (to the nearest $)   **(1 mark)**

(c)   Next week's production costs are likely to be approximately $ [   ] (to the nearest $)   **(1 mark)**

(d)

		True	False
(i)	There is very little correlation between weekly costs of production and production level.	☐	☐
(ii)	90% of the variation in weekly costs is attributable to the amount produced.	☐	☐
(iii)	Given the information, any forecast using the regression equation is likely to be very unreliable.	☐	☐

(2 marks)

(Total = 20 marks)

24 Spreadsheets

12 mins

1   Spreadsheets are useful for: (tick one)

☐ Business correspondence
☐ Presentation slides
☐ Preparing budgets

(1 mark)

2   A **macro** is an automated process that records key strokes and mouse clicks.

☐ True
☐ False

(1 mark)

3   A spreadsheet facility that allows the column and row reference to remain the same when the formula is copied to another cell is known as: (tick one)

☐ Absolute cell referencing
☐ Relative cell referencing

(1 mark)

The following data applies to questions 4 to 6:

	A	B	C	D	F	G
1		Jan	Feb	Mar	Apr	May
2	Sales	15,000	13,400	16,100	17,200	15,300
3	Cost of sales	11,090	10,060	12,040	13,000	11,100
4	Gross profit	3,910	3,340	4,060	4,200	4,200
5	Expenses	1,500	1,500	1,500	1,500	1,500
6	Net profit	2,410	1,840	2,560	2,700	2,700
7						
8	Net profit %					

4   What formula would be entered in cell C4? ☐

(2 marks)

5   What formula should be entered in cell B8? ☐

(2 marks)

6   What amount will =SUM(B5:G5) give? ☐

(2 marks)

(Total = 9 marks)

25 Material costs   11 mins

1   A company wishes to minimise its inventory costs. Order costs are $10 per order and holding costs are
     $0.10 per unit per month. Fall Co estimates annual demand to be 5,400 units.

     The economic order quantity is ☐ units.   **(2 marks)**

2   For a particular component, the re-order quantity is 6,000 units and the average inventory holding is 3,400
     units.

     The level of safety inventory is ☐ units (to the nearest whole unit).   **(2 marks)**

3   The following data relates to component L512:

     Ordering costs $100 per order
     Inventory holding costs $8 per unit per annum
     Annual demand   1,225 units

     The economic order quantity is ☐ units (to the nearest whole unit).   **(2 marks)**

4   The following data relate to inventory item A452:

     Average usage   100 units per day
     Minimum usage   60 units per day
     Maximum usage   130 units per day
     Lead time   20-26 days
     EOQ   4,000 units

     The maximum inventory level was ☐ units   **(2 marks)**

                                                                        (Total = 8 marks)

26 Labour costs   23 mins

1   (a)   The following data relate to work in the finishing department.

           Basic daily pay   8 hours × $6 per hour
           Standard time allowed to finish one unit   12 minutes
           Premium bonus payable at the basic rate   50% of time saved

           On a particular day an employee finishes 50 units. His gross pay for the day will be $ ☐ (to
           the nearest $)   **(2 marks)**

     (b)   An employee is paid according the following differential piecework scheme,

           | Weekly output | Rate of pay per unit |
Units	$
1–25	2.30
26–40	2.40
41 and above	2.60

           with only the additional units qualifying for the higher rates. In addition he receives a guaranteed
           weekly wage of $420. In a week when he produces 28 units, his gross wage will be $ ☐ (to
           the nearest penny).   **(2 marks)**

2   A factory's employees are paid according to the following incentive scheme.

Normal working day	8 hours
Basic rate of pay per hour	$7
Standard time allowed to produce 1 unit	3 minutes
Premium bonus	50% of time saved at basic rate

Overtime is paid at a rate of time and a half.

Employee A387 worked for 10 hours on Monday and produced 220 units.

Employee A387

	Basic pay $	Overtime premium $	Premium bonus $	Total pay $
Monday	**A**	**B**	**C**	**D**

In the above table, the values that would be entered for A, B, C and D are:

A   [   ]

B   [   ]

C   [   ]

D   [   ]

                                                                    (2 marks)

3   A company pays employees under a piecework scheme. An employee is paid whereby she receives $4 per piecework hour produced, plus a guaranteed weekly wage of $200. In week 12 she produces the following output.

	Piecework time allowance per unit Hours
50 units of product J	0.3
10 units of product W	4.0

The employee's gross pay for week 12 was $ [   ]

                                                                    (2 marks)

4   A team of five employees is rewarded by means of a group incentive scheme. The team receives a basic hourly rate for output up to and including 200 units per day.

The basic rate of pay for members of the team is:

	Number of employees	Hourly rate $
Team leader	1	14
Operatives	3	10
Junior operative	1	6

For outputs exceeding 200 units per day the hourly rate for all members of the team is increased, for all hours worked that day. The increases in hourly rates, above the basic hourly rate, are as follows.

Output per day Units	Increase in hourly rate %
201 to 250	10
251 to 280	12
281 to 300	15

Due to a limitation on machine capacity it is not possible to exceed an output of 300 units per day.

Output per day	Hourly group remuneration
Units	$
Up to 200	A
201 to 250	B
251 to 280	C
281 to 300	D

The values that would be entered in the table above for A, B, C and D are:

A ☐ (1 mark)

B ☐ (1 mark)

C ☐ (1 mark)

D ☐ (1 mark)

---

5 A manufacturing firm has temporary production problems and overtime is being worked.

The amount of overtime premium contained in direct wages would normally be classed as which one of the following:

☐ Direct expenses
☐ Production overheads
☐ Direct labour costs (1 mark)

---

6 A manufacturing firm has temporary production problems and overtime is being worked.

The amount of overtime premium contained in direct wages would normally be classed as which one of the following:

☐ Direct expenses
☐ Production overheads
☐ Direct labour costs
☐ Administrative overheads (2 marks)

---

7 In a typical cost ledger, the double entry for indirect labour cost incurred is:

☐	DR	Wages control	CR	Overhead control
☐	DR	Admin overhead control	CR	Wages control
☐	DR	Overhead control	CR	Wages control
☐	DR	Wages control	CR	Admin overhead control

(2 marks)

(Total = 17 marks)

27 Overheads and absorption costing   45 mins

1
Actual overheads	$496,980
Actual machine hours	16,566
Budgeted overheads	$475,200

Based on the data above, and assuming that the budgeted overhead absorption rate was $32 per hour, the number of machine hours (to the nearest hour) budgeted to be worked were ☐ hours. (2 marks)

2

Budgeted overheads	$690,480
Budgeted machine hours	15,344
Actual machine hours	14,128
Actual overheads	$679,550

Based on the data above, the machine hour absorption rate is (to the nearest $)

$ [   ] per machine hour.   **(2 marks)**

---

3   A company absorbs overheads on machine hours. In a period, actual machine hours were 22,435, actual overheads were $496,500 and there was over absorption of $64,375.

The budgeted overhead absorption rate was $ [   ] per machine hour (to the nearest $).   **(2 marks)**

---

4   The management accountant of a company is preparing the overhead analysis for the forthcoming year, 20X4. The company has two production cost centres, Machining and Assembly, and two service cost centres, Maintenance and Stores. Relevant information is as follows.

	Machining	Assembly	Maintenance	Stores
Number of employees	25	32	8	4
Number of stores requisitions	22,100	8,000	7,525	–
Area occupied (sq m)	5,000	3,000	1,000	800
Maintenance hours	9,200	2,800	1,450	1,050
Machine hours	31,000	9,000	1,000	1,000
Direct labour hours	8,000	15,000		

Using the information given above, complete the overhead analysis sheet shown below.

Overhead analysis sheet 20X4

Overhead item	Basis of apportionment	Machining $	Assembly $	Maintenance $	Stores $	Total $
Various	Allocation	84,000	71,000	28,000	31,000	214,000
Power	Machine hrs	A= [ ]				21,000
Rent	B= [ ]		C= [ ]			29,400
Canteen costs	D= [ ]					8,280

(2 marks each)

---

5   A company absorbs fixed production overheads in one of its departments on the basis of machine hours. There were 100,000 budgeted machine hours for the forthcoming period. The fixed production overhead absorption rate was $2.50 per machine hour.

During the period, the following actual results were recorded:

Standard machine hours	110,000
Fixed production overheads	$300,000

Fixed production overhead was [   ] absorbed by $ [   ]   **(2 marks)**

6   A company absorbs overheads on the basis of direct labour hours. The overhead absorption rate for the period has been based on budgeted overheads of $165,000 and 55,000 direct labour hours.

During the period, overheads of $180,000 were incurred and 60,000 direct labour hours were worked.

	True	False
Overhead was $15,000 over absorbed	☐	☐
Overhead was $15,000 under absorbed	☐	☐
No under or over absorption occurred	☐	☐
The overhead expenditure variance is $15,000 adverse	☐	☐

(2 marks)

7 | Budgeted machine hours | 17,000 |
|---|---|
| Actual machine hours | 21,250 |
| Budgeted overheads | $85,000 |
| Actual overheads | $110,500 |

Based on the data above:

(a)   The machine hour absorption rate is $ ☐ per hour.   (2 marks)

(b)   The overhead for the period was ☐ absorbed by $ ☐   (2 marks)

8   The accounting entries at the end of a period for production overhead under-absorbed would be (tick the correct boxes):

	Debit	Credit	No entry in this a/c
Overhead control account	☐	☐	☐
Work in progress account	☐	☐	☐
Income statement	☐	☐	☐

(2 marks)

9   A company absorbs overheads based on units produced. In one period 110,000 units were produced and the actual overheads were $500,000. Overheads were $50,000 over absorbed in the period.

The overhead absorption rate was $ ☐ (to 2 decimal places).

(2 marks)

10   A company operates a standard costing system and absorbs overheads on the basis of standard machine hours. Details of budgeted and actual figures are as follows.

	Budget	Actual
Overheads	$1,250,000	$1,005,000
Output	250,000 units	220,000 units
Machine hours	500,000 hours	450,000 hours

Overheads were ☐ absorbed by $ ☐

(2 marks)

11   The following information relates to a company's main cost centres.

	Machining	Assembly	Maintenance	Stores	Total
Total overheads	$130,000	$122,000	$39,150	$42,000	$333,150

The maintenance cost centre overhead is to be reapportioned to the other three cost centres on the basis of the number of maintenance hours.

The stores cost centre overhead is to be apportioned to the two production cost centres on the basis of the number of stores requisitions.

	Machining	Assembly	Maintenance	Stores
Number of employees	25	32	8	4
Number of stores requisitions	22,100	8,000	7,525	–
Area occupied (sq m)	5,000	3,000	1,000	800
Maintenance hours	9,200	2,800	1,450	1,050
Machine hours	31,000	9,000	1,000	1,000
Direct labour hours	8,000	15,000		

To the nearest cent, the overhead absorption rate for the machining department was $ ☐ for each machine hour.

(2 marks)

---

12   Which of the following statements about overhead absorption rates are *not* true?

Not true

(i)   They are predetermined in advance for each period   ☐

(ii)   They are used to charge overheads to products   ☐

(iii)   They are based on actual data for each period   ☐

(iv)   They are used to control overhead costs   ☐

(2 marks)

---

13   A company has three main departments – Casting, Dressing and Assembly – and for period 3 has prepared the following production overhead budgets.

Department	Casting	Dressing	Assembly
Production overheads	$225,000	$175,000	$93,000
Expected production hours	7,500	7,000	6,200

During period 3, actual results were as follows.

Department	Casting	Dressing	Assembly
Production overheads	$229,317	$182,875	$94,395
Production hours	7,950	7,280	6,696

(a)   The overhead absorption rate for the Casting department was $ ☐ per production hour.

(b)   The overhead in the Dressing department in period 3 was ☐ absorbed by $ ☐ .

(2 marks)

(Total = 34 marks)

28 Marginal and absorption costing   16 mins

1   The overhead absorption rate for product M is $8 per machine hour. Each unit of M requires 6 machine
    hours. Inventories of product M last period were:

	Units
Opening inventory	2,400
Closing inventory	2,700

    The absorption costing profit for the period for product M will be:

    ☐   higher

    ☐   lower   **(2 marks)**

    than the marginal costing profit. The difference between the two profit figures will be

    $ ☐   **(2 marks)**

2   In a period where opening inventories were 5,000 units and closing inventories 8,000 units, a firm had a
    profit of $130,000 using absorption costing. If the fixed overhead absorption rate was $4 per unit:

    The profit using marginal costing would be $ ☐   **(2 marks)**

3   A company produces a single product. The managers currently use absorption costing, but are considering
    using marginal costing in future.

    The fixed production overhead absorption rate is $68 per unit. There were 200 units of opening inventory for
    the period and 360 units of closing inventory.

    If marginal costing principles were applied, the profit for the period would be ☐ than the profit

    reported under absorption costing. The difference between the two profits figures would be $ ☐
                                                                         (2 marks each)

4   A company has opening inventories of 825 units and closing stocks of 1,800 units in a period. The profit
    based on marginal costing was $50,400 and profit using absorption costing was $60,150.

    The fixed overhead absorption rate per unit (to the nearest $) is $ ☐   **(2 marks)**

                                                                         (Total = 12 marks)

29 Process costing   24 mins

1   A food manufacturing process has a normal wastage of 10% of input. In a period, 3,000 kg of material were
    input and there was an abnormal loss of 75 kg. No inventories are held at the beginning or end of the
    process.

    The quantity of good production achieved was ☐ kg.   **(2 marks)**

2   A company makes a product, which passes through a single process.

    Details of the process for the last period are as follows:

Materials	5,000 kg at 50p per kg
Labour	$700
Production overheads	200% of labour

    Normal losses are 10% of input in the process, and without further processing any losses can be sold as
    scrap for 20c per kg.

    The output for the period was 4,200 kg from the process.

    There was no work in progress at the beginning or end of the period.

(a)   The value credited to the process account for the scrap value of the normal loss for the period will be
$ [   ] (to the nearest $)   **(2 marks)**

(b)   The value of the abnormal loss for the period is $ [   ] (to the nearest $)   **(2 marks)**

---

3   A company makes a product in a single process. The following data are available for the latest period.

Opening work in progress: 300 units		Closing work in progress: 150 units	
Valued as follows:	$	Degree of completion:	%
Material	3,600	Material	100
Labour	1,600	Labour	50
Overhead	400	Overhead	30

Units added and costs incurred during the period:

Material: 750 units	$11,625
Labour	$6,200
Overhead	$4,325
Losses	nil

WP Co uses the weighted average method of inventory valuation.

(a)   The cost per equivalent unit of material is $ [   ] (to 2 decimal places)   **(2 marks)**

(b)   The cost per equivalent unit of labour is $ [   ] (to 2 decimal places)   **(2 marks)**

(c)   The cost per equivalent unit of overheads is $ [   ] (to 2 decimal places)   **(2 marks)**

---

4   A company makes one product, which passes though a single process. The details of the process for period 2 were as follows.

There were 400 units of opening work-in-progress, valued as follows.

Material	$49,000
Labour	$23,000
Production overheads	$3,800

No losses were expected in the process.

During the period, 900 units were added to the process, and the following costs occurred.

Material	$198,000 (900 units)
Labour	$139,500
Production overheads	$79,200

There were 500 units of closing work-in-progress, which were 100% complete for material, 90% complete for labour and 40% complete for overheads. No losses were incurred in the process.

PP Co uses weighted average costing.

(a)   The number of equivalent units used when calculating the cost per unit in relation to labour is
[   ] equivalent units   **(2 marks)**

(b)   The value of completed output for the period was $ [   ] (to the nearest $)   **(2 marks)**

---

5   340 litres of Chemical X were produced in a period. There is a normal loss of 10% of the material input into the process. There was an abnormal loss in the period of 5% of the material input.

[   ] litres of material were input into the process during the period.

(2 marks)

(Total = 18 marks)

30 Process costing, joint products and by-products   16 mins

1   Chemicals A, B and C are produced from a single joint process. The information below relates to the month of January 20X2.

Input into process: Direct materials 16,000 litres, cost $120,000
                      Direct labour $240,000
                      Factory overheads are absorbed at 100% of prime cost

Output from process: Scrap normally accounts for 10% of input and can be sold for $20 per litre. Actual scrap in January 20X2 was 10% of input. Proceeds from the sale of scrap is credited to the process account.

                      Chemical A – 7,200 litres
                      Chemical B – 4,320 litres
                      Chemical C – 2,880 litres

The selling prices of the three chemicals are:

Chemical A $50 per litre
Chemical B $40 per litre
Chemical C $30 per litre

(a)   Using the relative sales value method for splitting joint costs, the total cost of chemicals A, B and C are as follows.

Chemical A = $ [   ]   **(2 marks)**

Chemical B = $ [   ]   **(2 marks)**

Chemical C = $ [   ]   **(2 marks)**

(b)   Using the volume method for splitting joint costs, the total cost of chemicals A, B and C are as follows.

Chemical A = $ [   ]   **(2 marks)**

Chemical B = $ [   ]   **(2 marks)**

Chemical C = $ [   ]   **(2 marks)**

                                                      (Total = 12 marks)

31 Job costing and service costing   14 mins

1   A technical writer is to set up her own business. She anticipates working a 40-hour week and taking four weeks' holiday per year. General expenses of the business are expected to be $10,000 per year, and she has set herself a target of $40,000 a year salary.

Assuming that only 90% of her time worked will be chargeable to customers, her charge for each hour of writing (to the nearest penny) should be $ [   ]   **(2 marks)**

2   Which of the following is/are characteristics of job costing?

[ ]   Customer-driven production
[ ]   Complete production possible within a single accounting period
[ ]   Homogeneous products   **(1 mark)**

3   A company operates a job costing system. The company's standard net profit margin is 20 per cent of sales value.

The estimated costs for job B124 are as follows.

Direct materials   3 kg @ $5 per kg
Direct labour   4 hours @ $9 per hour

Production overheads are budgeted to be $240,000 for the period, to be recovered on the basis of a total of 30,000 labour hours.

Other overheads, related to selling, distribution and administration, are budgeted to be $150,000 for the period. They are to be recovered on the basis of the total budgeted production cost of $750,000 for the period.

The total cost of job B124 is $ ☐ (to the nearest penny)   **(2 marks)**

---

4   Which of the following are characteristics of service costing?

☐   High levels of indirect costs as a proportion of total cost
☐   Cost units are often intangible
☐   Use of composite cost units
☐   Use of equivalent units   **(2 marks)**

---

5   Which of the following would be suitable cost units for a hospital?

☐   Patient/day
☐   Operating theatre hour
☐   Ward
☐   X-ray department
☐   Outpatient visit   **(2 marks)**

---

6   In which of the following situation(s) will job costing normally be used?

☐   Production is continuous
☐   Production of the product can be completed in a single accounting period
☐   Production relates to a single special order   **(1 mark)**

                                                            (Total = 10 marks)

---

32 Budgeting   **47 mins**

1   A principal budget factor is:

☐   The factor on which total annual expenditure is highest
☐   The factor with the highest unit cost
☐   A factor which limits the activities of an undertaking
☐   A factor common to all budget centres
☐   A factor controllable by the manager of the budget centre   **(2 marks)**

---

2   A carpet fitting firm estimates that it will take 3,520 actual active hours to carpet an office block. Unavoidable interruptions and lost time are estimated to take 20% of the operatives' time. If the wage rate is $7 per hour, the budgeted labour cost is $ ☐ (to the nearest $)   **(2 marks)**

---

3   A job requires 4,590 actual labour hours for completion and it is anticipated that there will be 10% idle time. If the wage rate is $8 per hour, the budgeted labour cost for the job is $ [   ] (to the nearest $)

(2 marks)

4   A company is currently preparing its production budget for product U for the forthcoming year.

Budgeted sales of product U are 140,000 units. Opening inventory is estimated to be 11,500 units and the company wishes to reduce inventory at the end of the year by 20%.

The budgeted number of units of product U to be produced is [   ] units.   (2 marks)

5   A company manufactures a single product and an extract from their flexed budget for production costs is as follows.

	Activity level	
	80%	90%
	$	$
Direct material	2,400	2,700
Direct labour	2,120	2,160
Production overhead	4,060	4,080
	8,580	8,940

The total production cost allowance in a budget flexed at the 83% level of activity would be $ [   ] (to the nearest $)   (2 marks)

6   A company budgets to make 4,000 units and estimates that the standard material cost per unit will be $6. In fact 4,800 units are produced at a material cost of $29,760. For the purposes of budgetary control of the expenditure on material cost, the two figures that should be compared are:

Actual $ [   ] (to the nearest $)

Budget $ [   ] (to the nearest $)   (2 marks)

7   The following cost per unit details have been extracted from the selling overhead cost budget for year 8.

Sales (units)	2,400	3,000
Selling overhead ($ per unit)	16.25	15.00

The budget cost allowance for selling overhead for a sales level of 2,800 units is $ [   ] (to the nearest $)

(2 marks)

8   For a passenger coach company, 8,000 passengers were carried during October and variable costs were in line with budget. The budgeted variable cost per passenger is $0.20 and the total cost of $22,100 meant that fixed costs were $4,500 below budget.

The budgeted level of fixed costs for October was $ [   ] (to the nearest $)   (2 marks)

9   Which one of the following statements about a fixed budget is/are correct? A fixed budget is:

☐   A budget which ignores inflation
☐   A budget for fixed assets
☐   A budget which is most generally used for planning purposes
☐   A budget for a single level of activity
☐   A budget for fixed costs   (2 marks)

10 A company plans to sell 1,800 units of product F next year. Opening inventory of F is budgeted to be 150 units and Lardy Co budgets to increase inventory by 10% by the end of the year. How many units of product F should be produced next year?

◻ units

(2 marks)

11 When preparing a materials purchases budget, the quantity to be purchased equals

materials usage ◻ opening inventory of materials ◻ closing inventory of materials

(1 mark)

12 The quantity of material in the material purchases budget is greater than the quantity of material in the material usage budget. Which of the following statements can be inferred from this situation?

◻ Wastage of material occurs in the production process
◻ Finished goods inventories are budgeted to decrease
◻ Finished goods inventories are budgeted to increase
◻ Raw materials inventories are budgeted to decrease
◻ Raw materials inventories are budgeted to increase

(2 marks)

13 A flexible budget is

◻ a budget which by recognising different cost behaviour patterns is designed to change as the volume of activity changes

◻ a budget for a defined period of time which includes planned revenues, expenses, assets, liabilities and cash flow

◻ a budget which is prepared for a period of one year which is reviewed monthly, whereby each time actual results are reported, a further forecast period is added and the intermediate period forecasts are updated

◻ a budget of semi-variable production costs only

(2 marks)

14 A company is currently preparing a material usage budget for the forthcoming year for material Z that will be used in product XX. The production director has confirmed that the production budget for product XX will be 10,000 units.

Each unit of product XX requires 4 kgs of material Z. Opening inventory of material Z is budgeted to be 3,000 kgs and the company wishes to reduce inventory at the end of the year by 25%.

The usage budget for material Z for the forthcoming year is ◻ kgs

(2 marks)

15 Which of the following would be included in the master budget?

◻ Budgeted income statement
◻ All functional budgets
◻ Budgeted cash flow
◻ Budgeted statement of financial position

(2 marks)

16   A company manufactures and sells one product which used 4kg of raw material.

Its budget for the next period shows:

	Units
Sales	9,500
Opening inventory (finished goods)	2,000
Closing inventory (finished goods)	1,500

	Kg
Opening inventory (raw materials)	12,500
Closing inventory (raw materials)	13,250

How many kg of raw material will it need to purchase? ☐ kg   (2 marks)

The following information relates to questions 17 and 18:

A company is preparing its budgets for the forthcoming year.

The estimated sales for the first four months of the forthcoming year are as follows:

Month 1	6,000 units
Month 2	7,000 units
Month 3	5,500 units
Month 4	6,000 units

40% of each month's sales units are to be produced in the month of sale and the balance is to be produced in the previous month.

50% of the direct materials required for each month's production will be purchased in the previous month and the balance in the month of production.

The direct material cost is budgeted to be $5 per unit.

17   The production budget in units for Month 1 will be ☐ units

(2 marks)

18   The material cost budget for Month 2 will be $ ☐

(2 marks)

(Total = 35 marks)

33 Standard costing   10 mins

1   A company is planning to make 120,000 units per period of a new product. The following standards have been set:

	Per unit
Direct material A	1.2 kgs at $11 per kg
Direct material B	4.7 kgs at $6 per kg
Direct labour:	
Operation 1	42 minutes
Operation 2	37 minutes
Operation 3	11 minutes

Overheads are absorbed at the rate of $30 per labour hour. All direct operatives are paid at the rate of $8 per hour. Attainable work hours are less than clock hours, so the 500 direct operatives have been budgeted for 400 hours each in the period.

Actual results for the period were:

Production	126,000 units
Direct labour	cost $1.7m for 215,000 clock hours
Material A	cost $1.65m for 150,000 kgs
Material B	cost $3.6m for 590,000 kgs

(a)   The standard cost for one unit is $ [ ]   **(2 marks)**

(b)   Attainable work hours per period are [ ] hours, which represents [ ] % of clock hours.   **(2 marks)**

(c)   (i)   The labour rate variance for the period is $ [ ].   **(1 mark)**

       (ii)   A realistic labour efficiency variance for the period is $ [ ].   **(2 marks)**

(Total = 7 marks)

34 Basic variance analysis   **38 mins**

1   A company has the following budget and actual data.

Budgeted fixed production overhead cost	$380,000
Budgeted production (units)	76,000
Budgeted labour hours	76,000
Actual fixed production overhead cost	$409,750
Actual production (units)	74,500
Actual labour hours	76,500

(a)   The fixed production overhead expenditure variance is $ [ ]   *Favourable* [ ]   *Adverse* [ ]   **(2 marks)**

(b)   The fixed production overhead volume efficiency variance is $ [ ]   *Favourable* [ ]   *Adverse* [ ]   **(2 marks)**

(c)   The fixed production overhead volume capacity variance is $ [ ]   *Favourable* [ ]   *Adverse* [ ]   **(2 marks)**

(d)   The fixed production overhead volume variance is $ [ ]   *Favourable* [ ]   *Adverse* [ ]   **(2 marks)**

2   Which of the following statements is correct with regard to the material price variance calculation?

The material price variance is calculated by comparing the:

[ ]   Actual quantity purchased at standard cost with the actual quantity used at standard cost
[ ]   Actual quantity purchased at actual cost with the actual quantity used at standard cost
[ ]   Actual quantity purchased at actual cost with the actual quantity purchased at standard cost

(1 mark)

3 A company has a standard direct labour cost of $18 for a single unit of production. The standard wage is $9 per hour.

During June, 1,100 units were produced. Direct labour was paid for 2,400 hours at a total cost of $20,400.

(a)

		Favourable	Adverse
The direct labour rate variance for June was	$		

(1 mark)

(b)

		Favourable	Adverse
The direct labour efficiency variance for June was	$		

(2 marks)

---

4 Extracts from a company's records from last period are as follows.

	Budget	Actual
Production	1,925 units	2,070 units
Variable production overhead cost	$13,475	$13,455
Labour hours worked	3,850	2,990

		Favourable	Adverse
The variable production overhead expenditure variance for last period is	$		

(2 marks)

---

5 A company operates a standard costing system for production and uses variance analysis to identify deviations from budget.

Information with regard to variable overhead costs for the period was as follows:

Budgeted cost	$180,000
Actual costs	$173,800
Labour hours:	
Budgeted	90,000 hours
Actual	82,650 hours

Variable overheads are absorbed on a direct labour hour basis.

The variable overhead expenditure variance was $ ☐

☐ Favourable

☐ Adverse

(2 marks)

---

6 A company's budgetary control report for last month is as follows:

	Fixed budget $	Flexed budget $	Actual results $
Direct costs	61,100	64,155	67,130
Production overhead	55,000	56,700	54,950
Other overhead	10,000	10,000	11,500
	126,100	130,855	133,580

		Favourable	Adverse
The volume variance for last month was $			

(2 marks)

7   A company's budgetary control report for last month is as follows:

	Fixed budget	Flexed budget	Actual results
	$	$	$
Direct costs	61,100	64,155	67,130
Production overhead	55,000	56,700	54,950
Other overhead	10,000	10,000	11,500
	126,100	130,855	133,580
		Favourable	*Adverse*

The expenditure variance for last month was $ [＿＿＿]   [＿＿＿] [＿＿＿]

(2 marks)

8   In a period 4,800 units were made and there was an adverse labour efficiency variance of $26,000. Workers were paid $8 per hour, total wages were $294,800 and there was a nil rate variance.

Standard hours per unit = [＿＿＿]   (2 marks)

9   In a period, there was an adverse labour efficiency variance of $27,000. The standard wages rate per hour was $6 and 30 hours were allowed for each unit as standard. Actual labour hours worked were 52,500.

The number of units produced in the period was [＿＿＿]   (2 marks)

10   A company purchased 6,850 kgs of material at a total cost of $32,195. The material price variance was $1,370 adverse.

The standard price per kg was $ [＿＿＿] (to the nearest cent)   (2 marks)

11   If a more expensive material than the standard material is used in the production of product A, there will be an adverse material price variance. Which of the following might be an interrelated variance? Put a tick in all boxes that apply.

[＿＿＿]   A favourable sales volume variance

[＿＿＿]   A favourable labour efficiency variance

[＿＿＿]   A favourable material usage variance

[＿＿＿]   A favourable sales price variance

(2 marks)

(Total = 28 marks)

35 Further variance analysis

36 mins

1   Last period, the actual output of 22,000 units and the actual fixed costs of $42,000 were exactly as budgeted. However, the total actual expenditure of $140,000 was $10,000 higher than the budget.

The budgeted variable cost per unit was $ [   ] (to the nearest $)   **(2 marks)**

2   A company has prepared the following standard cost information for one unit of product Orange.

Direct materials	2kg @ $13/kg	$26.00
Direct labour	3.3 hours @ $4/hour	$13.20
Fixed overheads	4 hours @ $2.50	$10.00

Actual results for the period were recorded as follows:

Production	4,820 units
Materials – 9,720 kg	$121,500
Labour – 15,800 hours	$66,360
Fixed overheads	$41,700

All of the materials were purchased and used during the period.

(a)   The direct material price and usage variances are:

		Favourable	Adverse
Material price	$ [ ]	[ ]	[ ]
Material usage	$ [ ]	[ ]	[ ]

(2 marks)

(b)   The direct labour rate and efficiency variances are:

		Favourable	Adverse
Labour rate	$ [ ]	[ ]	[ ]
Labour efficiency	$ [ ]	[ ]	[ ]

(2 marks)

(c)   The total fixed production overhead variance is

	Favourable	Adverse
$ [ ]	[ ]	[ ]

(2 marks)

3   A company manufactures a single product. An extract from a variance control report together with relevant standard cost data is shown below.

Standard selling price per unit	$140
Standard direct material cost (10 kg × $4 per kg)	$40 per unit
Budgeted total material cost of sales	$4,600 per month
Budgeted profit margin	$9,775 per month

Actual results for January

Sales revenue $12,400   Production   100 units

There was no change in inventory levels during the month.

(a)   The selling price variance for January was $ [   ]   **(1 mark)**

(b)   The sales volume variance for January was $ [   ]   **(2 marks)**

4   A company is reviewing actual performance to identify any significant differences against budget.

The following standard cost information is relevant.

	$ per unit
Selling price	75
Direct materials	10
Direct labour	15
Fixed production overheads	4
Variable production overheads	2
Fixed selling costs	4
Variable selling costs	3
	38

Budgeted sales units   7,200   Actual sales units   8,400

The favourable sales volume variance using marginal costing is $ [   ]   **(2 marks)**

---

5   Standard cost and selling price data for a product are as follows.

	$ per unit	$ per unit
Selling price		32.00
Direct cost	16.20	
Fixed overhead cost	4.80	
		21.00
Profit		11.00

Data for the latest period were as follows.

	Budget	Actual
Sales units	780	830
Sales revenue		$26,480

(a)   *Favourable*   *Adverse*

The selling price variance for
last period is $ [   ]   [   ]   [   ]

(2 marks)

(b)   *Favourable*   *Adverse*

The sales volume profit variance
for last period is $ [   ]   [   ]   [   ]

(2 marks)

---

6   Product X has a standard direct material cost as follows.

10 kilograms of material Y at $10 per kilogram = $100 per unit of X.

During period 4, 1,000 units of X were manufactured, using 11,700 kilograms of material Y which cost $98,600.

Required

Calculate the following variances.

	Favourable	*Adverse*
The direct material price variance	[ ] [ ]	[ ]
The direct material usage variance	[ ] [ ]	[ ]

(2 marks)

7   A company is planning to make 120,000 units per period of a new product. The following standards have been set for direct materials.

	Per unit
Direct material A	1.2 kgs at $11 per kg
Direct material B	4.7 kgs at $6 per kg

Actual results for the period were:

Production	126,000 units
Material A	cost $1.65m for 150,000 kgs
Material B	cost $3.6m for 590,000 kgs

The material cost variances for the period are:

	Material price variance	Material usage variance
Material A	$ ▢	$ ▢
Material B	$ ▢	$ ▢

(2 marks)

8   In a period, there was an adverse labour efficiency variance of $27,000. The standard wages rate per hour was $6 and 30 hours were allowed for each unit as standard. Actual labour hours worked were 52,500.

The number of units produced in the period was ▢

(2 marks)

9   In a period 4,920 units were made with a standard labour allowance of 6.5 hours per unit at $5 per hour. Actual wages were $6 per hour and there was a favourable efficiency variance of $36,000.

The number of labour hours actually worked was ▢

(2 marks)

10 The variable overhead production cost of product X is as follows.

2 hours at $1.50 = $3 per unit

During the month, 400 units of product X were made. The labour force worked 820 hours, of which 60 hours were recorded as idle time. The variable overhead cost was $1,230.

		Favourable	Adverse
The variable overhead expenditure variance is $ ▢		▢	▢
The variable overhead efficiency variance is $ ▢		▢	▢

(2 marks)

(Total = 27 marks)

36 Cost-volume-profit (CVP) analysis   22 mins

1   A company sells a single product. In the coming month, it is budgeted that this product will generate a total revenue of $300,000 with a contribution of $125,000. Fixed costs are budgeted at $100,000 for the month.

The margin of safety is ⬚ %   **(2 marks)**

2   A company makes and sells a single product which has a selling price of $26, prime costs are $10 and overheads (all fixed) are absorbed at 50% of prime cost. Fixed overheads are $50,000.

The breakeven point (to the nearest whole unit) is ⬚ units   **(2 marks)**

3

Profit/loss
($)

A

L

C   Level of activity

D

B

In the above profit-volume chart, the contribution at level of activity L can be identified as ⬚ (insert A, B, C or D as appropriate).   **(2 marks)**

4   A company manufactures a product which has a selling price of $14 and a variable cost of $6 per unit. The company incurs annual fixed costs of $24,400. Annual sales demand is 8,000 units.

New production methods are under consideration, which would cause a 30% increase in fixed costs and a reduction of $1 in the variable cost per unit. The new production methods would result in a superior product and would enable the sales price to be increased to $15 per unit.

(a)   If the organisation implements the new production methods and wishes to achieve the same profit as that under the existing method, the number of units to be produced and sold annually would reduce by ⬚ % (to one decimal place).   **(2 marks)**

(b)   If the change in production methods were to take place, the margin of safety as a percentage of the original budgeted annual sales would be ⬚ % (to one decimal place)   **(2 marks)**

5   A company has calculated its margin of safety as 25% on budgeted sales. Budgeted sales are 10,000 units per month, and budgeted contribution is $40 per unit.

The budgeted fixed costs = $ ⬚   **(2 marks)**

6   A company wishes to make a profit of $400,000. It has fixed costs of $200,000 with a P/V ratio of 0.8 and a selling price of $15 per unit.

In order to make a profit of $400,000, Twenty Co will need to earn $ ⬚ sales revenue.   **(2 marks)**

7   A company sells product V, for which data is as follows.

	$ per unit
Selling price	108
Variable cost	73

Period fixed costs amount to $196,000, and the budgeted profit is $476,000 per period.

If the selling price and variable cost per unit increase by 10% and 7% respectively, the sales volume will need to [_____] to [_____] units in order to achieve the original budgeted profit for the period.

(2 marks)

(Total = 16 marks)

37 Relevant costing and decision-making   27 mins

1   A company is about to tender for a one off contract. Requirements for this contract have been established as follows:

		$
Labour:	Skilled workers (100 hours at $9/hour)	900
	Semi skilled workers (200 hours at $5/hour)	1,000
	Management (20 hours at $20/hour)	400
Materials:	N (100 litres at $4.50/litre)	450
	T (300kg at $7/kg)	2,100
		4,850

The skilled workers will be diverted from production of product P with resulting loss of sales. Each unit of P generates a contribution of $7 and takes two skilled labour hours to make. Semi skilled workers will be hired as required. The management cost represents an allocated amount for hours expected to be spent. At the moment the management team has spare capacity.

Current inventories of material N are 200 litres and it is in continuous use by the business. It cost $4.50/litre originally but new supplies now cost $4.00/litre due to improved negotiating by the purchasing department. It could be sold as scrap for $2/litre.

The current inventories of material T are 200 kg which cost $7/kg some years ago but has not been used by the business for some time. If not used for the contract it would be scrapped for $4/kg. The current purchase price is $8/kg.

(a)   The relevant cost of labour is $ [_____]   **(2 marks)**

(b)   The relevant cost of materials is $ [_____]   **(2 marks)**

2   A firm has some material which originally cost $45,000. It has a scrap value of $12,500 but if reworked at a cost of $7,500, it could be sold for $17,500. There is no other foreseen use for the material.

The relevant cost of using the material for a special job is $ [_____]   **(2 marks)**

3   A company makes three products, all of which use the same machine which is available for 50,000 hours per period.

The standard costs of the products per unit are as follows.

	Product A $	Product B $	Product C $
Direct materials	70	40	80
Direct labour:			
Machinists ($8 per hour)	48	32	56
Assemblers ($6 per hour)	36	40	42
Total variable cost	154	112	178
Selling price per unit	$200	$158	$224
Maximum demand (units)	3,000	2,500	5,000

Fixed costs are $300,000 per period.

(a)   The deficiency in machine hours for the next period is ☐ hours   **(2 marks)**

(b)   In order to determine the priority ranking of the products, it is necessary to calculate the contribution per machine hour (as machine hours are the limiting factor).

(i)   Contribution per machine hour (Product A) = $ ☐   **(2 marks)**

(ii)   Contribution per machine hour (Product B) = $ ☐   **(2 marks)**

(iii)   Contribution per machine hour (Product C) = $ ☐   **(2 marks)**

State your answers to 2 decimal places.

(c)   If the optimum production plan includes manufacturing 2,500 units of product B, this product will generate a contribution of $ ☐ (to the nearest $)   **(2 marks)**

---

4   A company is considering its options with regard to a machine which cost $120,000 four years ago.

If sold, the machine would generate scrap proceeds of $150,000. If kept, this machine would generate net income of $180,000.

The current replacement cost for this machine is $210,000.

The relevant cost of the machine is:

☐ $120,000   ☐ $180,000

☐ $150,000   ☐ $210,000   **(2 marks)**

---

5   A company manufactures three products, the selling price and cost details of which are as follows.

	Product M $ per unit	Product F $ per unit	Product S $ per unit
Selling price	129	137	141
Direct material ($8/kg)	32	16	40
Direct labour ($6/hour)	30	36	24
Variable overhead	10	12	8
Fixed overhead	15	20	14

In a period when direct labour is restricted in supply, the most and least profitable use of direct labour are:

Most profitable product   ☐

Least profitable product   ☐   **(2 marks)**

(Total = 20 marks)

38 Linear programming

1 In graphing the constraints $4X + 5Y \le 6$:

    (a)   The line cuts the x axis at   X = [ ]

    (b)   The line cuts the y axis at   Y = [ ]

    State your answers to 1 decimal place.   **(2 marks)**

2 A farmer wants to find the possible amounts of two different chemicals, A and B, to use on arable land, and is using linear programming. He must use at least 50 kg of A per hectare. The weight of B per hectare may be between two and five times the weight of A per hectare. The total weight of chemicals per hectare must not exceed 1,000 kg.

If a = kg per hectare of chemical A, and b = kg per hectare of chemical B, complete the following constraints.

    (a) $a \ge$ [ ]

    (b) $b \ge$ [ ] a

    (c) $b \le$ [ ] a

    (d) $a + b \le$ [ ]   **(2 marks)**

3 (a) A company is using linear programming to decide how many units of each of its two products to make each week. Weekly production will be x units of product X and y units of product Y. At least 100 units of X must be produced each week, and at least three times as many units of Y as of X must be produced each week. Each unit of X requires 45 minutes of labour, and each unit of Y requires 4 hours of labour. There are 10,000 hours of labour available each week. Complete the following constraints.

    [ ] X + [ ] y $\le$ 10,000

            X $\ge$ [ ]

            y $\ge$ [ ] X

    (2 marks)

    (b) The company also wishes to minimise the cost of telephone calls made. 50% of calls in peak hours cost $1 each and the remainder of such calls cost $1.50 each. 40% of calls at other times cost 80p each, 50% of them cost 90p each, and 10% of them cost $1 each. These proportions cannot be varied, though the total number of calls made in peak hours and of calls made at other times can be. If x = the number of calls made each day in peak hours, and y = the number of calls made each day at other times, the office manager's objective is to minimise:

    [ ] X + [ ] y

    (2 marks)

(Total = 8 marks)

Mixed Bank questions

Mixed Bank Questions

Mixed Bank 1

1   The following data relate to Product D.

Material cost per unit	$20.00
Labour cost per unit	$69.40
Production overhead cost per machine hour	$12.58
Machine hours per unit	14
General overhead absorption rate	8% of total production cost

What is the total cost per unit of Product D, to the nearest $0.01?

A $176.12
B $265.52
C $286.76
D $300.12

2   A product is made in two consecutive processes. Data for the latest period are as follows:

	Process 1	Process 2
Input (kg)	47,000	42,000
Normal loss (% of input)	8	5
Output (kg)	42,000	38,915

No work in progress is held at any time in either process.

The abnormal loss or abnormal gain arising in each process during the period was:

	Process 1	Process 2
A	Abnormal loss	Abnormal loss
B	Abnormal loss	Abnormal gain
C	Abnormal gain	Abnormal loss
D	Abnormal gain	Abnormal gain

3   The following information is available for a company in the latest period.

	Original budget	Flexed budget	Actual results
Sales and production (units)	11,200	9,500	9,500
	$'000	$'000	$'000
Sales revenue	224.0	190.0	209.0
Direct material	56.0	47.5	57.0
Direct labour	66.0	57.5	56.1
Overhead	27.4	24.0	28.0
Profit	74.6	61.0	67.9

Which of the following statements is correct?

A   Budgeted production volumes were achieved during the period.
B   Direct labour is a variable cost
C   The actual selling price per unit exceeded the standard selling price per unit
D   Direct material cost savings were achieved against the budget cost allowance.

4   Variable costs are conventionally deemed to

A   be constant per unit of output
B   vary per unit of output as production volume changes
C   be constant in total when production volume changes
D   vary, in total, from period to period when production is constant

5

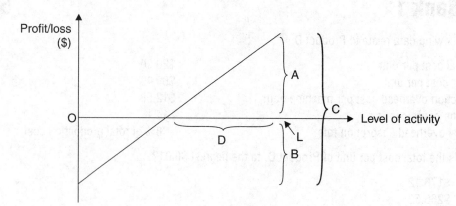

In the above profit-volume chart, the contribution at level of activity L can be read as:

A   distance A
B   distance B
C   distance C
D   distance D

6   In a period, 28,644 kg of material were used at a total standard cost of $114,576. The material usage variance was $1,140 favourable.

What was the standard allowed weight of material for the period?

| | kg

7   Which of the following is/are classified as direct materials?

| | Cleaning materials used to clean the factory floor

| | Component parts ordered for a specific job

| | Part finished goods transferred into a process from an earlier process

| | Maintenance materials used to repair machines

8   Which of the following is/are descriptions of a semi-variable cost?

| | Rental of a photocopier; the rent cost is $250 per month if the number of copies taken is less than 8,000. If the number of copies exceeds 8,000 the monthly rental increases to $300

| | Hire of a delivery vehicle: the hire cost is $800 per month, plus $0.07 per mile travelled

| | A piecework scheme with a guaranteed day rate

9   The laundry operation of a major hospital wishes to develop a model to predict its total costs in a period. The following costs have been recorded at two activity levels in the past.

	Number of items laundered (L)	Total cost (TC) $
Period 1	10,400	4,880
Period 2	11,650	5,130

The total cost model for a period could be represented as:

TC = $[_____] + $[_____] L

10   Which of the following are advantages of job costing for service department costs?

[_____] Realistic apportionment of expenses to responsible department

[_____] Improved information for the budget process

[_____] Formal contracts must be drawn up by service users

11   An internet service provider operates a customer service centre to deal with domestic and industrial customers' enquiries about their internet connection.

A standard time is allowed for dealing with each enquiry and employees are paid a bonus for any time saved compared with the standard allowance

The following data relates to the bonus scheme.

Basic daily pay for each employee   8 hours @ $15 per hour
Standard time allowed to deal with one enquiry   10 minutes
Bonus payable at basic hourly rate   30% of time saved

The bonus payable to an employee who deals with 60 enquiries in a single day would be $[_____].

12   The standard price of material K is $3 per kg.

Inventories of material K are recorded at standard price. During June, 30,000 kg of K were purchased for $105,000 on 12 June, of which 20,000 kg were issued to production on 28 June. The correct entries to record the issue to production are:

		$
[_____]	Debit work-in-progress account	60,000
[_____]	Debit material price variance account	15,000
[_____]	Debit work-in-progress account	70,000
[_____]	Debit material price variance account	10,000
[_____]	Credit material stores account	70,000
[_____]	Credit payables control account	15,000
[_____]	Credit material stores account	15,000
[_____]	Credit material stores account	60,000

13 A company makes and sells two products, Alpha and Beta. The following information is available for period 1.

	Production Units	Sales Units
Alpha	2,500	2,300
Beta	1,750	1,600

	Product	
	Alpha	Beta
	$	$
Unit selling price	90	75
Unit variable costs		
Direct materials	15	12
Direct labour ($6/hr)	18	12
Variable production overheads	12	8

Fixed costs for the company in total were $110,000 in period 1 and are recovered on the basis of direct labour hours.

The profit reported for period 1 using marginal costing principles is $ [   ] .

14 Which of the following would be best described as a short term tactical plan?

    A   Reviewing cost variances and investigate as appropriate
    B   Comparing actual market share to budget
    C   Lowering the selling price by 15%
    D   Monitoring actual sales to budget

15 When you copy a formula in a spreadsheet, the program automatically changes the references to any cells affected by this. The function which enables it to do this is known as:

    A   Absolute cell referencing
    B   Relative cell referencing
    C   A macro
    D   An 'IF' statement

16 A company uses the Economic Order Quantity (EOQ) model to establish reorder quantities.

The following information relates to the forthcoming period:
Order costs = $25 per order
Holding costs = 105 of purchase price = $4/unit
Annual demand = 20,000 units
Purchase price = $40 per unit
EOQ = 500 units
No safety inventory are held

What are the total annual costs of inventory (ie the total purchase cost plus total order cost plus total holding costs)?

    A $22,000
    B $33,500
    C $802,000
    D $803,000

17   Which of the following criticisms of standard costing apply in all circumstances?

   (i)   Standard costing can only be used where all operations are repetitive and output is homogeneous.

   (ii)   Standard costing systems cannot be used in environments which are prone to change. They assume stable conditions.

   (iii) Standard costing systems assume that performance to standard is acceptable. They do not encourage continuous improvement.

   A   Criticism (i)
   B   Criticism (ii)
   C   Criticism (iii)
   D   None of them

18   A company is considering accepting a one-year contract which will require four skilled employees. The four skilled employees could be recruited on a one-year contract at a cost of $40,000 per employee. The employees would be supervised by an existing manager who earns $60,000 per annum. It is expected that supervision of the contract would take 10% of the manager's time.

   Instead of recruiting new employees the company could retrain some existing employees who currently earn $30,000 per year. The training would cost $15,000 in total. If these employees were used they would need to be replaced at a total cost of $100,000.

   The relevant labour cost of the contract is

   A $115,000
   B $135,000
   C $160,000
   D $275,000

19   For a set of six data pairs for the variable x (profit) and y (sales) the following values have been found.

   $\Sigma x = 2$
   $\Sigma y = 15$
   $\Sigma x^2 = 30$
   $\Sigma y^2 = 130$
   $\Sigma xy = 14$

   The correlation coefficient is [   ] to 2 decimal places.

20   A company wants to calculate the total cost of a job. The estimated cost for the job is as follows.

   Direct materials   10 kg @ $10 per kg
   Direct labour   20 hours @ $5 per hour

   Variable production overheads are recovered at the rate of $2 per labour hour.

   Fixed production overheads for the company are budgeted to be $100,000 each year and are recovered on the basis of labour hours. There are 10,000 budgeted labour hours each year.

   Other costs in relation to selling, distribution and administration are recovered at the rate of $50 per job.

   The total cost of the job is $ [   ] (to the nearest $)

Mixed Bank 2

1   Product S is produced in two production cost centres. Budgeted data for Product S are as follows.

	Cost centre Alpha	Cost centre Beta
Direct material cost per unit	$20.00	$10.10
Direct labour hours per unit	1.5	1
Direct labour rate per hour	$7.75	$7.35
Production overhead absorption rate per direct labour hour	$4.08	$4.98

General overhead costs are absorbed into product costs at a rate of ten per cent of production cost. The total **production cost** per unit of Product S is, to the nearest $0.01:

A $30.10
B $60.18
C $68.10
D $70.12

2   Gross wages incurred in department 1 in June were $54,000. The wages analysis shows the following summary breakdown of the gross pay.

	Paid to direct labour $	Paid to indirect labour $
Ordinary time	25,185	11,900
Overtime: basic pay	5,440	3,500
premium	1,360	875
Shift allowance	2,700	1,360
Sick pay	1,380	300
	36,065	17,935

What is the direct wages cost for department 1 in June?

A $25,185
B $30,625
C $34,685
D $36,065

3   The following data have been collected for four cost types – W, X, Y, Z – at two activity levels:

Cost type	Cost @ 100 units $	Cost @ 140 units $
W	8,000	10,560
X	5,000	5,000
Y	6,500	9,100
Z	6,700	8,580

Where V = variable, SV = semi-variable and F = fixed, assuming linearity, the four cost types W, X, Y and Z are respectively

	W	X	Y	Z
A	V	F	SV	V
B	SV	F	V	SV
C	V	F	V	V
D	SV	F	SV	SV

4   What is a by-product?

A   A product produced at the same time as other products which has no value

B   A product produced at the same time as other products which requires further processing to put it in a saleable state

C   A product produced at the same time as other products which has a relatively low volume compared with the other products

D   A product produced at the same time as other products which has a relatively low value compared with the other products

5   In a situation where there are no production resource limitations, which of the following must be available for the material usage budget to be completed?

☐ Standard material usage per unit

☐ Budgeted production volume

☐ The budgeted average lead time for delivery of materials

☐ Budgeted change in materials inventory

6   The standard selling price of product X is $15. Actual sales in the year were 2,000 units at $15.30 per unit.

Calculate the selling price variance for the year:

		Favourable	*Adverse*
Selling price variance	☐	☐	☐

The following information relates to questions 7 – 9:

A company makes one product, which passes through a single process.

Details of the process are as follows:

Materials	5,000 kg at 50c per kg
Labour	$800
Production overheads	200% of labour

Normal losses are 20% of input in the process, and without further processing any losses can be sold as scrap for 30c per kg.

The output for the period was 3,800 kg from the process.

There was no work in progress at the beginning or end of the period.

7   The value of the normal loss is $ ☐

8   The value of the abnormal ☐ is $ ☐ . This value will be:

☐ debited to the income statement

☐ credited to the income statement

9   The value of the output from the process is $ ☐

10   An extract from the production overhead control account for a company for the last period is as follows.

PRODUCTION OVERHEAD CONTROL

	$'000		$'000
Payables	48	Work in progress	58
Wages and salaries	12		
Provision for depreciation	4		
	64		

The production overhead for the last period was:

☐ under absorbed

☐ over absorbed

11   A company operates a differential piece-rate system and the following weekly rates have been set:

1 – 500 units	$0.20 per unit in this band
501 – 600 units	$0.25 per unit in this band
601 units and above	$0.55 per unit in this band

Details relating to Employee A are shown below:

Employee A

| Actual output achieved | 800 units |
| Actual hours worked | 45 hours |

There is a guaranteed minimum wage of $5 per hour for a 40-hour week paid to all employees.

The amount payable (to the nearest $) to employee A is $ ☐

12   The management accountant of a company has used the following data to draw the contribution breakeven chart shown.

Fixed costs of sale = $10,000
Variable costs of sale = $0.50 per $ of sale
Variable selling costs = $0.10 per $ of sale
Sales revenue = $90,000
Fixed administration cost = $15,000

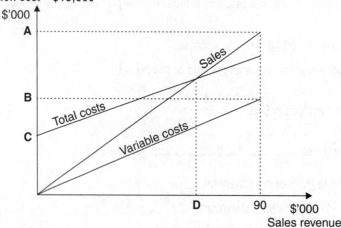

The monetary values indicated by A, B, C and D on the contribution breakeven chart shown above are:

A $ [_____]

B $ [_____]

C $ [_____]

D $ [_____]

13   Which of the following statements about a standard hour is/are correct? A standard hour is:

[_____] Always equivalent to a clock hour

[_____] Useful for monitoring output in a standard costing system

[_____] Any hour during which no idle time occurs

[_____] The quantity of work achievable at standard performance in an hour

[_____] A basis for measuring output when dissimilar products are manufactured

[_____] An hour throughout which units of the same type are made

14   A hotel company is developing a cost accounting system. Initially it has been decided to create four cost centres: Residential and Catering deal directly with customers while Housekeeping and Maintenance are internal service cost centres.

The management accountant has completed the initial overhead allocation and apportionment exercise and has derived the following total cost centre overheads.

	Residential	Catering	Housekeeping	Maintenance	Total
	$	$	$	$	$
Total	85,333	68,287	50,370	23,010	227,000

Housekeeping works 70% for Residential and 30% for Catering, and Maintenance works 20% for Housekeeping, 30% for Catering and 50% for Residential.

After the apportionment of the service cost centres the total overhead for the Residential cost centre will be

$ [_____] .

15   The relationship between expenditure in $ on advertising (X) in one time period and sales (in $) (Y) in the next period has been found to be Y = 50 + 7X. Which of the following interprets the value '7' correctly?

A   For every $1 spent on advertising, sales increase by $7 on average

B   For every $1 increase in sales, $7 must on average be spent on advertising

C   For every $1 spent on advertising, sales increase by $8

D   When advertising is zero, sales are $50/7

16   A company made 17,500 units at a total cost of $16 each. Three quarters of the costs were variable and one quarter fixed. 15,000 units were sold at $25 each. There were no opening inventories.

By how much will the profit calculated using absorption costing principles differ from the profit if marginal costing principles had been used?

A   The absorption costing profit would be $10,000 less

B   The absorption costing profit would be $10,000 greater

C   The absorption costing profit would be $30,000 greater

D   The absorption costing profit would be $40,000 greater

17 Job 198 requires 380 active labour hours to complete. It is expected that there will be five per cent idle time. The wage rate is $6 per hour. The labour cost of Job 198 is:

A $2,166
B $2,280
C $2,394
D $2,400

18 Which of the following would help to explain a favourable direct material price variance?

(i)   The standard price per unit of direct material was unrealistically high
(ii)   Output quantity was greater than budgeted and it was possible to obtain bulk purchase discounts
(iii)   The material purchased was of a higher quality than standard

A   (i), (ii) and (iii)
B   (i) and (ii) only
C   (ii) and (iii) only
D   (i) and (iii) only

19 In a period 12,250 units were made and there was a favourable labour efficiency variance of $11,250. If 41,000 labour hours were worked and the standard wage rate was $6 per hour, how many standard hours (to two decimal places) were allowed per unit?

A   3.19
B   3.35
C   3.50
D   6.00

20 A company wishes to maximise its annual profit. It has two products, F and G. F sells for $20 a unit, and costs are 60% of selling price. G costs $15 per unit to make, and is sold at a profit of 40% of cost. There are no other costs. The company is using linear programming to determine the best sales mix. If f is the number of units of F sold each year, and g is the number of units of G sold each year, which of the following is the correct objective?

A   Maximise 6f + 8g
B   Maximise 8f + 9g
C   Maximise 6f + 9g
D   Maximise 8f + 6g

Answers to multiple choice questions

1 Information for management

1   C   Complete accuracy is not necessarily an **essential** quality of good information. It needs to be **sufficiently accurate** for its purpose, and often there is no need to go into unnecessary detail for pointless accuracy.

Relevance (**option A**) is an essential quality of good information. Busy managers should not be forced to waste their time reading pages of unnecessary information.

Communication of the information to the right person (**option B**) is essential. Individuals who are given the authority to do certain tasks must be given the information they need to do them.

The correct timing of information (**option D**) is essential. Information which is not available until after a decision is made will be useful only for comparisons and longer-term control, and may serve no purpose even then. Information prepared too frequently can also be a waste of time and resources.

2   D   Data collected by survey for a particular project are a primary data source.

Historical records of transport costs were not collected specifically for the preparation of forecasts, therefore these are secondary data.

The *Annual Abstract of Statistics* is a source of secondary external data.

3   B   Tactical planning is used by middle management to decide how the resources of the business should be employed to achieve specific objectives in the most efficient and effective way.

Strategic planning (**option A**) is planning for the achievement of long-term objectives, and corporate planning (**option D**) is another name for this.

Operational planning (**option C**) is concerned with the very short term, day to day planning that is carried out by 'front line' managers such as supervisors and head clerks.

4   D   Management accounts often incorporate non-monetary measures. Therefore **statement (i)** is incorrect.

There is no legal requirement to prepare management accounts. Therefore **statement (ii)** is incorrect.

Management accounts do serve as a future planning tool, but they are also useful as an historical record of performance. Therefore **statement (iii)** is incorrect.

5   D   **Statement (i)** is a description of a management information system, not a management control system.

Statement (ii) is the 'wrong way round'. The strategy is the course of action that a business might pursue in order to achieve its objectives.

Statement (iii) is correct. Data is the 'raw material' which is processed into useful information.

6   B   Profit centre managers are normally responsible for costs and revenues only.

7   A   Monthly variance reports are an example of tactical management information.

2 Cost classification

1   B   The royalty cost can be traced in full to the product, ie it has been incurred as a direct consequence of making the product. It is therefore a direct expense. **Options A, C and D** are all overheads or indirect costs which cannot be traced directly and in full to the product.

2   B   The wages paid to the stores assistant cannot be traced in full to a product or service, therefore this is an indirect labour cost.

             The assembly workers' wages can be traced in full to the televisions manufactured (**option A**), therefore this is a direct labour cost.

             The wages paid to plasterers in a construction company can be traced in full to the contract or building they are working on (**option C**). This is also a direct labour cost.

3   B   Overtime premium is always classed as factory overheads unless it is:

- Worked at the specific request of a customer to get his order completed.

- Worked regularly by a production department in the normal course of operations, in which case it is usually incorporated into the direct labour hourly rate.

4   D   Indirect costs are those which **cannot be easily identified** with a specific cost unit. Although the staples could probably be identified with a specific chair, the cost is likely to be relatively insignificant. The expense of tracing such costs does not usually justify the possible benefits from calculating more accurate direct costs. The cost of the staples would therefore be treated as an indirect cost, to be included as a part of the overhead absorption rate.

             Options A, B and C all represent significant costs which can be traced to a specific cost unit. Therefore they are classified as direct costs.

5   B   Prime cost is the total of direct material, direct labour and direct expenses. Therefore the correct answer is B.

             Option A describes total production cost, including absorbed production overhead. **Option C** is only a part of prime cost.

6   D   The manager of a profit centre usually has control over how revenue is raised, ie selling prices (item (i)) and over the controllable costs incurred in the centre (item (ii)).

             Apportioned head office costs (item (iii)) are uncontrollable from the point of view of the profit centre manager. A responsibility centre manager does not have control over the capital investment in the centre (item (iv)) unless the centre is designated an investment centre.

7   C   Controllable costs are items of expenditure which can be directly influenced by a given manager within a given time span.

             Option A describes a committed cost. A cost which can be easily analysed in terms of its cost behaviour (**option B**) would indeed be easier to monitor in terms of flexible budget comparisons, but this would not necessarily make it controllable. **Option D** describes an avoidable cost.

8   D   It would be appropriate to use the cost per customer account and the cost per cheque received and processed for control purposes. Therefore **items (ii) and (iii)** are suitable cost units.

             Stationery costs, **item (i)**, is an expense of the department, therefore it is not a suitable cost unit.

9   A   A period cost is charged against the sales for the period. It is not carried forward in stock to a future period.

             Many period costs can be easily allocated to a period (**option B**) and are incurred regularly (**option D**). However the major distinguishing feature of a period cost in the context of cost accounting is that it is not included in the stock valuation for the period. Hence option A is the better description.

             Option C describes a product cost, which is carried forward in the stock valuation until the relevant cost unit is sold.

10　C　The supervisors are engaged in the production activity, therefore **option D** can be eliminated. They supervise the production of all products, therefore their salaries are indirect costs because they cannot be specifically identified with a cost unit. This eliminates **options A and B**. The salaries are indirect production overhead costs, therefore **option C** is correct.

11　A

> **ACCA examiner's comments**
>
> This question tested sections B1(a) and (c) in the Study Guide. It was a little surprising to discover the poor performance to a question on this topic. Perhaps it is one that students tend to skip over in their studies.

Remember you are only looking for costs that are **directly related** to getting the finished goods from the production line to your customers. Before they can be distributed, finished goods may have to be temporarily **stored** in a warehouse therefore the **rental** of the warehouse will be regarded as a **distribution cost**. In addition, you will need **delivery vehicles** for distribution purposes – any costs related to these vehicles will be classed as distribution costs. Hence both **(i) and (ii)** are distribution costs (**option A**). Commission paid to sales staff is a **selling cost**.

> **ACCA examiner's solution**
>
> The correct answer was A. Distribution costs are those costs incurred in making completed products ready for dispatch and their delivery to customers. Thus the warehouse rental and depreciation of delivery vehicles are distribution costs but the sales commission is clearly a selling cost.

3 Cost behaviour

1　B　Within the relevant range, fixed costs are not affected by the level of activity, therefore **option B** is correct.

Option A describes a linear variable cost. **Option C** could apply to any type of cost, not just to fixed costs.

2　B　Variable overhead $= \dfrac{97,850 - 84,865}{15,950 - 13,500} = \dfrac{12,985}{2,450}$
$= \$5.30$ per square metre

Fixed overhead $= 84,865 - (\$5.30 \times 13,500)$
$= \$84,865 - \$71,550 = \$13,315$

Overheads on 18,300 square metres $= \$13,315 + (5.30 \times 18,300)$
$= \$13,315 + \$96,990$
$= \$110,305$

If you selected **option A** you calculated the correct amount of variable cost but you forgot to add on the fixed cost. If you selected **options C or D** you calculated a total unit rate from one of the two activity levels given. However, this makes no allowance for the constant amount of fixed costs that is included in each of the total cost figures provided.

3　B　Graph 2 shows that costs increase in line with activity levels

4　A　Graph 1 shows that fixed costs remain the same whatever the level of activity

5　A　Graph 1 shows that cost per unit remains the same at different levels of activity

6　C　Graph 4 shows that semi-variable costs have a fixed element and a variable element

7　A　Graph 3 shows that the step fixed costs go up in 'steps' as the level of activity increases

8   C

	Units	$
High output	1,100	18,300
Low output	700	13,500
Variable cost of	400	4,800

Variable cost per unit $4,800/$400 = $12 per unit

Fixed costs = $18,300 − ($12 × 1,100) = $5,100

Therefore the correct answer is C.

Option A is the total cost for an activity of 700 units
Option B is the total variable cost for 1,100 units (1,100 × $12)
Option D is the difference between the costs incurred at the two activity levels recorded

9   D   The salary is part fixed ($650 per month) and part variable (5 pence per unit). Therefore it is a semi-variable cost and answer D is correct.

If you chose **option A or B** you were considering only part of the cost.

Option C, a step cost, involves a cost which remains constant up to a certain level and then increases to a new, higher, constant fixed cost.

10   D   The cost described will increase in **steps**, remaining fixed at each step until another supervisor is required. Such a cost is known as a **step cost**.

11   A   Independent Variable x = advertising expenditure

Dependent variable y = sales revenue

Highest x = month 6 = $6,500
Highest y = month 6 = $225,000

Lowest x = month 2 = $2,500
Lowest y = month 2 = $125,000
Using the high-low method:

	Advertising expenditure $	Sales revenue $
Highest	6,500	225,000
Lowest	2,500	125,000
	4,000	100,000

Sales revenue generated for every $1 spent on advertising = $\dfrac{\$100,000}{\$4,000}$ = $25 per $1 spent.

∴ If $6,500 is spent on advertising, expected sales revenue = $6,500 × $25 = $162,500

∴ Sales revenue expected without any expenditure on advertising = $225,000 − $162,500 = $62,500

∴ Sales revenue = 62,500 = (25 × advertising expenditure)

12   D   The cost described is a stepped fixed cost. A stepped fixed cost is fixed in nature but only within certain levels of activity.

13   B

	Activity level $	Cost $
Highest	10,000	400,000
Lowest	5,000	250,000
	5,000	150,000

Variable cost per unit = $\dfrac{\$150,000}{5,000\ \text{units}}$ = $30

14   A   The diagram shown depicts annual factory power cost where the electricity supplier sets a tariff based on a fixed charge plus a constant unit cost for consumption but subject to maximising arrival charge.

15   C   Using the high-low method:

Units	Cost $
20,000	40,000
4,000	20,000
16,000	20,000

$$\text{Variable cost per unit} = \frac{\$20,000}{16,000 \text{ units}}$$

$$= \$1.25$$

16   A   Graph A shows that up to 30,000 units, each unit costs a constant price per unit. After 30,000 units, the gradient of the new variable cost line is more gentle which indicates that the cost per unit is lower than the cost when 0 – 30,000 units are purchased.

17   C

	Production Units	Total cost $
Level 2	5,000	9,250
Level 1	3,000	6,750
	2,000	2,500

$$\text{Variable cost per unit} = \frac{\$2,500}{2,000 \text{ units}}$$

$$= \$1.25 \text{ per unit}$$

Fixed overhead = $9,250 – ($1.25 × 5,000) = $3,000

4 Correlation and regression

1   C   From the data given, it is clear that the correlation is **positive** and **strong**. The correlation coefficient describing a positive strong relationship is 0.98.

2   A   Y = 20 – 0.25X
X = 12
∴ Y = 20 – 0.25(12) = 17%

3   D   (i)   A correlation coefficient close to +1 or –1 indicates a strong linear relationship between X and Y. The regression equation is therefore more reliable for forecasting.

(ii)   Working to a high number of decimal places gives spurious accuracy unless both the data itself is accurate to the same degree and the methods used lend themselves to such precision.

(iii)   Forecasting for values of X outside the range of the original data leads to unreliable estimates, because there is no evidence that the same regression relationships hold for such values.

(iv)   The regression equation is worthless unless a sufficiently large sample was used to calculate it. In practice, samples of about ten or more are acceptable.

(i) and (iv) increase the reliability of forecasting.

4   A   The formula for the correlation coefficient is provided in your exam. There are no excuses for getting this question wrong.

$$\text{Correlation coefficient, } r = \frac{n\Sigma XY - \Sigma X \Sigma Y}{\sqrt{[n\Sigma X^2 - (\Sigma X)^2][n\Sigma Y^2 - (\Sigma Y)^2]}}$$

$$= \frac{(4 \times 157) - (12 \times 42)}{\sqrt{[4 \times 46 - 12^2][4 \times 542 - 42^2]}}$$

$$= \frac{628 - 504}{\sqrt{(184 - 144) \times (2{,}168 - 1{,}764)}}$$

$$= \frac{124}{\sqrt{40 \times 404}}$$

$$= \frac{124}{127.12}$$

$$= 0.98 \text{ (to 2 decimal places)}$$

5   C   (i)   High levels of correlation do not prove that there is cause and effect.

            (ii)   A correlation coefficient of 0.73 would generally be regarded as indicating a strong linear relationship between the variables.

            (iii) The coefficient of determination provides this information and is given by squaring the correlation coefficient, resulting in 53% in this case.

            (iv) The coefficient of determination provides this information and not the correlation coefficient. Remember that you must square the correlation coefficient in order to obtain the coefficient of determination.

        Statements (ii) and (iii) are relevant and the correct answer is therefore C.

6   C   The value X = 10 does not lie between 15 and 45 so we do not know whether or not the relationship between the variables still holds for this value of X. We therefore cannot rely upon the estimate.

        The sample size is quite large for this type of analysis and will provide reliable estimates. **Option A** will not therefore reduce the reliability of the estimate.

        The correlation coefficient is very close to –1, indicating a very strong relationship between the variables which will provide reliable estimates. **Option B** will not therefore reduce the reliability of the estimate.

        The fact that the correlation coefficient is negative tells us that Y decreases as X increases but it says nothing about the strength of the relationship between the variables nor the reliability of the estimates. **Option D** is therefore an incorrect answer.

7   D   When X = 20, we don't know anything about the relationship between X and Y since the sample data only goes up to X = 10. (i) is therefore true.

        Since a correlation coefficient of 0.8 would be regarded as strong (it is a high value) the estimate would be reliable. (ii) is therefore not true.

        With such a small sample and the extrapolation required, the estimate is unlikely to be reliable. (iii) is therefore not true.

        The sample of only six pairs of values is very small and is therefore likely to reduce the reliability of the estimate. (iv) is therefore true.

        The correct answer is therefore D.

8   B   The least squares method of linear regression analysis involves using the following formulae for a and b in Y = a + bX.

$$b \quad = \frac{n\Sigma XY - \Sigma X\Sigma Y}{n\Sigma X^2 - (\Sigma X)^2}$$

$$= \frac{(5 \times 8,104) - (100 \times 400)}{(5 \times 2,040) - 100^2}$$

$$= \frac{40,520 - 40,000}{10,200 - 10,000}$$

$$= \frac{520}{200}$$

$$= 2.6$$

At this stage, you can eliminate options A and C.

$$a \quad = \frac{\Sigma Y}{n} - b\frac{\Sigma X}{b}$$

$$= \frac{400}{5} - 2.6 \times (\frac{100}{5})$$

$$= 28$$

9   C   The independent variable is denoted by X and the dependent one by Y.

The variable to be forecast must always be Y. **Option A** is therefore incorrect.

In calculating the correlation coefficient, it does matter which variable is X and which is Y, and a totally different regression line equation will result if X and Y are interchanged. **Option B** is therefore incorrect.

The scatter diagram is used to show whether or not there is a relationship between X and Y and it does not matter which variable is associated with a particular axis. **Option D** is therefore incorrect.

10   A $a = \frac{\Sigma y}{n} - b\frac{\Sigma x}{n}$

where b = 17.14

$$\Sigma x = 5.75$$
$$\Sigma y = 200$$
$$n = 4$$

$$a = \frac{200}{4} - 17.14 \times \frac{5.75}{4}$$

$$= 50 - (17.14 \times 1.4375)$$
$$= 50 - 24.64$$
$$= 25.36 \text{ (to 2 decimal places)}$$

11   A   Statements (i) and (ii) only are correct with regard to regression analysis.

12   C

$$a = \frac{\Sigma y}{n} - b\frac{\Sigma x}{n}$$

$$= \frac{330}{11} - b\frac{\times 440}{11}$$

$$b = \frac{n\Sigma xy - \Sigma x\Sigma y}{n\Sigma x^2 - (\Sigma x)^2}$$

$$= \frac{(11 \times 13,467) - (440 \times 330)}{(11 \times 17,986) - 440^2}$$

$$= \frac{148,137 - 145,200}{197,846 - 193,600}$$

$$= \frac{2,937}{4,246}$$

$$= 0.6917$$

$$\therefore \ a \ = \ \frac{330}{11} - \left(0.6917 \times \frac{440}{11}\right)$$

$$= 30 - 27.668$$

$$= 2.332$$

$$= 2.33 \ \text{(to 2 decimal places)}$$

13 C The correlation coefficient can take on any value from -1 to $+1$.

14 B

Month	Activity level (x) Units	Total cost (y) $
7	300	17,500
8	360	19,500
9	400	20,500
10	320	18,500
11	280	17,000
	$\Sigma x = 1,660$	$\Sigma y = 93,000$

$$a = \frac{\Sigma y}{n} - \frac{b \Sigma x}{n}$$

$$= \frac{93,000}{5} - \frac{29.53 \times 1,660}{5}$$

$$= 18,600 - 9,803.96$$

$$= 8,796.04$$

$$= \$8,796 \ \text{(to the nearest \$)}$$

15 A

Examiner's comments. This question examined Section C1(a) of the syllabus – the calculation of an expected value. This short calculation caused many candidates a lot of problems. Less than 30% of candidates answered this correctly. Both choices B and D were very popular. Choice B weighted the two profits equally and not in the ratio described in the question. Choice D simply divided $180,000 by 2 and added $75,000. This indicates a poor understanding of what an expected value is, namely a **weighted** average.

Probability of $75,000 = 2 \times$ probability of $180,000

Expected value = sum of (profit $\times$ probability)

Expected value = [($180,000 $\times$ 1) + ($75,000 $\times$ 2)]/(1 + 2)

= $110,000

ACCA Examiner's solution.

The correct answer was A ($110,000). The correct calculation is:

[(180,000 $\times$ 1) + (75,000 $\times$ 2)]/(1 + 2) = $110,000

> **Examiner's comments**. Less than 30% of candidates answered this correctly. The requirement asked for the most likely level of profit – that is, the one of the three possibilities with the highest probability of occurring.

$$\text{Probability of outcome} = \frac{\text{Profit x probability}}{\text{Profit}}$$

Outcome $\dfrac{\text{Profit x probability}}{\text{Profit}}$

High $\dfrac{10,000}{25,000}$ = 40%

Medium $\dfrac{8,000}{16,000}$ = 50%

Low $\dfrac{1,000}{10,000}$ = 10%

The most likely level of profit is the one with the highest probability of occurring. In this case, the medium outcome has a 50% likelihood of occurrence which is the highest of the three possibilities.

> **ACCA Examiner's solution**. The correct answer was A ($16,000). The question stated that there were just three possible outcomes for profit in a decision situation. The requirement asked for the most likely level of profit, that is the one of the three possibilities with the highest probability of occurring. The probability of a $25,000 profit was 0.40 (10,000/25,000) and that of a $16,000 profit was 0.50 (8,000/16,000).

5 Spreadsheets

1   B   Data is entered into a cell.

2   B   Spreadsheets are not useful for word processing

3   B   C4

4   C   =D4-D5

5   A   =G6/G2*100

6   D

> **ACCA examiner's comments**
>
> This question tested sections C3(b) and E2(b) of the Study Guide. The most popular answer was A – selected by over 30% of candidates. Answers B or C were selected by almost 40% of the candidates, which was surprising, as in both the 10% element of April's sales were being **deducted** in arriving at the March production – a fundamental error.
>
> The poor performance in this question may relate more to the spreadsheet element in it rather than the budgeting element.

Budgeted production = budgeted sales + closing inventory – opening inventory. In March, 10% of March's sales (found in cell F3) will still be inventory at the beginning of the month and 10% of April's sales (cell F4) will be in inventory at the end of the month. Production for March will therefore be

March's sales (F3) + 10% of April's sales (F4) – 10% of March's sales (F3)

Or

$=[(0.9*F3) + (0.1*F4)]$

ACCA examiner's solution

The correct answer was D. Basic budget preparation indicates that budgeted production for a period = budgeted sales for the period + closing inventory of finished goods for the period – opening inventory of finished goods for the period. For this question, this translates into a budgeted production for March of: F3 + 10% of F4 – 10% of F3. This can be simply rearranged into the spreadsheet formula shown in D.

---

6 Material costs

1   A   Among other things, the GRN is used to update the inventory records and to check that the quantity invoiced by the supplier was actually received. The GRN does not usually contain price information. Therefore the correct answer is A.

2   A   Free inventory balance   =   units in inventory + units on order from suppliers – units outstanding on customers' orders

        13,000   =   units in inventory + 27,500 – 16,250

        ∴ Units in inventory   =   13,000 – 27,500 + 16,250 = 1,750

    Option B is simply the difference between the units outstanding on customers' orders and the free inventory balance.

    If you selected **option C** you have interchanged inventory on order and the outstanding orders. If you selected **option D** you have simply added the free inventory to the units outstanding on existing orders.

3   C   Reorder level = maximum usage × maximum lead time
                    = 95 × 18
                    = 1,710 units

    If you selected **option A** you have used the minimum figures for usage and lead time. **Option B** uses the average figures and **option D** is simply the reorder quantity.

4   C   Maximum level   =   reorder level + reorder quantity – (minimum usage ×minimum lead time)
                         =   1,710 + 1,750 – (50 × 12) = 2,860 units

    If you selected options A, C or D you have used the correct formula, but used the incorrect reorder level as calculated in the previous question.

5   C $EOQ = \sqrt{\dfrac{2CoD}{C_h}} = \dfrac{2 \times \$80 \times 2,500}{\$15} = 163$

    If you selected **option A** you have interchanged Co and C_h.

    If you selected **option B**, you have omitted the 2.

    If you selected **option D** you forgot to take the square root.

6   D   Stock-outs arise when too little inventory is held (i); safety inventories are the level of units maintained in case there is unexpected demand (ii); and a reorder level can be established by looking at the maximum usage and the maximum lead-time (iii). Therefore, they are all correct statements with regards to inventories.

7   C   The economic batch quantity is used to establish the cumulative production quantity.

8   D $EOQ = \sqrt{\dfrac{2C_oD}{C_H}}$

Where C_o = 20

D   = 12,500 × 4 = 50,000

C_H = 10% × $15 = 1.50

$EOQ = \sqrt{\dfrac{2 \times 20 \times 50,000}{1.50}}$

$= \sqrt{1,333,333}$

= 1,155 units

9   D   If there is a decrease in the cost of ordering a batch of raw material, then the EOQ will also be lower (as the numerator in the EOQ equation will be lower). If the EOQ is lower, than average inventory held (EOQ/2) with also be lower and therefore the total annual holding costs will also be lower.

10   C   Reorder level = maximum usage × maximum lead time

= 520 × 15

= 7,800 units

11   C   Statement (i) is not correct. A debit to stores with a corresponding credit to work in progress (WIP) indicates that **direct materials returned** from production were $18,000.

Statement (ii) is correct. **Direct costs of production** are 'collected' in the WIP account.

Statement (iii) is correct. **Indirect costs of production or overhead** are 'collected' in the overhead control account.

Statement (iv) is correct. The purchases of materials on credit are credited to the creditors account and debited to the material stores control account.

Therefore the correct answer is C.

12   C

Examiner's comments. Less than one third of candidates answered this question correctly. Option A was a popular choice with candidates. However this answer ignores the annual cost of holding the permanent buffer inventory. Answers B or D were chosen by approximately 40% of the candidates.

Annual holding cost

= [buffer (safety) inventory + reorder level/2)] x holding cost per unit

= [500 + (2,000/2)] x $2

= $3,000

ACCA Examiner's solution

The correct answer was C ($3,000). This can be calculated as follows:

[Buffer inventory + (EOQ/2)] × Annual holding cost per component

= [500 + (2,000/2)] × $2 = $3,000

---

7 Labour costs

1   D   Budgeted hours = 3,000 + 8,000 + 7,000 + 9,000 = 27,000

$$\text{Capacity ratio} = \frac{\text{actual hours worked}}{\text{budgeted hours}} = \frac{29,000}{27,000} \times 100\% = 107.4\%$$

If you selected **option A** you had your formula upside down, and **option B** is the production volume ratio. If you selected **option C** you based your calculation on units, rather than standard hours. Units of dissimilar products cannot be meaningfully added together; a more meaningful measure is to convert the production units to a number of standard hours produced.

2   A

Product	Units	Standard hours	
W	12,000	(× 0.2)	2,400
X	25,000	(× 0.4)	10,000
Y	16,000	(× 0.5)	8,000
Z	5,000	(× 1.5)	7,500
			27,900

$$\text{Efficiency ratio} = \frac{\text{Standard hours produced}}{\text{Actual hours worked}} = \frac{27,900}{29,000} \times 100\% = 96.2\%$$

Options B and D are the production volume and capacity ratios respectively. If you selected **option C** you had your formula for the efficiency ratio upside down.

3   A   The graph shows a constant wage up to a certain level of output, which is payable even at zero output. This is the minimum guaranteed wage. Above a certain output the wage cost rises at a constant rate. This is the piece rate payable in addition to the minimum wage.

Graphs for the other options would look like this:

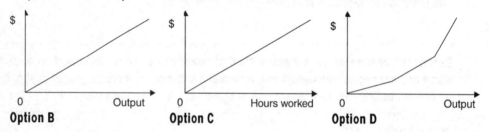

Option B   **Option C**   **Option D**

4   B

	Hours
Standard time for 180 units (× 4/60)	12
Actual time taken	7
Time saved	5

	$
Basic pay 7 hours × $5	35
Bonus: 60% × 5 hours saved × $5 per hour	15
	50

Option A is the basic daily pay, without consideration of any bonus. If you selected **option C**, you simply added 60 per cent to the basic daily pay, so you have misunderstood how to calculate the bonus.

Option D is based on the standard time allowance for 180 units, without considering the basic pay for the seven-hour day.

5	A	Number of units qualifying for payment	= 210 – 17
			= 193

Piecework payment to be made:

	$
First 100 units @ $0.20	20.00
Last 93 units @ $0.30	27.90
	47.90

Option B is not correct because it includes payment for the 17 rejected units. If you selected **option C** you calculated the correct number of units qualifying for payment, but you evaluated all of them at the higher rate of $0.30 per unit. **Option D** is incorrect because it includes the 17 rejected units, and evaluates them all at the higher rate of $0.30 per unit.

6   C   The overtime premium paid at the specific request of a customer would be treated as a direct cost because it can be traced to a specific cost unit.

The four hours of machine breakdown is idle time. It cannot be traced to a specific cost unit therefore it is an indirect cost.

The direct wages cost is as follows.

	$
Basic pay for active hours (38 hours × $3.60)	136.80
Overtime premium re: customer request (2 hours × $1.80)	3.60
	140.40

Option A is incorrect because it is the employee's total wages for the week, both direct and indirect.

Option B is the basic pay for a 36 hour week, making no allowance for the overtime worked at the customer's request.

If you selected **option D** you calculated the basic pay for all of the hours worked, but you made no allowance for either the idle time or the overtime premium.

7   C   Group bonus schemes are useful to reward performance when production is integrated so that all members of the group must work harder to increase output, for example in production line manufacture. **Statement (i)** is therefore true.

Group bonus schemes are not effective in linking the reward to a particular individual's performance. Even if one individual makes a supreme effort, this can be negated by poor performance from other members of the group. Therefore **statement (ii)** is not true.

Non-production employees can be included in a group incentive scheme, for example when all employees in a management accounting department must work harder to produce prompt budgetary control reports. **Statement (iii)** is therefore true, and the correct option is C.

8   B   The overtime was not worked for any specific job and is therefore an **indirect wages cost** to be 'collected' in the overhead control account. Similarly, the holiday pay is an **indirect cost**, therefore the total **debit to the overhead control account** is $2,500. The **direct wages** of $70,800 is **debited to the work in progress account** and the total wages cost is **credited to the wages control account**.

If you selected **option C** you identified the correct accounts but your entries were reversed.

If you selected **option A** you treated the overtime premium as a direct cost, and if you selected **option D** you made the same mistake and your entries were reversed.

9	B	Reduction in number of employees	= 30 – 20 = 10
		Number of employees leaving	= 15
		∴ Number of employees replaced	= 15 – 10 = 5

Labour turnover rate $= \dfrac{\text{replacements}}{\text{average no. of employees in period}} \times 100\%$

$= \dfrac{5}{(30 + 20) \div 2} \times 100\%$

$= 20\%$

If you selected **options A or C** you calculated the correct number of replacements as five, but you expressed this as a percentage of 30 and 20 respectively, instead of as a percentage of the average number of employees.

If you selected **option D** you used 15 employees leaving as the numerator in your calculation. However, the labour turnover rate is calculated based on the number of employees replaced.

10　A

	Hours
Standard time for 80 units ($\times$ 9/60)	12
Actual time taken	8
Time saved	4

Group bonus : 70% $\times$ 4 hours saved $\times$ \$6 per hour = \$16.80

Jane's share of bonus　= 50% $\times$ (\$16.80 $\times$ 60%)
= \$5.04

If you selected **option B** you took all of the time saved as the bonus hours, instead of only 70 per cent. **Option C** is the bonus payable to Jane and her team-mate combined. If you selected **option D** you have calculated the group bonus correctly but have not taken the final step to calculate Jane's share of the bonus.

11　C　Maintenance workers in a shoe factory would be classified as indirect labour.

8 Overheads and absorption costing

1　D　Number of employees in packing department = 2 direct + 1 indirect = 3

Number of employees in all production departments = 15 direct + 6 indirect = 21

Packing department overhead

Canteen cost apportioned to packing department	=	$\dfrac{\$8,400}{21} \times 3$
	=	\$1,200
Original overhead allocated and apportioned	=	\$8,960
Total overhead after apportionment of canteen costs	=	\$10,160

If you selected **option A** you forgot to include the original overhead allocated and apportioned to the packing department. If you selected **option B** you included the four canteen employees in your calculation, but the question states that the basis for apportionment is the number of employees in each **production** cost centre.

If you selected **option C** you based your calculations on the direct employees only.

2　D　Department 1 appears to undertake primarily machine-based work, therefore a machine-hour rate would be most appropriate.

$\dfrac{\$27,000}{45,000} = \$0.60$ per machine hour

Therefore the correct answer is D.

Option A is not the most appropriate because it is not time-based, and most items of overhead expenditure tend to increase with time.

Options B and C are not the most appropriate because labour activity is relatively insignificant in department 1, compared with machine activity.

3 C Department 2 appears to be labour-intensive therefore a direct labour-hour rate would be most appropriate.

$$\frac{\$18,000}{25,000} = \$0.72 \text{ per direct labour hour}$$

Option B is based on labour therefore it could be suitable. However differential wage rates exist and this could lead to inequitable overhead absorption. **Option D** is not suitable because machine activity is not significant in department 2.

4 A **Statement (i)** is correct because a constant unit absorption rate is used throughout the period. **Statement (ii)** is correct because 'actual' overhead costs, based on actual overhead expenditure and actual activity for the period, cannot be determined until after the end of the period. **Statement (iii)** is incorrect because under/over absorption of overheads is caused by the use of predetermined overhead absorption rates.

5 A **Description B** could lead to under-absorbed overheads if actual overheads far exceeded both budgeted overheads and the overhead absorbed. **Description C** could lead to under-absorbed overheads if overhead absorbed does not increase in line with actual overhead incurred.

6 B Budgeted absorption rate for fixed overhead   = $360,000/8,000
                                                     = $45 per unit

Fixed overhead absorbed   = 9,000 units × $45

                          = $405,000

If you selected **option A** you based your absorption calculations on sales units instead of production units.

If you selected **option C** you calculated the correct figure for fixed overhead absorbed but also added the variable overheads.

Option D is the figure for actual total overhead incurred.

7 A

Actual fixed overhead incurred = $432,000
Fixed overhead absorbed   = $405,000 (from question 6)
Fixed overhead under absorbed $27,000

If you selected **option B** you simply calculated the difference between the budgeted and actual fixed overhead. If you selected **option C** you based your absorption calculations on sales units instead of production units. If you selected **option D** you performed the calculations correctly but misinterpreted the result as an over absorption.

8 C The insurance cost is likely to be linked to the cost of replacing the machines, therefore the most appropriate basis for apportionment is the value of machinery.

Options A, B and D would all be possible apportionment bases in the absence of better information, but **option C** is preferable.

9 A All of the overhead absorption methods are suitable, depending on the circumstances.

Method 1, direct labour hours, is suitable in a labour-intensive environment.

Method 2, machine hours, is suitable in a machine-intensive environment.

Method 3, a percentage of prime costs, can be used if it is difficult to obtain the necessary information to use a time-based method. **Method 4**, a rate per unit, is suitable if all cost units are identical.

10   C   Statement (i) is correct. The cost of indirect material issued is 'collected' in the overhead control account **pending absorption into work in progress**.

Statement (ii) is incorrect. The overhead cost **incurred** was $210,000. The overhead **absorbed into work in progress** during the period was $404,800.

Statement (iii) is incorrect. The $8,400 is **debited to profit and loss**, indicating an extra charge to compensate for the overhead **under absorbed.**

Statement (iv) is correct. The indirect wage cost is 'collected' in the overhead control account **pending absorption into work in progress**.

Therefore the correct answer is C.

11   A   Only production related costs should be considered when considering the allocation, apportionment and reapportionment of overhead in an absorption costing situation.

12   A

	$
Actual fixed production overheads	×
Absorbed fixed production overheads (4,500 × $8)	36,000
Over-absorbed fixed production overheads	6,000

Actual fixed production overheads   = $36,000 – $6,000

                           = $30,000

13   D

	Production cost centre	
	Primary	*Finishing*
Allocated and apportioned	$96,000	$82,500
Total direct labour hours	9,600 hours	6,875 hours
Fixed overhead absorption rate	$10 per hour	$12 per hour

Workings

(W1)

Total direct labour hours – Primary = (6,000 × 36/60) hours + (7,500 × 48/60) hours

                                    = (3,600 + 6,000) hours

                                    = 9,600 hours

(W2)

Total direct labour hours – Finishing = (6,000 × 25/60) hours + (7,500 × 35/60) hours

                                    = (2,500 + 4,375) hours

                                    = 6,875 hours

Budgeted fixed overhead cost per unit for Product Y

Primary   = 48 minutes/60 minutes × $10 per hour

                = $8 per unit

Finishing   = 35 minutes/60 minutes × $12 per hour

                = $7 per unit

Total   = $8 + $7

                = $15 per unit of Product Y

14   A

	$
Absorbed overhead (30,000 hours × $3.50)	105,000
Actual overhead	108,875
Under-absorbed overhead	3,875

15   D   Using simultaneous equations:

Let P   = overheads for department P after reapportionment
X   = overheads for department X after reapportionment
Y   = overheads for department Y after reapportionment

P   = 95,000 + 0.4X + 0.3Y
X   = 46,000 + 0.1Y
Y   = 30,000 + 0.2X

X   = 46,000 + 0.1 (30,000 + 0.2X)
X   = 46,000 + 3,000 + 0.02X
X   = 49,000 + 0.02X
X   − 0.02X = 49,000
0.98X = 49,000
X   = 49,000/0.98
    = 50,000

If X   = 50,000
Y   = 30,000 + (0.2 × 50,000)
Y   = 30,000 + 10,000
Y   = 40,000
∴ X   = 50,000 and Y = 40,000

∴ P   = 95,000 + 0.4X + 0.3Y
    = 95,000 + (0.4 × 50,000 + (0.3 × 40,000)
    = 95,000 + 20,000 + 12,000
    = 127,000

16   D   Production overhead absorption rate = $150,000/60,000
                                            = $2.50 per machine hour

Production overhead absorbed   = $2.50 × 55,000 hours
                                  = $137,500

Production overhead incurred   = $150,000

Production overhead under absorbed = $ 12,500

9 Marginal and absorption costing

1   D   We know that the profit using marginal costing would be higher than the absorption costing profit, because inventories are decreasing. However, we cannot calculate the value of the difference without the fixed overhead absorption rate per unit.

Difference in profit = $\dfrac{\text{2,000 units inventory reduction}}{} \times \dfrac{\text{fixed overhead absorption rate per unit}}{}$

2   B   Difference in profit   = change in inventory level × fixed overhead per unit
                              = (2,400 − 2,700) × ($4 × 3)
                              = $3,600

The absorption profit will be higher because inventories have increased, and fixed overheads have been carried forward in inventories.

If you selected **option A or C** you used $4 per unit as the fixed overhead absorption rate, but this is the absorption rate per machine hour. If you selected **option D** you calculated the correct monetary value of the profit difference but you misinterpreted its 'direction'.

3   A   Difference in profit   = change in inventory level × fixed overhead per unit
                              = (15,000 − 20,000) × $8
                              = $40,000

The inventory level increased during the period therefore the absorption costing profit is higher than the marginal costing profit.

Marginal costing profit = $130,000 − $40,000 = $90,000

If you selected **option B** you decided there would be no difference in the reported profits. If inventory levels change there will always be a difference between the marginal and absorption costing profits.

If you selected **option C** you calculated the correct monetary value of the profit difference but you misinterpreted its 'direction'.

4	A	Contribution per unit	= $30 − $(6.00 + 7.50 + 2.50)
			= $14
		Contribution for month	= $14 × 5,200 units
			= $72,800
		Less fixed costs incurred	= $27,400
		Marginal costing profit	= $45,400

If you selected **option B** you calculated the profit on the actual sales at $9 per unit. This utilises a unit rate for fixed overhead which is not valid under marginal costing.

If you selected **option C** you used the correct method but you based your calculations on the units produced rather than the units sold.

If you selected **option D** you calculated the correct contribution but you forgot to deduct the fixed overhead.

5   D

	$	$
Sales (5,200 at $30)		156,000
Materials (5,200 at $6)	31,200	
Labour (5,200 at $7.50)	39,000	
Variable overhead (5,200 at $2.50)	13,000	
Total variable cost		(83,200)
Fixed overhead ($5 × 5,200)		(26,000)
Over-absorbed overhead (W)		1,600
Absorption costing profit		48,400

Working	$
Overhead absorbed (5,800 × $5)	29,000
Overhead incurred	27,400
Over-absorbed overhead	1,600

If you selected **option A** you calculated all the figures correctly but you subtracted the over-absorbed overhead instead of adding it to profit.

Option B is the marginal costing profit.

If you selected **option C** you calculated the profit on the actual sales at $9 per unit, and forgot to adjust for the over-absorbed overhead.

6   B   Inventory levels increased by 3,000 units and absorption costing profit is $105,000 higher ($955,500 − $850,500).

∴ Fixed production cost included in inventory increase:

$$= \frac{\$105,000}{3,000} = \$35 \text{ per unit of inventory}$$

$$\frac{\text{Budgeted fixed costs}}{\text{Fixed cost per unit}} = \frac{\$1,837,500}{£35} = 52,500 \text{ units}$$

Option A is an average of the opening and closing inventories.

Option C is the total of the opening and closing inventories. If you selected **option D** you simply calculated the difference between the two stated profit figures.

7   D   Decrease in inventory levels = 48,500 − 45,500 = 3,000 units

Difference in profits   = $315,250 − $288,250 = $27,000

Fixed overhead per unit $= \dfrac{\$27,000}{3,000} = \$9$ per unit

If you selected one of the other options you attempted various divisions of all the data available in the question!

8   C   All of the methods are acceptable bases for absorbing production overheads. However, the **percentage of prime cost has serious limitations** and the rate per unit can only be used if all cost units are identical.

9   D   Absorption costing is concerned with including in the total cost of a product an appropriate share of **overhead**, or **indirect cost**. Overheads can be fixed or variable costs, therefore option D is correct. **Option A** and **option B** are incorrect because they relate to direct costs. **Option C** is incorrect because it does not take account of variable overheads.

10   C   If inventory levels increase in a period, absorption costing will show a higher profit than marginal costing.

Difference in profit = change in inventory levels × overhead absorption rate per unit

= (750 units − 300 units) × $5 per unit

= 450 units × $5

= $2,250

	$
Marginal costing profit	72,300
Increase in profit	2,250
Absorption costing profit	74,550

11   B
Contribution per unit	= selling price − variable cost
	= $10 − $6
	= $4 per unit

Total contribution	= 250,000 units × $4 per unit = $1,000,000
Total fixed costs	= 200,000 units × $2 per unit
	= $400,000

Marginal costing profit	= total contribution − total fixed costs
	= $1,000,000 − $400,000
	= $600,000

12   D   Breakeven sales revenue $= \dfrac{\text{Fixed costs} + \text{target profit}}{\text{C/St ratio}}$

$= \dfrac{\$75,000 + \$150,000}{0.75}$

$= \dfrac{\$225,000}{0.75}$

= $300,000

If selling price = $10 per unit

$\dfrac{\$300,000}{\$10}$ = 30,000 units must be sold

13 **C** If inventory levels increase in a period, absorption costing will show a higher profit than marginal costing.

Difference in profit = change in inventory levels × overhead absorption rate per unit

= (350 – 100) units × $4 per unit
= 250 units × $4
= $1,000

	$
Marginal costing profit	37,500
Increase in profit	1,000
Absorption costing profit	38,500

14 **B**

$$\text{Fixed production overhead absorption rate} = \frac{\$48,000}{12,000\,\text{units}}$$

$$= \$4 \text{ per unit}$$

Increase in inventory levels = (12,000 – 11,720) units

= 280 units

∴ Difference in profit = 280 units × $4 per unit

= $1,120

Marginal costing profits are lower than absorption costing profits when stock levels increase in a period, therefore marginal costing profit will be $1,120 lower than absorption costing profits for the same period.

15 **C** If budgeted fixed overhead expenditure = 100%

Actual fixed overhead expenditure = 110%

∴ Variance = 10%

If variance = $36,000 = 10% × budgeted fixed overhead expenditure

Budgeted fixed overhead expenditure = $36,000/0.1

= $360,000

∴ Actual fixed overhead expenditure = 110% × $360,000

= $396,000

16 **B** Increase in inventory = (18,000 – 16,500) units
= 1,500 units
∴ Difference in profit = 1,500 units × $10
= $15,000

Profits under marginal costing will be $15,000 less than profits under absorption costing ie $40,000 – $15,000 = $25,000.

17 **D**

ACCA examiner's comments

This question tested section D4(d) of the Study Guide. Significantly less than 50% of candidates selected the correct answer to this question.

Choice A (7,500 units) could be obtained by deducting the 2,500 from the 10,000 in the final step. Nearly 15% of candidates selected A. More than 40% of candidates selected either B or C which probably meant that they had taken the initial difference in 'profits' as $1,000 which gave an inventory change of 500 units.

Any difference between marginal and absorption costing profit is due to changes in inventory.

	$
Absorption costing profit	2,000
Marginal costing loss	(3,000)
Difference	5,000

Change in inventory = Difference in profit/fixed product cost per unit

= $5,000/$2 = 2,500 units

Marginal costing loss is lower than absorption costing profit therefore inventory has gone up – that is, production was greater than sales by 2,500 units.

Production = 10,000 units (sales) + 2,500 units = 12,500 units

---

ACCA examiner's solution

The correct answer was D (12,500 units).

The difference between the marginal costing loss and the absorption costing profit was $5,000. This equates with the change in inventory (in units) evaluated at $2 (the fixed production cost per unit). Therefore the change in inventory last month was 2,500 units (5,000/2). As the marginal costing 'profit' outcome was lower than the absorption costing profit then production was greater than sales last month – by 2,500 units. Therefore last month's production was (10,000 + 2,500) = 12,500 units.

---

10 Process costing

1   A   Good production = input – normal loss – abnormal loss
                 = (2,500 – (2,500 × 10%) – 75)kg
                 = 2,500 – 250 – 75
                 = 2,175 kg

If you selected **option B** you did not deduct the abnormal loss. If you selected **option C** you treated the abnormal loss as a gain and you added it to the input instead of deducting it. If you selected **option D** you did not deduct the normal loss.

2   C   Work in progress = 300 litres input – 250 litres to finished goods
                 = 50 litres

Equivalent litres for each cost element are as follows.

	Material		Conversion costs	
	%	Equiv. litres	%	Equiv. litres
50 litres in progress	100	50	50	25

Option A is incorrect because it assumes that the units in progress are only 50 per cent complete with respect to materials. **Option B** has transposed the information concerning the two cost elements. If you selected **option D** you calculated the correct number of litres in progress but you did not take account of their degree of completion.

3   A   There is no mention of a scrap value available for any losses therefore the normal loss would have a zero value. The normal loss does not carry any of the process costs therefore **options B, C and D** are all incorrect.

4   D   Expected output = 2,000 units **less** normal loss (5%) 100 units = 1,900 units

In situation (i) there is an **abnormal loss** of 1,900 – 1,800 = 100 units
In situation (ii) there is an **abnormal gain** of 1,950 – 1,900 = 50 units
In situation (iii) there is an **abnormal gain** of 2,000 – 1,900 = 100 units

Therefore the correct answer is D.

5 B Abnormal losses are valued at the same unit rate as good production, so that their occurrence does not affect the cost of good production.

The scrap value of the abnormal loss **(option A)** is credited to a separate abnormal loss account; it does not appear in the process account. **Option C** is incorrect because abnormal losses also absorb some conversion costs.

6 D The total loss was 15% of the material input. The 340 litres of good output therefore represents 85% of the total material input.

Therefore, material input = $\dfrac{340}{0.85}$ = 400 litres

Options A and B are incorrect because they represent a further five per cent and ten per cent respectively, added to the units of good production.

If you selected **option C** you simply added 15 per cent to the 340 litres of good production. However, the losses are stated as **a percentage of input**, not as a percentage of output.

7 C **Step 1.** **Determine output and losses**

| Input | Output | | | Equivalent units | | |
Units		Total Units	Materials Units	%	Labour and overhead Units	%
	Finished units (balance)	400	400	100	400	100
500	Closing inventory	100	100	100	80	80
500		500	500		480	

Step 2. **Calculate the cost per equivalent unit**

Input	Cost	Equivalent production in units	Cost per unit
	$		$
Materials	9,000	500	18
Labour and overhead	11,520	480	24
			42

Step 3. **Calculate total cost of output**

Cost of completed units = $42 × 400 units = $16,800

If you selected **option A** you omitted the absorption of overhead at the rate of 200 per cent of direct wages. If you selected **option B** you did not allow for the fact that the work in progress was incomplete. **Option D** is the total process cost for the period, some of which must be allocated to the work in progress.

8 B Using the data from answer 7 above, extend **step 3** to calculate the value of the work in progress.

	Cost element	Number of equivalent units	Cost per equivalent unit	Total
			$	$
Work in progress:	Materials	100	18	1,800
	Labour & overhead	80	24	1,920
				3,720

If you selected **option A** you omitted the absorption of overhead into the process costs. If you selected **option C** you did not allow for the fact that the work in progress was incomplete. **Option D** is the total process cost for the period, some of which must be allocated to the completed output.

9　C　STATEMENT OF EQUIVALENT UNITS

	Total Units		Materials		Equivalent units Labour		Overheads
Output to process 2*	600		600		600		600
Closing WIP	100	(100%)	100	(50%)	50	(30%)	30
	700		700		650		630

*500 units input + opening WIP 200 units – closing WIP 100 units.

Option A is incorrect because it is the number of units input to the process, taking no account of opening and closing work in progress. **Option B** is the completed output, taking no account of the work done on the closing inventory.

Option D is the total number of units worked on during the period, but they are not all complete in respect of overhead cost.

10　B　STATEMENT OF COSTS PER EQUIVALENT UNIT

	Materials $	Labour $	Overheads $	Total
Opening stock	2,400	1,200	400	
Added during period	6,000	3,350	1,490	
Total cost	8,400	4,550	1,890	
Equivalent units	700	650	630	
Cost per equivalent unit	$12	$7	$3	$22

Value of units transferred to process 2 = 600 units × $22 = $13,200

Option A is incorrect because it represents only the material cost of the units transferred. **Option C** is all of the costs incurred in the process during the period, but some of these costs must be allocated to the closing work in progress. **Option D** is the value of 700 completed units: but only 600 units were transferred to the next process.

11　D

	Total Units		Equivalent units Materials Units		Conversion costs Units
Opening inventory	300		300		300
Fully worked units*	9,550		9,550		9,550
Output to finished goods	9,850		9,850		9,850
Closing inventory	450	(100%)	450	(30%)	135
	10,300		10,300		9,985

* Fully worked units = input – closing inventory
$$= (10,000 - 450) \text{ units}$$
$$= 9,550 \text{ units}$$

12　B　Input costs = 2,000 units × $4.50 = $9,000

Conversation costs 　　　　　= $13,340

Normal loss 　　　　　= 5% × 2,000 units × $3 = $300

Expected output 　　　　　= 2,000 units – 100 units = 1,900 units

Cost per unit of output = $\dfrac{\text{Input costs}}{\text{Expected output}}$

$$= \frac{\$9,000 + \$13,340 - \$300}{1,800 \text{ units}} = \frac{\$22,040}{1,900 \text{ units}} = \$11.6 \text{ (to one decimal point)}$$

13 D

	$
Material	9,000
Conversion costs	11,970
Less: scrap value of normal loss (300 × $1.50)	(450)
Cost of process	20,520

Expected output = 3,000 − (10% × 3,000)
= 3,000 − 300 = 2,700 units

$$\text{Costs per unit} = \frac{\text{Input costs} - \text{scrap value of normal loss}}{\text{Expected output}} = \frac{\$20,520}{2,700} = \$7.60$$

Value of output = 2,900 × $7.60 = $22,040

If you selected option B, you calculated the input costs less the scrap value of normal loss. You forgot to calculate a cost per unit and then to multiply this by the actual output. If you selected option C, you simply calculated the input costs. You need to take account of scrap proceeds and to calculate a cost per unit also.

14 B   Abnormal gain = 276 units − 112 units = 164 units

Cost per unit of good production = $29,744/5,408 = $5.50

∴ Value of abnormal gain = 164 units × $5.50 = $902

The value of the input can be found as the balancing figure in the value columns of the process account.

Polishing process account

	$		$
Input (balancing figure)	29,532	Output	29,744
Abnormal gain	902	Normal loss (276 × $2.50)	690
	30,434		30,434

15 D   Statement (i) is incorrect. Units of normal loss are valued at their scrap value (which may be nil).

Statement (ii) is incorrect. Units of abnormal loss are valued at the same rate as good units.

Therefore the correct answer is D, statements (i) and (ii) both being incorrect.

11 Process costing, joint products and by-products

1 C   **Total production inventory**

	$
Opening stock	1,000
Direct materials added	10,000
Conversion costs	12,000
	23,000
Less closing inventory	3,000
Total production cost	20,000

	Production Units		Sales value $		Apportioned cost $
P	4,000	(× $5)	20,000	($20,000 × 20/80)	5,000
R	6,000	(× $10)	60,000	($20,000 × 60/80)	15,000
			80,000		20,000

Product R cost per unit = $15,000/6,000 = $2.50 per unit.

Option A is the cost per unit for product P, and if you selected **option B** you apportioned the production costs on the basis of units sold.

If you selected **option D** you made no adjustment for inventories when calculating the total costs.

2   A   From the previous answer, total production cost to be apportioned = $20,000.

	Production		Apportioned cost
	Units		$
P	4,000	($20,000 × 4/10)	8,000
R	6,000	($20,000 × 6/10)	12,000
	10,000		20,000

If you selected **option B** you made no adjustment for inventories when calculating the total costs.

If you selected **option C** you apportioned the production costs on the basis of the units sold. **Option D** is the total cost of product R.

3   D   **Statement (i)** is incorrect because the value of the product described could be relatively high even though the output volume is relatively low. This product would then be classified as a joint product.

Statement (ii) is incorrect. Since a by-product is not important as a saleable item, it is not separately costed and does not absorb any process costs.

Statement (iii) is correct. These common or joint costs are allocated or apportioned to the joint products.

4   B   **Net process costs**

	$
Raw material input	216,000
Conversion costs	72,000
Less by-product revenue	(4,000)
Net process cost	284,000

	Production		Sales value			Apportioned cost
	Units		$			$
E	21,000	(× $15)	315,000	($284,000 × 315/495)		180,727
Q	18,000	(× $10)	180,000	($284,000 × 180/495)		103,273
			495,000			284,000

If you selected **option A** you apportioned some of the net process costs to the by-product. **Option C** makes no allowance for the credit of the by-product revenue to the process account, and **option D** is the production cost of product E.

5   C   No costs are apportioned to the by-product. The by-product revenue is credited to the sales account, and so does not affect the process costs.

	Units		Sales value			Apportioned cost
			$			$
L	3,000	(× $32)	96,000	($230,000 × 96/332)		66,506
M	2,000	(× $42)	84,000	($230,000 × 84/332)		58,193
N	4,000	(× $38)	152,000	($230,000 × 152/332)		105,301
			332,000			230,000

If you selected **option A** you credited the by-product sales revenue to the process account, but the question states that by-product revenue is credited to the sales account.

If you selected **option B** you apportioned some of the process costs to the by-product. **Option D** is the production cost for product L.

6　A　Total production units = 412,000 + 228,000

$$= 640,000 \text{ units}$$

Joint costs apportioned to Product H = $\dfrac{228,000}{640,000} \times \$384,000 = \$136,800$

Further processing costs = $159,600

∴ Total product cost of Product H = $(136,800 + 159,600) = $296,400

∴ Closing inventory value of Product H = $\dfrac{28,000}{228,000} \times \$296,400 = \$36,400$

7　D

Examiner's comments. This question examined Section D6(k) of the syllabus. Less than 30% of candidates answered this question correctly. Both B and C were popular choices by candidates. Choice B split the joint production costs on the basis of sales **prices** and choice C used the sales value **of sales** to apportion joint production costs.

Sales value of production

W	(12,000 units × $10)	$120,000
X	(10,000 units × $12)	$120,000

Joint production costs will be apportioned equally between the two products as the sales value of production is the same for each product.

Joint production costs allocated to X = $776,160/2 = $388,080

Value of closing inventory = $\dfrac{2,000}{10,000} \times \$388,080 = \$77,616$

ACCA Examiner's solution.

The correct answer was D ($77,616).

The correct approach is as follows:

Sales value of **production**:

Product W:	(12,000 × $10)	= $120,000
Product X	(10,000 × $12)	= $120,000

Therefore joint production costs are apportioned W : X in the ratio 1 : 1.

Amount apportioned to product X is ($776,160/2) = $388,080

20% of X's production is in closing inventory, therefore value of closing inventory

= (0.2 × $388,080) = $77,616

---

12 Job, batch and service costing

1　D　**Process costing** is a costing method used where it is not possible to identify separate units of production, or jobs, usually because of the continuous nature of the production process. The manufacture of liquid soap is a **continuous production process.**

			$
2	B	Selling price of job	1,690
		Less profit margin (30/130)	390
		Total cost of job	1,300
		Less overhead	694
		Prime cost	606

If you selected **option A** you deducted 30 per cent from the selling price to derive the total cost of the job. **Option C** is the result of deducting the overhead from the selling price, but omitting to deduct the profit margin. **Option D** is the total cost of the job; you needed to deduct the overhead to derive the prime cost.

			$
3	A	Direct materials (5 × $20)	100
		Direct labour (14 × $8)	112
		Variable overhead (14 × $3)	42
		Fixed overhead (14 × $5*)	70
		Other overhead	80
		Total cost of job 173	404

$$\text{*Fixed production overhead absorption rate} = \frac{\$200,000}{40,000}$$

$$= \$5 \text{ per direct labour hour}$$

4   C   The most logical basis for absorbing the overhead job costs is to use a percentage of direct labour cost.

$$\text{Overhead} = \frac{\$24,600}{\$(14,500+3,500+24,600)} \times \$126,000$$

$$= \frac{\$24,600}{\$42,600} \times \$126,000$$

$$= \$72,761$$

If you selected **option A** you used the materials cost as the basis for overhead absorption. This would not be equitable because job number BB15 incurred no material cost and would therefore absorb no overhead. **Option B** is based on the prime cost of each job (material plus labour) and therefore suffers from the same disadvantage as **option A**. **Option D** is the total overhead for the period, but some of this cost should be charged to the other two jobs.

			WIP
5	C	*Job number*	$
		AA10 (26,800 + 17,275 + 14,500) + ($\frac{14,500}{42,600} \times 126,000$)	101,462
		CC20 (18,500 + 24,600 + 72,761)	115,861
			217,323

Option A is the direct cost of job AA10, with no addition for overhead. **Option B** is the direct cost of both jobs in progress, but with no addition for overhead. **Option D** is the result of charging all of the overhead to the jobs in progress, but some of the overhead must be absorbed by the completed job BB15.

6   C   The actual material and labour costs for a batch **((i) and (iv))** can be determined from the material and labour recording system. Actual manufacturing overheads cannot be determined for a specific batch because of the need for allocation and apportionment of each item of overhead expenditure, and the subsequent calculation of a predetermined overhead absorption rate. Therefore **item (ii)** is incorrect and **item (iii)** is correct.

7   B   Cost per cake would be very small and therefore not an appropriate cost unit. The most appropriate cost unit would be cost per batch.

8   B   The vehicle cost per passenger-kilometre (i) is appropriate for cost control purposes because it **combines** the distance travelled and the number of passengers carried, **both of which affect cost**.

The fuel cost for each vehicle per kilometre (ii) can be useful for control purposes because it **focuses on a particular aspect** of the cost of operating each vehicle.

The fixed cost per kilometre (iii) is not particularly useful for control purposes because it **varies with the number of kilometres travelled**.

9   B   Number of occupied room-nights = 40 rooms × 30 nights × 65%

= 780

Room servicing cost per occupied room-night = $\dfrac{\$3,900}{780}$ = $5

Option A is the cost per available room-night. This makes no allowance for the 65% occupancy achieved. If you selected **option C** you simply divided $3,900 by 40 rooms. This does not account for the number of nights in the period, nor the percentage occupancy achieved. If you selected **option D** you calculated the cost per **occupied room**, rather than the cost per **occupied room-night**.

10   D
Weeks during year	= 52 – 4 = 48
Hours worked per year	= 48 × 35 hours
	= 1,680 hours
Hours chargeable to clients	= 1,680 × 90% = 1,512
Hourly charge rate	= $\dfrac{\$3,000 + \$18,000}{1,512} = \dfrac{\$21,000}{1,512}$
	= $13.89 per hour
Price for 3-hour 'colour and cut'	= $13.89 × 3 = $41.67

If you selected **option A** you calculated the correct hourly charge rate but you forgot to multiply by three to determine the correct total charge.

If you selected **option B** you did not add on the $3,000 required to cover the materials costs. **Option C** makes no allowance for the ten per cent of time which is not chargeable to clients.

11   A   For most services it is difficult to identify many attributable direct costs. A high level of indirect costs must be shared over several cost units, therefore **option A** is not a characteristic of service costing.

Many services are intangible, for example an accountancy practice offers an intangible service, therefore **option B** is a characteristic of service costing.

Composite cost units such as tonne-kilometre or room-night are often used, therefore **characteristic C** does apply. Service costing can also be used to establish a cost for an internal service such as a maintenance department which does work for other departments. Therefore **option D** is a characteristic of service costing.

12   B   A college and a hotel are likely to use service costing. A plumber works on separately identifiable jobs and is therefore more likely to use job costing.

13   C   An airline company, a railway company and a firm of accountants are **all** considered to be service industries.

14   C   **Assignment 789**

	$
Senior consultant – 54 hours × $40	2,160
Junior consultant – 110 hours × $25	2,750
Overhead absorption – 164 hours × $20	3,280
Total cost	8,190
40% × total cost = 40% × $8,190	3,276
Final fee	11,466

15 A **Total cost – job number 1012**

	$
Direct materials	45
Direct labour	30
Prime cost	75
Production overheads (30/7.5 × $12.50)	50
Total production cost	125
Non-production overheads (0.6 × $75)	45
Total cost – job number 1012	170

13 Budgeting

1 B **Coordination** (i) is an objective of budgeting. Budgets help to ensure that the **activities of all parts of the organisation are coordinated towards a single plan.**

Communication (ii) is an objective of budgeting. The budgetary planning process **communicates targets** to the managers responsible for achieving them, and it should also provide a **mechanism for junior managers to communicate to more senior staff** their estimates of what may be achievable in their part of the business.

Expansion (iii) is not in itself an objective of budgeting. Although a budget may be set **within a framework of expansion plans**, it is perfectly possible for an organisation to **plan for a reduction in activity.**

Resource allocation (iv) is an objective of budgeting. Most organisations face a situation of **limited resources** and an objective of the budgeting process is to ensure that these resources are allocated among budget centres in the most efficient way.

2 B The production cost budget would not be contained in a budget manual. The budget manual provides **guidelines and information about the budget process**; the production cost budget is part of the result of the budgetary planning process.

A timetable (option A), an organisation chart (option C) and specimen budgetary control reports (option D) are all useful information about the budget process and would therefore usually be contained in the budget manual.

3 B The **master budget** is the summary budget into which all subsidiary budgets are consolidated. It usually comprises the **budgeted income statement**, **budgeted balance sheet** and **budgeted cash flow statement**.

The master budget is used **in conjunction with the supporting subsidiary budgets**, to plan and control activities. The subsidiary budgets are not in themselves a part of the master budget. Therefore option D is not correct.

4 C The **principal budget factor** is the factor which limits the activities of an organisation.

Although cash and profit are affected by the level of sales (options A and B), sales is not the only factor which determines the level of cash and profit.

5 D A functional budget is a budget prepared for a particular function or department. A cash budget is **the cash result of the planning decisions included in all the functional budgets**. It is not a functional budget itself. Therefore the correct answer is D.

The production budget (option A), the distribution cost budget (option B) and the selling cost budget (option C) are all prepared for specific functions, therefore they are functional budgets.

6 D The annual budget is set **within the framework of the long-term plan.** It acts as the first step towards the **achievement of the organisation's long-term objectives.** Therefore the long term objectives must be established before any of the other budget tasks can be undertaken and the correct answer is D.

The principal budget factor (option A) may be affected by the organisation's long-term objectives. Although it must be identified before the other budgets can be prepared, it is not the first task in the list provided.

Since sales are often the limiting factor the sales demand (option B) must be established early in the planning process. However, the establishment of the long-term objectives must come first because, for example, the objectives may affect the decision about which markets to enter.

The predetermined overhead absorption rate (option C) cannot be calculated until the level of activity is known, which in turn will be affected by the principal budget factor and the long-term objectives.

7   B   Since there are no production resource limitations, sales would be the principal budget factor and the sales budget (2) would be prepared first. Budgeted inventory changes included in the finished goods inventory budget (4) would then indicate the required production for the production budget (5). This would lead to the calculation of the material usage (1) which would then be adjusted for the budgeted change in material inventory (6) to determine the required level of budgeted material purchases (3). Therefore the correct answer is B.

If you selected option A you began with production as the principal budget factor. However, there are no production resource limitations so production output is not a limiting factor. If you selected option C or D you correctly identified sales as the principal budget factor, but you did not identify the correct flow through the inventory adjustments to determine the required production and material purchases.

8   C   Since there are no production resource limitations, sales would be the principal budget factor therefore the sales budget must be prepared before the production budget (i). The budgeted change in finished goods inventory (iii) would then indicate the required volume for the production budget. Therefore the correct answer is C.

Item (ii), the material purchases, would be information derived **from** the production budget after adjusting for material inventory changes, and item (iv), the standard direct labour cost per unit, would be required for the **production cost budget**, but not for the production budget, which is **expressed in volume terms.**

9   B   Any opening inventory available at the beginning of a period will **reduce** the additional quantity required from production in order to satisfy a given sales volume. Any closing inventory required at the end of a period will **increase** the quantity required from production in order to satisfy sales and leave a sufficient volume in inventory. Therefore we need to **deduct** the opening inventory and **add** the required closing inventory.

10   C   Once the material usage budget has been prepared, based on the budgeted production volume, the usage is adjusted for the budgeted change in materials inventories in order to determine the required budgeted purchases. If purchases exceed production requirements this means that raw material inventories are being increased, and the correct answer is C.

Option A is incorrect because wastage would have been allowed for in determining the material usage budget. Option B is incorrect because a budgeted increase in finished goods inventory would have been allowed for in determining the production budget and hence the material usage budget.

11   C

	Units
Required for sales	24,000
Required to increase inventory (2,000 × 0.25)	500
	24,500

If you selected option A you subtracted the change in inventory from the budgeted sales. However, if inventories are to be increased then **extra units must be made for inventory**.

Option B is the budgeted sales volume, which would only be equal to budgeted production if there were no planned changes to inventory volume.

If you selected option D you increased the sales volume by 25 per cent, instead of adjusting inventory by this percentage.

12   B

	Units
Required increase in finished goods inventory	1,000
Budgeted sales of Alpha	60,000
Required production	61,000

	kg
Raw materials usage budget (× 3 kg)	183,000
Budgeted decrease in raw materials inventory	(8,000)
Raw materials purchase budget	175,000

If you selected option A you made no allowance for the increase in finished goods inventory. If you selected option C you did not adjust for the budgeted decrease in raw materials inventory, and option D adjusts for an increase in raw materials inventory, rather than a decrease.

13   D

	Units
Budgeted sales	18,000
Budgeted reduction in finished goods	(3,600)
Budgeted production of completed units	14,400
Allowance for defective units (10% of output = 1/9 of input)	1,600
Production budget	16,000

If you selected option A you deducted a ten per cent allowance for defective units, instead of adding it, and option B makes no allowance for defective units at all. If you selected option C you added ten per cent to the required completed units to allow for the defective units, but the ten per cent **should be based on the total number of units output**, ie ten per cent of 16,000 = 1,600 units.

14   D

	Hours
Active hours required for production = 200 × 6 hours =	1,200
Allowance for idle time (20% of total time = 25% of active time)	300
Total hours to be paid for	1,500
× $7 per hour	
Direct labour cost budget	$10,500

If you selected option A you deducted 20% from the active hours for idle time, instead of **adding an allowance of 20% of total time paid for**. Option B makes no allowance for idle time, while option C calculates the allowance based on the active hours rather than on the hours paid for.

15   D

	Units
Planned increase in inventories of finished goods	4,600
Budgeted sales	36,800
Budgeted production (to pass quality control check)	41,400

This is 92% of total production, allowing for an 8% rejection rate.

Budgeted production = $\dfrac{100}{92}$ × 41,400 = 45,000 units

Budgeted direct labour hours = (× 5 hours per unit) 225,000 hours

If you selected option A you deducted eight per cent from the budgeted production, instead of **adding a rejection allowance of eight per cent of the final output**. Option B makes no allowance for rejects while option C calculates the number of rejects based on the budgeted good production rather than on the total output.

16   D

> **ACCA examiner's comments**
>
> This question tested section E2(b) in the Study Guide.
>
> The most popular choice by candidates was option C which is obtained by multiplying $240,000 by 1.20 – an incorrect adjustment of adding 20% for the idle time. Option A ($240,000 x 0.80) was chosen by more than 25% of the candidates.

Before you can work out the total cost, you have to determine how many labour hours are required. You can calculate the number of hours required for the units quite easily: 4,800 x 5 = 24,000 hours. However 20% of labour time is idle, which means that 24,000 hours is only 80% of the total hours required to produce 4,800 units. Total hours = 24,000 x (100/80) = 30,000 hours.

Total cost = 30,000 hours x $10 per hour = $300,000 (which is option D)

ACCA examiner's solution

The correct answer was D.

The manufacturing time to produce 4,800 units is 24,000 (4,800 x 5) which at $10 per hour gives option B ($240,000). This was chosen by more than 20% of candidates. However the question asks for the budgeted **total** labour cost, therefore the $240,000 needs to be adjusted for the idle time. The $240,000 represents payment for 80% of the total time and therefore the total cost is $300,000 ($240,000/0.80 or $240,000 x 100/80).

The most popular choice by candidates was option C which is obtained by multiplying $240,000 by 1.20 – an incorrect adjustment of adding 20% for the idle time. Option A ($240,000 x 0.80) was chosen by more than 25% of the candidates.

---

14 Standard costing

1   B

		$ per unit	$ per unit
Material P	7kg × $4	28	
Material S	3kg × $9	27	
			55
Direct labour 5hr × $7			35
Standard prime cost of product J			90

Option A is the **standard material cost** and **option C** is the **standard total production cost**, including overheads which are not part of prime cost.

Option D includes the absorption of **general overhead**; always **read the question carefully**!

2   C   A personnel manager would usually keep information concerning the expected rates of pay for employees with a given level of experience and skill.

Option A is incorrect because although the trade union is involved in negotiating future rates of pay for their members, they do not take decisions on the standard rate to be paid in the future.

A production manager (**option B**) would provide information concerning the number of employees needed and the skills required, but they would not have the latest information concerning the expected rates of pay.

3   B   An attainable standard assumes efficient levels of operation, but includes **allowances** for normal loss, waste and machine downtime.

Option A describes an ideal standard.
Option C describes a current standard.
Option D describes a basic standard.

4   C   It is generally accepted that the use of **attainable standards** has the optimum motivational impact on employees. Some allowance is made for unavoidable wastage and inefficiencies, but the attainable level can be reached if production is carried out efficiently.

Option A and **option D** are not correct because employees may feel that the goals are **unattainable** and will not work so hard.

Option B is not correct because standards set at a minimal level will not provide employees with any incentive to work harder.

5   B   The volume of output would influence the total number of labour hours required, but it would not be directly relevant to the standard labour time per unit.

The type of performance standard (**option A**) would be relevant. For example, if an ideal standard is used there would be no extra time allowed for inefficiencies. **Option C** would be relevant because it would provide information about the tasks to be performed and the time that those tasks should take.

6   D   Required liquid input = 1 litre $\times \dfrac{100}{80}$ = 1.25 litres

If you selected **option A** you **deducted** 20 per cent from the required output, instead of **adding extra** to allow for losses, whereas **option B** makes **no allowance** for losses.

Option C simply adds an extra 20 per cent to the completed output, but the wastage is 20 per cent of the liquid **input**, not 20 per cent of output.

7   C   When management by exception is operated within a standard costing system, only the variances which exceed acceptable tolerance limits need to be investigated by management with a view to control action. Adverse and favourable variances alike may be subject to investigation, therefore **option A** is incorrect.

Any efficient information system would ensure that only managers who are able to act on the information receive management reports, even if they are not prepared on the basis of management by exception. Therefore **option B** is incorrect.

8   A   Standard costing provides targets for achievement, and yardsticks against which actual performance can be monitored (**item (i)**). It also provides the unit cost information for evaluating the volume figures contained in a budget (**item (ii)**). Inventory control systems are simplified with standard costing. Once the variances have been eliminated, all inventory units are valued at standard price (**item (iii)**).

Item (iv) is incorrect because standard costs are an **estimate** of what will happen in the future, and a unit cost target that the organisation is aiming to achieve.

9   D   Standard labour cost per unit = 9 hours $\times \dfrac{100}{90} \times \$9 = \$90$

You should have been able to eliminate **option A** because it is less than the basic labour cost of $81 for 9 hours of work. Similar reasoning also eliminates **option B**. If you selected **option C** you simply added 10% to the 9 active hours to determine a standard time allowance of 9.9 hours per unit. However the idle time allowance is given as 10% of the total labour time.

15 Basic variance analysis

1   C   Since inventories are valued at standard cost, the material price variance is based on the materials purchased.

	$
12,000 kg material purchased should cost (×$3)	36,000
but did cost	33,600
Material price variance	2,400 (F)

800 units manufactured should use (× 14 kg)	11,200 kg
but did use	11,500 kg
Usage variance in kg	300 kg (A)
× standard price per kg	× $3
Usage variance in $	$900 (A)

If you selected **option A or B** you based your calculation of the material price variance on the material actually used, and if you selected **option B** you forgot to evaluate the usage variance in kg at the standard price per kg. If you selected **option D** you evaluated the usage variance at the actual price per kg, rather than the standard price per kg.

2   C

	$
2,300 hours should have cost (× $7)	16,100
but did cost	18,600
Rate variance	2,500 (A)

Option A is the total direct labour cost variance. If you selected **option B** you calculated the correct money value of the variance but you misinterpreted its direction. If you selected **option D** you based your calculation on the 2,200 hours worked, but **2,300 hours were paid for** and these hours should be the basis for the calculation of the rate variance.

3   D

260 units should have taken (× 10 hrs)	2,600 hrs
but took (active hours)	2,200 hrs
Efficiency variance in hours	400 hrs (F)
× standard rate per hour	× $7
Efficiency variance in $	$2,800 (F)

Option A is the total direct labour cost variance. If you selected **option B** you based your calculations on the 2,300 hours paid for; but efficiency measures should be based on the **active hours only**, ie 2,200 hours.

If you selected **option C** you calculated the correct money value of the variance but you misinterpreted its direction.

4   B   Idle time hours (2,300 − 2,200) × standard rate per hour = 100 hrs × $7
$$= \$700 \text{ (A)}$$

If you selected **option A** you calculated the correct money value of the variance but you misinterpreted its direction. The idle time variance is always adverse.

If you selected **option C or D** you evaluated the idle time at the actual hourly rate instead of the standard hourly rate.

5   C   Standard variable production overhead cost per hour = $11,550 ÷ 5,775 = $2

	$
8,280 hours of variable production overhead should cost (× $2)	16,560
but did cost	14,904
Variable production overhead expenditure variance	1,656 (F)

Standard time allowed for one unit = 5,775 hours ÷ 1,925 units = 3 hours

2,070 units should take (× 3 hours)	6,210 hours
but did take	8,280 hours
Efficiency variance in hours	2,070 hours (A)
× standard variable production overhead cost per hour	× $2
Variable production overhead efficiency variance	$4,140 (A)

If you selected **option A** you calculated the correct efficiency variance in hours but you omitted to evaluate it at the standard variable overhead cost per hour. If you selected **option B** you evaluated the efficiency variance at the actual variable overhead rate per hour, instead of at the standard rate per hour. If you selected **option D** you calculated the expenditure variance as the difference between the budget and actual expenditure. However this does not compare like with like. The actual expenditure should be compared with the expected expenditure for the number of hours actually worked.

6   C   **Fixed overhead expenditure variance**

	$
Budgeted fixed overhead expenditure (4,200 units × $4 per unit)	16,800
Actual fixed overhead expenditure	17,500
Fixed overhead expenditure variance	700 (A)

The variance is adverse because the actual expenditure was higher than the amount budgeted.

Fixed overhead volume variance

	$
Actual production at standard rate (5,000 × $4 per unit)	20,000
Budgeted production at standard rate (4,200 × $4 per unit)	16,800
Fixed overhead volume variance	3,200 (F)

The variance is favourable because the actual volume of output was greater than the budgeted volume of output.

If you selected an incorrect option you misinterpreted the direction of one or both of the variances.

7   A   **Capacity variance**

Budgeted hours of work	9,000 hours
Actual hours of work	9,400 hours
Capacity variance in hours	400 hours (F)
× standard fixed overhead absorption rate per hour *	× $4
Fixed production overhead capacity variance	$1,600 (F)

* $36,000/9,000 = $4 per hour

If you selected **option B or C** you performed the calculations correctly but misinterpreted the variance as adverse. Since the labour force worked 400 hours longer than budgeted, there is the potential for output to be 400 standard hours (or 80 units of production) higher than budgeted and hence the variance is favourable.

Efficiency variance

1,900 units of product should take (× 9,000/1,800 hrs)	9,500 hours
but did take	9,400 hours
Efficiency variance in hours	100 hours (F)
× standard fixed overhead absorption rate per hour *	× $4
Fixed production overhead efficiency variance in $	$400 (F)

* $36,000/9,000 = $4 per hour

If you selected **option B or D** you performed the calculations correctly but misinterpreted the variance as adverse. Time was saved compared to the standard time allowed for 1,900 units and so the efficiency variance is favourable.

8   C   **Statement (i)** is not consistent with a favourable labour efficiency variance. Employees of a lower skill level are likely to work less efficiently, resulting in an **adverse efficiency variance**.

Statement (ii) is consistent with a favourable labour efficiency variance. **Time would be saved in processing** if the material was easier to process.

Statement (iii) is consistent with a favourable labour efficiency variance. **Time would be saved in processing** if working methods were improved.

Therefore the correct answer is C.

9   D   Direct material cost variance = material price variance + material usage variance

The adverse material usage variance could be larger than the favourable material price variance. The total of the two variances would therefore represent a net result of an adverse total direct material cost variance.

The situation in **option A** would sometimes arise, but not always, because of the possibility of the situation described in option D.

Option B could sometimes be correct, depending on the magnitude of each of the variances. However it will not **always** be correct as stated in the wording.

Option C is incorrect because the sum of the two favourable variances would always be a larger favourable variance.

10 B

	$
53,000 kg should cost (× $2.50)	132,500
but did cost	136,000
Material price variance	3,500 (A)

11 A

	$
27,000 units should use (× 2 kg)	54,000 kg
but did use	53,000 kg
	1,000 kg (F)
× standard cost per kg	2.5
Material usage variance	2,500 (F)

12 A

	$
9,200 hours should have cost (× $12.50)	115,000
but did cost	110,750
Direct labour rate variance	4,250 (F)

13 D

2,195 units should have taken (× 4 hours)	8,780 hours
but did take	9,200 hours
Direct labour efficiency variance (in hours)	420 hours (A)
× standard rate pre hour	× 12.50
	5,250 (A)

14 D **Labour rate variance**

	$
14,000 hours should have cost (× $10 per hour)	140,000
but did cost	176,000
Labour rate variance	36,000 (A)

Labour efficiency variance

	$	
5,500 units should have taken (× 3 hours per unit)	16,500	hrs
but did take	14,000	hrs
Labour efficiency variance (in hours)	2,500	hrs (F)
× standard rate per unit	× $10	
	$25,000	(F)

15 A

ACCA examiner's comments

This question tested section E4(a) in the Study Guide.

Almost as many candidates selected option B as selected the correct choice A. Candidates selecting a variance value of $10,000 had presumably calculated the volume variance rather than the capacity variance, which was $10,000 favourable.

A one mark written question on this topic with just two choices (A or B) was also set in the June 2008 examination. A comparable outcome occurred then as the candidates opted for A and B in almost equal proportions.

Standard fixed overhead absorption rate per hour = $125,000/25,000 = $5 per hour

Fixed overhead volume capacity variance

Budgeted hours of work	25,000 hrs
Actual hours of work	24,000 hrs
Fixed overhead volume capacity variance	1,000 hrs (A)
× standard fixed overhead absorption rate per hour	× $5
Fixed overhead volume capacity variance in $	$5,000 (A)

16 Further variance analysis

1   B   The only fixed overhead variance in a marginal costing statement is the fixed overhead expenditure variance. This is the difference between budgeted and actual overhead expenditure, calculated in the same way as for an absorption costing system.

There is no volume variance with marginal costing, because under or over absorption due to volume changes cannot arise.

2   D   Raising prices in response to higher demand would result in a favourable selling price variance.

Market penetration pricing (**option A**) is a policy of low prices. This would result in an adverse selling price variance, if the original planned policy had been one of market skimming pricing, which involves charging high prices.

Early payment discounts (**option B**) are financial accounting items which do not affect the recorded selling price.

Reducing selling prices (**option C**) is more likely to result in an adverse selling price variance.

3   A

	$
Total actual direct material cost	2,400
Add back variances: direct material price	(800)
direct material usage	400
Standard direct material cost of production	2,000
Standard material cost per unit	$10
Number of units produced (2,000 ÷ $10)	200

Option B is the actual sales revenue divided by the standard selling price. This does not lead to a **production** figure, and it does not allow for any selling price variance which may have arisen.

If you selected **option C** you divided the actual material cost by $10 without adjusting first for the material cost variances.

If you selected **option D** you had the right idea about adjusting the variances, but you got the additions and subtractions the wrong way round. An adverse variance must be deducted from the actual cost to derive the standard cost, and vice versa with a favourable variance.

4   A   Since there was no change in inventories, the usage variance can be used to calculate the material usage.

Saving in material used compared with standard $= \dfrac{\$400(F)}{\$2\,per\,kg} = 200\ kg$

Standard material usage for actual production (200 units × 5kg)	1,000 kg
Usage variance in kg	200 kg (F)
Actual usage of material	800 kg

Option B is the standard usage for the output of 200 units

If you selected **option C** you added the 200 kg usage variance instead of subtracting it.

5 D

		$
200 units should sell for (× $70)		14,000
but did sell for		15,200
Selling price variance		1,200 (F)

Option A is 1/10 of the correct value – did you miss off a zero?

Option B is the sales volume variance.

If you selected **option C** you calculated the correct value for the variance, but misinterpreted it as adverse.

6 C

Budgeted sales volume per month $= \dfrac{\text{Budgeted material cost of sales}}{\text{Standard material cost per unit}}$

$= \dfrac{\$2,300}{\$10} = 230$ units

Budgeted profit margin per unit $= \dfrac{\text{Budgeted monthly profit margin}}{\text{Budgeted monthly sales volume}}$

$= \dfrac{\$6,900}{230} = \$30$ per unit

Budgeted sales volume	230 units
Actual sales volume	200 units
Sales volume variance in units	30 units (A)
Standard profit per unit	× $30
Sales volume variance in $	$900 (A)

If you selected **option A** you calculated the correct value for the variance, but misinterpreted it as favourable.

Option B is the selling price variance.

If you selected **option D** you evaluated the sales volume variance in units at the standard selling price per unit, instead of using the standard profit per unit. Remember that the volume variance highlights the margin lost or gained as a result of achieving a lower or higher sales volume than budgeted.

7 B

Actual expenditure = $(48,000 + 2,000) = $50,000

Overhead absorbed = $(50,000 − 8,000) = $42,000

Overhead absorption rate per unit = $48,000 ÷ 4,800 = $10

∴ Number of units produced = $42,000 ÷ $10 = 4,200

If you selected **option A** you **subtracted** the **adverse** expenditure variance from the budgeted fixed production overhead cost. If the expenditure variance is adverse the actual expenditure must be greater than the budget.

Option C is the budgeted output, and if you selected **option D you added the under-absorbed** overhead to the actual expenditure to determine the overhead absorbed. If overhead is **under absorbed then the actual overhead must be greater than the overhead absorbed.**

8 D

Total standard cost of material purchased – actual cost of material purchased = Price variance

Total standard cost $= \$21,920 + \$1,370$

$= \$23,290$

Standard price per kg $= \dfrac{\$23,290}{6,850}$

$= \$3.40$

Option A is the favourable price variance per kg. This should have been added to the actual price to determine the standard price per kg. If you selected **option B** you subtracted the price variance from the actual cost. If the price variance is favourable then the standard price per kg must be higher than the actual price paid. **Option C** is the actual price paid per kg.

BPP
LEARNING MEDIA

9   B

Actual sales	2,550 units
Budgeted sales	2,400 units
Variance in units	150 units (F)
× standard contribution per unit ($(27 – 12))	× $15
Sales volume variance in $	$2,250 (F)

	$
Revenue from 2,550 units should have been (× $27)	68,850
but was	67,320
Selling price variance	1,530 (A)

If you selected **option A** you evaluated the sales volume variance at the standard profit per unit. This would be the sales volume variance as calculated in an absorption costing system.

If you selected **option C or D** you calculated the variances correctly but you misinterpreted the direction of the volume variance and price variance respectively.

10   C

	$	
Budgeted sales volume	10,000	units
Actual sales volume	9,800	units
Sales volume variance (units)	200	units (A)
× standard profit per unit	× $5	
Sales volume profit variance (in $)	$1,000	(A)

11   B   Direct material price variance

	$
12,000 litres should have cost (× $2.50)	30,000
But did cost (12,000 × $2.50 × 1.04)	31,200
Direct material price variance	1,200 (A)

12   C   Standard cost per unit = 10.5 litres × $2.50 per litre

$$= \$26.25 \text{ per unit}$$

Standard cost of actual production = standard cost + variance
= $(12,000 litres × $2.50) + 1,815
= $(30,000 + 1,815)
= $31,815

∴ Actual production = standard cost of actual production/standard cost per unit

$$= 31,815/\$26.25$$

$$= 1,212 \text{ units}$$

13   C

	$
Sales revenue for 9,000 units should have been (× $12.50)	112,500
but was	117,000
Sales price variance	4,500 (F)

14   C

	$
8,500 units should have cost (× $15)	127,500
but did cost (8,500 × $17)	144,500
	17,000 (A)

15   B

	$
Absorbed overhead (12,400 × 1.02 × $4.25)	53,754
Actual overhead	56,389
Under-absorbed overhead	2,635

16   D

Standard contribution	$10,000
Sales price variance	$500
Variable cost variance	$(2,000)
	$8,500

ACCA Examiner's solution

The correct answer is obtained as follows:

	$
Standard contribution on actual sales	10,000
Add Favourable sales price variance	500
Subtract Adverse total variable costs variance	(2,000)
Actual contribution	8,500

The most popular choice made by candidates was B. Those choosing B had overlooked the fact that the 'standard contribution on actual sales' (given in the question) would have been obtained by adjusting the budgeted contribution by the sales volume contribution variance, therefore this variance should have been **ignored** in answering the specific question set.

17   A

Standard contribution	$50,000
Variable cost variance	$(3,500)
	$46,500

ACCA Examiner's solution

The correct answer is obtained as follows:

	$
Standard contribution on actual sales	50,000
Subtract adverse total variable cost variance	(3,500)
Actual contribution	46,500

No adjustment is required for the favourable sales volume contribution variance as it will have **already been added** to the budgeted contribution to arrive at the standard contribution from actual sales ($50,000) given in the question. The total fixed costs variance, along with the budgeted fixed costs, appears in a reconciliation statement below the actual contribution.

17 Cost-volume-profit (CVP) analysis

1   D   Breakeven point $= \dfrac{\text{Fixed costs}}{\text{Contribution per unit}}$

$$= \frac{10{,}000 \times (\$4.00 + 0.80)}{(\$6.00 - (\$1.20 + \$0.40))} = \frac{\$48{,}000}{\$4.40} = 10{,}909 \text{ units}$$

If you selected **option A** you divided the fixed cost by the selling price, but the **selling price also has to cover the variable cost. Option B** ignores the selling costs, but these are costs that **must be covered before the breakeven point is reached. Option C** is the budgeted sales volume, which happens to be below the breakeven point.

2   C

	$ per unit
New selling price ($6 × 1.1)	6.60
New variable cost ($1.20 × 1.1) + $0.40	1.72
Revised contribution per unit	4.88
New fixed costs ($40,000 × 1.25) + $8,000	$58,000

Revised breakeven point $= \dfrac{\$58{,}000}{\$4.88} = 11{,}885 \text{ units}$

If you selected **option A** you divided the fixed cost by the selling price, but the **selling price also has to cover the variable cost. Option B** fails to allow for the increase in variable production cost and **option D** increases all of the costs by the percentages given, rather than the production costs only.

3   B   P/V ratio $= \dfrac{\text{Contribution per unit}}{\text{Selling price per unit}}$

$$= \frac{\$(20 - 4 - 3 - 2 - 1)}{\$20} \times 100\% = 50\%$$

If you selected **option A** you calculated profit per unit as a percentage of the selling price per unit. **Option C** excludes the variable selling costs from the calculation of contribution per unit and **option D** excludes the variable production overhead cost, but **all variable costs must be deducted from the selling price to determine the contribution.**

4   C   Contribution per unit = $90 – $40 = $50. The sale of 6,000 units just covers the annual fixed costs, therefore the fixed costs must be $50 × 6,000 = $300,000.

If you selected **option A** you calculated the correct contribution of $50 per unit, but you then divided the 6,000 by $50 instead of multiplying. **Option B** is the total annual variable cost and **option D** is the annual revenue.

5   A   Breakeven point $= \dfrac{\text{Fixed costs}}{\text{P/V ratio}} = \dfrac{\$76{,}800}{0.40} = \$192{,}000$

Actual sales	= $224,000
Margin of safety in terms of sales value	$32,000
÷ selling price per unit	÷ $16
Margin of safety in units	2,000

If you selected **option B** you calculated the breakeven point in units, but forgot to take the next step to calculate the margin of safety. **Option C** is the actual sales in units and **option D** is the margin of safety in terms of sales value.

6	A	Currently weekly contribution = 12% × $280,000 = $33,600	

	$
Extra contribution from 5% increase in sales = 5% × $33,600	1,680
Loss on product Z each week 3,000 × $(1.90 – 2.20 – 0.15)	(1,350)
Weekly increase in profit	330

If you selected **option B** you forgot to allow for the variable cost of distributing the 3,000 units of Z. **Option C** is based on a five per cent increase in **revenue** from the other products; however extra variable costs will be incurred, therefore the gain will be a five per cent increase in **contribution**. If you selected **option D** you made no allowance for the variable costs of either product Z or the extra sales of other products.

7   B   **Statement (i)** is correct. The line which passes through the origin indicates the sales revenue at various levels of activity. The sales revenue is $100,000 for 10,000 units therefore the selling price is $10 per unit.

Statement (ii) is incorrect. The sloping line which intercepts the vertical axis at $30,000 shows the total cost at various levels of activity. The **total cost** for 10,000 units is $80,000. The fixed costs of $30,000 (the cost at zero activity) must be subtracted from this to derive the variable cost of 10,000 units, which is $50,000. Therefore the variable cost per unit is $5.

Statement (iii) is correct. The fixed cost is the cost incurred at zero activity and is shown as a horizontal line at $30,000.

Statement (iv) is incorrect. The profit for 10,000 units is the difference between the sales value ($100,000) and the total cost ($80,000) which amounts to $20,000.

Therefore the correct answer is B.

8   B   The distance H is the total cost at zero activity, ie the fixed cost. **Option A**, contribution, is the distance between the sales line and the variable cost line, which are the two lines that pass through the origin. Sales value (**option C**) is represented by the steepest of the two lines passing through the origin. Variable cost (**option D**) is represented by the less steep of the two lines passing through the origin.

9   A   The chart shows the variable cost line and the contribution can be read directly as the distance between this and the sales value line. Therefore this is a contribution breakeven chart.

A conventional breakeven chart (**option B**) shows the fixed cost line instead of the variable cost line. A profit-volume chart (**option C**) plots a single line to indicate the profit at any level of activity. **Option D** is not a generally recognised description of a chart used for breakeven analysis.

10   A   **Statement (i)** is correct. The point where the profit-volume line crosses the x axis is the point of zero profit and zero loss, ie the breakeven point.

Statement (ii) is correct. The profit can be read from the y axis at any point beyond the breakeven point.

Statement (iii) is incorrect. The starting point of the profit-volume line is the point on the y axis representing the loss at zero activity, which is the fixed cost incurred.

Therefore the correct answer is A, **statements (i) and (ii)** are correct.

11   D   Profits will be maximised at the point where the iso-profit line is furthest from the origin (but within the feasible region).

12   D   Line 'T' = Total fixed costs
Line 'V' = Contribution

13   C   Breakeven point = $\dfrac{\text{Fixed costs}}{\text{Contribution per unit}}$

Fixed costs = 2,400 units × $30 per unit = $72,000

Contribution per unit = Selling price – variable costs = (60 – 15 –5) = $40

$$\therefore \text{Breakeven point} = \frac{\$72,000}{\$40} = 1,800 \text{ units}$$

14 C

$$\text{Sales revenue at breakeven point} = \frac{\text{Fixed costs}}{\text{C/S ratio}} = \frac{\$60,000}{0.4} = \$150,000$$

Budgeted/planned sales revenue = $150,000 + margin of safety

= $150,000 + $64,000 = $214,000

$$\text{Budgeted/planned activity level} = \frac{\$214,000}{\$40} = 5,350 \text{ units}$$

15 A The breakeven chart shows that both selling price per unit and variable cost per unit are constant; this is shown graphically by each line having a constant gradient.

16 D $\text{Selling price} = \dfrac{\text{Contribution per unit}}{\text{C/S ratio}} = \dfrac{\$27}{0.45} = \$60$

Margin of safety (revenue) = $13,500

$\text{Margin of safety (units)} = \dfrac{\$13,500}{\$60} = 225 \text{ units}$

$\therefore$ Breakeven point = (1,000 – 225 units) = 775 units

$\text{Breakeven point} = \dfrac{\text{Fixed costs}}{\text{Contribution on per unit}}$

$775 = \dfrac{\text{Fixed costs}}{\$27}$

$\therefore$ Fixed costs = 775 units × $27 = $20,925

17 C **Budgeted breakeven sales revenue**

Budgeted contribution – fixed costs = budgeted profit

$200,000 – fixed costs = $50,000

Fixed costs = $200,000 – $50,000

$\text{Budgeted breakeven sales revenue} = \dfrac{\text{Fixed costs}}{\text{C/S ratio}^*} = \dfrac{\$150,000}{0.4} = \$375,000$

$^*\text{C/S ratio} = \dfrac{\text{Contribution}}{\text{Sales revenue}} = \dfrac{\$200,000}{\$500,000}$

18 C

ACCA examiner's comments

This question tested section F1(c) in the Study Guide which refers to the identification of elements in profit-volume charts. Only one third of the candidates selected the correct answer to this question. Choice B was the most popular selection by candidates for this question. This was possibly based on the calculation of $140,000 as a percentage of $500,000 or just a pure guess.

The profit/volume graph shows levels of profit at different levels of sales. In order to answer the question, you must determine **contribution** for $500,000 sales revenue.

Remember that **profit = contribution – fixed costs**.

When sales revenue = 0, contribution = 0 and the graph shows a loss of $60,000 at zero sales revenue. This means that fixed costs must be $60,000.

Contribution at $500,000 sales revenue   = $140,000 (profit) + $60,000 (fixed costs)

                                                    = $200,000

Contribution to sales ratio = contribution/sales revenue = ($200,000/$500,000) = 0.4 or 40%

ACCA examiner's solution

The correct answer was C (40%). The diagram shows that at an activity level of $500,000 worth of sales, the profit was $140,000. It also shows that the loss at zero activity is $60,000 which also represents the total fixed costs. Therefore the contribution at $500,000 of sales is $200,000 ($140,000 + $60,000) and the contribution to sales ratio is: (200,000/500,000 x 100) = 40%.

---

18 Relevant costing and decision-making

1   D   An opportunity cost is the value of the benefit sacrificed when one course of action is chosen, in preference to another.

            A sunk cost (**option A**) is a **past cost** which is not relevant to the decision. An incremental cost (**option B**) is an **extra cost** to be incurred in the future as the result of a decision taken now. The salary cost forgone is certainly relevant to the decision therefore **option C** is not correct.

2   C   The **material is in regular use** and so 1,000 kg will be purchased. 500 kg of this will replace the 500 kg in inventory that is used, 100 kg will be purchased and used and the remaining 400 kg will be kept in inventory until needed. The relevant cost is therefore 600 × $3.25 = $1,950.

            If you selected **option A** you valued the inventory items at their resale price. However, the items are in regular use therefore they would not be resold.

            Option B values the inventory items at their original purchase price, but this is a sunk or past cost. **Option D** is the cost of the 1,000 kg that must be purchased, but since the material is in regular use the excess can be kept in inventory until needed.

3   B   When calculating the relevant cost of an asset, use the following diagram.

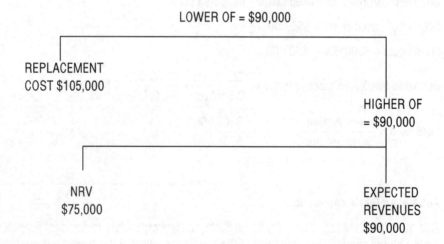

4   D

	Product	
	X	Y
	$	$
Selling price per unit	20	40
Variable cost per unit	12	30
Contribution per unit	8	10
Contribution per skilled labour hour required	(÷2) 4	(÷4) 2.5
Ranking	1st	2nd

Manufacture and sell: 800 units of Product X (using 800 × 2 hours = 1,600 hours); 100 units of Product Y (using the remaining 400 hours* (2,000 – 1,600).

* 400 hours ÷ 4 hours skilled labour per unit = 100 units.

5   B   The cost of special material which will be purchased is a relevant cost in a short-term decision making context.

6   A

	$
Contribution per unit – current $(3.70 – 2.50)	1.20
Contribution per unit – revised $(2.95 – 2.50)	0.45
	$
Total contribution – new business (6,000 × $0.45)	2,700
Lost contribution – current business (6,000/15 × 2 × $1.20)	(960)
Increase in monthly profit	1,740

7   B   Total relevant cost of materials

	$
Material T	
500kg × $45	22,500
Material V	
200kg × $40	8,000
200kg × $52	10,400
Total relevant cost of materials	40,900

8   D

	$
Opportunity cost (net realisable value)	1,200
Cost of disposal in one year's time	800
Total relevant cost of machine	2,000

9   C

500	Hours are required
400	Hours are available as spare labour capacity
100	Hours are required but not available as spare capacity

(1)   If the 100 hours are from worked overtime, then the cost

= 100 hours × 1½ × $12 = 31,800

(2)   If labour is diverted from the production of Product X, then the cost =

100 hours × $12 + (100/2 × $4)

= $1,200 + $200

= $1,400

Option (2) is cheaper and therefore the relevant cost of labour for the contract is $1,400.

	I	II	III	Total
10	B			
Optimal production plan (units)	2,000	1,500	4,000	
Kgs required per unit	6	4	2.5	
Kgs material available	12,000	6,000	10,000	28,000

19 Linear programming

1   A   The total labour usage per week in hours is $0.5x + 2y$, since each unit of X uses 30 minutes (half an hour) of labour and each unit of Y uses 2 hours of labour. This must not exceed 5,000 hours, so the labour constraint is $0.5x + 2y \leq 5,000$.

The requirement to produce at least 50 units of X each week gives $x \geq 50$.

The requirement to produce at least twice as many units of Y as of X each week gives $y \geq 2x$. Therefore the correct answer is A.

2   D   A sketch graph of the feasible region and the objective ($3x + y = 450$) is as follows.

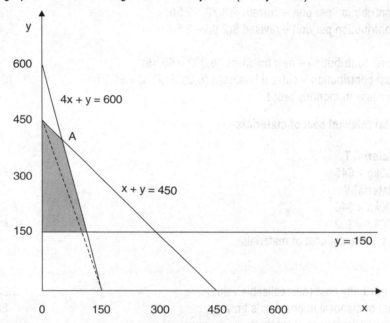

The optimum is at point A, the intersection of $x + y = 450$ and $4x + y = 600$.

At this point,

	$4x$	$+$	y	$=$	600	(1)
	x	$+$	y	$=$	450	(2)
	$3x$			$=$	150	(1) – (2)
	x			$=$	50	
Substituting in (2)	50	$+$	y	$=$	450	
			y	$=$	400	

The value of the objective function is therefore $(3 \times 50) + 400 = 550$, and the correct answer is D.

3   A   Use simultaneous equations to solve this problem.

Let G be the number of batches of golf balls
     T be the number of batches of teddy bears

Labour constraint:	$5G + 10T = 20,000$	(1)
Machine time constraint	$10G + 2T = 25,000$	(2)

Multiply equation (2) by –0.5:
–5G – 1T = -12,500 (3)

Add equation (3) to equation (1)
9T = 8,500
T = 833

Substitute T = 833 into either equation (we will use equation (1))
5G + (10 × 833) = 20,000
5G = 20,000 – 8,330
G = 1,670/5
G = 2,334

The company should manufacture 2,334 batches of golf balls and 833 batches of teddy bears.

4　A　Firstly, we must formulate the constraints and the objective function and then draw a graph in order to determine the optimum point, and find the total cost at this point.

Let　l = number of large posters
　　　s = number of small posters

The constraints are as follows.

l	$\geq 0.5s$
l	≥ 50
l + s	≥ 100
s	≤ 150

The objective is to **minimise** 4l + 2s.

A sketch graph of the feasible region and the objective (4l + 2s = 400) is shown below.

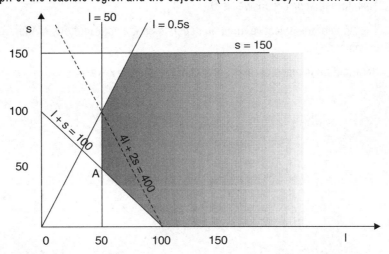

The **optimum** is at point A, at the intersection of the lines l = 50 and l + s = 100.

At this point,

l	= 50
l + s	= 100
50 + s	= 100
s	= 50

The cost at this point, which is the **minimum total cost**, is (50 × $4) + ($50 × $2) = $300.

The correct answer is therefore A.

5　C　The expected cost of a call in peak hours is ($1 × 40%) + ($1.50 × 60%) = $1.30 = 130p. The expected cost of a call at other times is (80p × 30%) + (90p × 50%) + ($1 × 20%) = 89p. The objective is therefore: minimise 130x + 89y.

6   C   The constraint requires that $X \leq \dfrac{(X + Y)}{4}$

Therefore $4X \leq X + Y$
$$4X - X \leq Y$$
$$3X \leq Y$$

Option C is therefore correct.

If you selected **option A**, you have stated the inequality that the number of managers must at most equal a quarter of non-managerial numbers instead of total staff numbers.

If you selected **option B**, you stated the inequality that the number of managers must at most equal four times the number of non-managerial staff. You have confused four with one quarter and non-managerial staff with total staff.

If you selected **option D**, you have stated the inequality that a quarter of the number of the managers must be less than or equal to the number of staff. This translates into $0 \leq 3X + 4Y$ which is true since X and Y cannot be negative, but this does not represent the correct constraint.

7   D   The minimum weight of 50 kg of P per hectare gives $p \geq 50$.

The requirement that the weight of Q per hectare be between two and five times the weight of P per hectare gives:

$q \geq 2p$
$q \leq 5p$

The maximum total weight of 500 kg per hectare gives $p + q \leq 500$.

Therefore the correct answer is D.

8   D   The slope of the objective function depends on the contributions of the products – this is the correct statement.

9   D   Contribution is maximised at Constraint (1) and the x – axis.

Answers to objective test questions

20 Information for management

1   Information

2   ☑ Complete
    ☐ Extensive
    ☑ Relevant
    ☑ Accurate

Good information is not necessarily extensive. Too much information may tend to obscure the important points.

3   Decision making.

4   ☑ False

Strategic planning is carried out by senior management. Front line managers will be concerned with **operational planning**.

5   Financial accounting systems

    ☑ **Management accounting systems**

Financial accounting systems provide information to **external** users.

6   ☑ True

The management accountant may frequently have to take into account non-financial information.

21 Cost classification

1   ☑ Direct expense

The royalty cost can be traced in full to the company's product, therefore it is a direct expense.

2   ☑ Constant in total when activity changes

3   ☑ A function or location for which costs are ascertained

A cost centre acts as a 'collecting place' for costs before they are analysed further.

4   ☑ Not a cash cost
    ☑ Part of production overheads

The depreciation on production equipment is an indirect expense incurred in the factory and is therefore included in production overheads.

5   ☑ A stores assistant in a factory store

The stores assistant's wages cannot be charged directly to a product, therefore the stores assistant is part of the indirect labour force.

22 Cost behaviour

1   The variable cost per X-ray is $ ⟨15.50⟩

	X-rays	Overheads
	No	$
	4,750	273,625
	4,500	269,750
Variable cost of	250	3,875

Variable cost per X-ray = $3,875/250 = $15.50

2   The delivery costs for a sales volume of 700 units will be $ ⟨11,500⟩

Using the high-low method

	Units	Total costs
		$
High	800	12,000
Low	400	10,000
	400	2,000

Variable cost per unit = $\dfrac{\$2,000}{400}$ = $5

Total costs	= fixed costs + variable costs
Let x	= fixed costs
$12,000	= x + (800 × $5)
$12,000	= x + $4,000
x	= $12,000 − $4,000
	= $8,000

For a sales volume of 700 units

Total costs	= fixed costs + variable costs
	= $8,000 + (700 × $5)
	= $8,000 + $3,500 = $11,500

3   ☑   Graph 1

4   ☑   Graph 2

5   ☑   Graph 1

        ☑   Graph 3

        ☑   Graph 4

A semi-variable or mixed cost is a cost which contains both fixed and variable components and which is therefore partly affected by a change in the level of activity.

6   (a)   The cost of sales consists of a fixed cost of $ [10,000] and a variable cost of $ [0.50] per $ of sale.

Cost of sales

	$
High level	55,000
Low level	50,000
Variable cost of sales of $10,000 sales	5,000

∴ Variable cost per $ of sales $0.50

∴ Substituting at low level,

   Fixed costs of sales   = $50,000 – (0.50 × $80,000)

                          = $10,000

(b)   The selling and distribution cost is a [variable] cost of $ [0.10] per $ of sale.

Selling and distribution costs

	$
High level	9,000
Low level	8,000
Variable distribution cost of $10,000 sales	1,000

∴ Variable cost per $ of sales $0.10

∴ Substituting at low level,

   Fixed selling and distribution costs = $8,000 – (0.10 × $80,000)

                                        = $0

(c)   [fixed]

23 Correlation and regression

1   ☑ False

The coefficient of determination (r^2) explains the percentage variation in the **dependent** variable which is explained by the **independent** variable.

2   Lowest value = [0]

     Highest value = [1]

The correlation coefficient, r, must always fall within the range –1 to +1, therefore the coefficient of determination, r^2, must always fall in the range 0 to 1 ($-1^2 = +1$).

3

a = [43.333]

b = [10]

Workings

Let   X = output ('000 units)
       Y = costs ($'000)
       n = 12 (there are 12 pairs of data for X and Y values)

X	Y	XY	X^2	Y^2
16	170	2,720	256	28,900
20	240	4,800	400	57,600
23	260	5,980	529	67,600
25	300	7,500	625	90,000
25	280	7,000	625	78,400
19	230	4,370	361	52,900
16	200	3,200	256	40,000
12	160	1,920	144	25,600
19	240	4,560	361	57,600
25	290	7,250	625	84,100
28	350	9,800	784	122,500
12	200	2,400	144	40,000
$\Sigma X = 240$	$\Sigma Y = 2,920$	$\Sigma XY = 61,500$	$\Sigma X^2 = 5,110$	$\Sigma Y^2 = 745,200$

$$b = \frac{n\Sigma XY - \Sigma X \Sigma Y}{n\Sigma X^2 - (\Sigma X)^2}$$

$$= \frac{(12 \times 61,500) - (240 \times 2,920)}{(12 \times 5,110) - (240)^2}$$

$$= \frac{738,000 - 700,800}{61,320 - 57,600}$$

$$= \frac{37,200}{3,720}$$

$$= 10$$

$$a = \frac{\Sigma Y}{n} - b\frac{\Sigma X}{n}$$

$$\frac{\Sigma Y}{n} = \frac{2,920}{12} = 243.333$$

$$\frac{\Sigma X}{n} = \frac{240}{12} = 20$$

$$a = 243.333 - (10 \times 20)$$

$$= 243.333 - 200$$

$$= 43.333$$

(Note. It is always best to calculate a value for b first since this value is needed in order to calculate a value for a.)

4 $\boxed{11.00}$

$Y = a + bX$

If intercept (a) is \$248, then $Y = 248 + bX$

If the value of Y is \$523 and X is 25, then using the equation $Y = 248 + bX$ we can determine the unknown value of b (ie the slope) as follows.

$$
\begin{aligned}
523 &= 248 + (b \times 25) \\
523 - 248 &= 25b \\
275 &= 25b \\
b &= \frac{275}{25} = +11.00
\end{aligned}
$$

5 $y = \boxed{2 + 2.2x}$

x	y	x^2	xy
1	4	1	4
2	6	4	12
3	10	9	30
4	10	16	40
10	30	30	86

$n = 4$

$$
b = \frac{n\sum xy - \sum x \sum y}{n\sum x^2 - (\sum x)^2}
$$

$$
= \frac{(4 \times 86) - (10 \times 30)}{4 \times 30 - 10^2} = \frac{44}{20} = 2.2
$$

$$
a = \bar{y} - b\bar{x} = \frac{30}{4} - \left(2.2 \times \frac{10}{4}\right) = 2
$$

Therefore $y = 2 + 2.2x$.

6 $x = \boxed{7.72 + 0.71y}$

Since the question asks for the regression line of x on y; x and y must therefore be interchanged in the formula.

x	y	y^2	xy
9	2	4	18
10	3	9	30
9	1	1	9
8	1	1	8
9	2	4	18
45	9	19	83

$n = 5$

$$
b = \frac{n\sum xy - \sum x \sum y}{n\sum y^2 - (\sum y)^2}
$$

$$
= \frac{(5 \times 83) - (45 \times 9)}{(5 \times 19) - 9^2} = \frac{10}{14} = 0.71
$$

$$
a = \bar{x} - b\bar{y} = \frac{45}{5} - \left(0.71 \times \frac{9}{5}\right) = 7.722 = 7.72 \text{ (to 2 decimal places)}
$$

Therefore, the equation is $x = 7.72 + 0.71y$

BPP
LEARNING MEDIA

7 | 0.4624 |

The coefficient of determination, r^2, measures the proportion of the total variation in the value of one variable that can be explained by variations in the value of the other variable.

r^2 $= 0.68^2$

    $= 0.4624$

Therefore, only just under half of the variation in one variable can be explained by variation in the other.

8   (a)   Weekly fixed costs are approximately $ | 1,500 |.

    (b)   Variable costs per unit are on average $ | 15 | (to the nearest $).

    (c)   Next week's production costs are likely to be approximately $ | 9,000 |.

    Workings

    A linear equation of the form y = a + bx has fixed costs of a and variable costs per unit of b.

    ∴ Fixed costs = $1,500

      Variable costs = $15 per unit

    If output = 500, total costs = $1,500 + ($15 × 500)

                    = $1,500 + $7,500

                    = $9,000

    (d)

		True	False
(i)	There is very little correlation between weekly costs of production and production level.	☐	☑
(ii)	90% of the variation in weekly costs is attributable to the amount produced.	☐	☑
(iii)	Given the information, any forecast using the regression equation is likely to be very unreliable.	☐	☑

If r = 0.9, there is a high degree of correlation between weekly costs of production and production level. Statement (i) is not correct.

If r = 0.9, r^2 (coefficient of determination) = 81% (0.9^2) and 81% of the variation in weekly costs can be explained by the amount produced. Statement (ii) is not correct.

If r = 0.9 and a linear pattern is evident, forecasts are likely to be reliable, not unreliable. Statement (iii) is not correct.

24 Spreadsheets

1   ☑   Preparing budgets

2   ☑   True

3   ☑   Absolute cell referencing

4 | = C2+C3 |

5 | =B6/B2*100 |

6 | 7,500 |

25 Material costs

1   The economic order quantity is ⌑ 300 ⌑ units.

The formula for the economic order quantity (EOQ) is

$$EOQ = \sqrt{\frac{2C_o D}{C_h}}$$

With C_o = $10

   D = 5,400 ÷ 12 = 450 per month

   C_h = $0.10

$$EOQ = \sqrt{\frac{2 \times \$10 \times 450}{\$0.10}}$$

$$= \sqrt{90,000}$$

$$= 300 \text{ units}$$

2   The level of safety inventory is ⌑ 400 ⌑ units (to the nearest whole unit).

Let x = safety inventory

$$\text{Average stock} = \text{safety inventory (x)} + \frac{\text{reorder quantity}}{2}$$

$$3,400 \quad = \quad x + \frac{6,000}{2}$$

$$3,400 \quad = \quad x + 3,000$$

$$x \quad = \quad 3,400 - 3,000$$

$$\therefore x \quad = \quad \underline{400} \text{ units}$$

3   The economic order quantity is ⌑ 175 ⌑ units (to the nearest whole unit).

$$EOQ = \sqrt{\frac{2C_o D}{C_h}}$$

$$= \sqrt{\frac{2 \times \$100 \times 1,225}{\$8}}$$

$$= \sqrt{30,625}$$

$$= 175 \text{ units}$$

4   The maximum inventory level was ⌑ 6,180 ⌑ units

Reorder level = maximum usage × maximum lead time

          = 130 × 26 = 3,380 units

Maximum level = reorder level + reorder quantity − (minimum usage × minimum lead time)

          = 3,380 + 4,000 − (60 × 20)

          = 6,180 units

26 Labour costs

1   (a)   His gross pay for the day will be $ [54] (to the nearest $)

	Hours
Standard time for 50 units (× 12/60)	10
Actual time taken	8
Time saved	2

Bonus = 50% × 2 hours saved × $6 =	$6
Basic daily pay = 8 hours × $6 =	$48
Total gross pay	$54

(b)   In a week when he produces 28 units, his gross wage will be $ [484.70] (to the nearest penny)

	$
Piecework earnings:	
1-25 units = 25 × $2.30	57.50
26-28 units = 3 × $2.40	7.20
Total piecework earnings	64.70
Guaranteed weekly wage	420.00
Gross wage	484.70

2

A   [$70.00]

B   [$7.00]

C   [$3.50]

D   [$80.50]

Workings

Standard time for 220 units (× 3/60 hours)	11 hours
Actual time	10 hours
Time saved	1 hour

		$
A	Basic pay 10 hours × $7	70.00
B	Overtime premium 2 hours × $3.50	7.00
C	Bonus = 50% × 1 hour × $7	3.50
D	Total pay	80.50

3   The employee's gross pay for week 12 was $ [420]

	Piecework hours
Piecework hours produced:	
Product J (50 × 0.3 hours)	15
Product W (10 × 4.0 hours)	40
	55

Employee's pay = $200 + (55 × $4) = $420

4

A $50.00

B $55.00

C $56.00

D $57.50

Basic hourly rate = (1 × $14) + (3 × $10) + (1 × $6) = $50.

Output per day	Increase	Hourly group remuneration
Units	%	$
Up to 200	–	50.00
201 to 250	10	55.00
251 to 280	12	56.00
281 to 300	15	57.50

5   ✓   Production overheads

Overtime premium is always classed as production overheads unless it is: worked at the specific request of a customer to get his order completed; or worked regularly by a production department in the normal course of operations, in which case it is usually incorporated into the direct labour hourly rate.

6   ✓   Production overheads

Overtime premium is always classed as production overheads unless it is: worked at the specific request of a customer to get his order completed; or worked regularly by a production department in the normal course of operations, in which case it is usually incorporated into the direct labour hourly rate.

7   ✓   DR   Overhead control   CR   Wages control

Indirect wages are 'collected' in the overhead control account, for subsequent absorption into work in progress.

27 Overheads and absorption costing

1   The number of machine hours (to the nearest hour) budgeted to be worked were   14,850   hours.

Budgeted hours $= \dfrac{\text{Budgeted overheads}}{\text{Budgeted overhead absorption rate}}$

$= \dfrac{\$475{,}200}{£32}$

$= 14{,}850$

2   The machine hour absorption rate is (to the nearest $) $ 45   per machine hour.

Machine hour absorption rate $= \dfrac{\text{Budgeted overheads}}{\text{Budgeted machine hours}}$

$= \dfrac{\$690{,}480}{15{,}344}$

$=$ $45 per machine hour

BPP)))
LEARNING MEDIA

3 The budgeted overhead absorption rate was $ [25] per machine hour (to the nearest $).

	$
Actual overheads incurred	496,500
Over-absorbed overhead	64,375
Actual overheads absorbed	560,875

$$\frac{\text{Actual overheads absorbed}}{\text{Actual machine hours}} = \text{Amount absorbed per machine hour}$$

$$\frac{\$560,875}{22,435} = \$25 \text{ per machine hour}$$

4

Overhead analysis sheet 20X4

Overhead item	Basis of apportionment	Machining $	Assembly $	Maintenance $	Stores $	Total $
Various	Allocation	84,000	71,000	28,000	31,000	214,000
Power	Machine hrs	A= [4,500]				21,000
Rent	B= [Area occupied]			C= [3,000]		29,400
Canteen costs	D= [3,000]					8,280

Workings

A: 9,000/42,000 × $21,000 = $4,500
C: 1,000/9,800 × $29,400 = $3,000
D: based on number of employees 25/69 × $8,280 = $3,000

5 Fixed production overhead was [under] absorbed by $ [25,000]

	$
Overhead absorbed (110,000 std hours × $2.50)	275,000
Overhead incurred	300,000
Overhead under absorbed	25,000

The overhead is under absorbed because the overhead absorbed was less than the overhead incurred.

6

	True	False
Overhead was $15,000 over absorbed		✓
Overhead was $15,000 under absorbed		✓
No under or over absorption occurred	✓	
The overhead expenditure variance is $15,000 adverse	✓	

Workings

Overhead absorption rate = $165,000/55,000

= $3 per direct labour hour

Overhead incurred $180,000
Overhead absorbed ($3 × 60,000 hrs) $180,000
Under/over absorption   nil

Overhead expenditure variance = $165,000 budget – $180,000 actual

= $15,000 adverse

7   (a)   The machine hour absorption rate is $ | 5 | per hour.

$$\text{Overhead absorption rate} = \frac{\text{Budgeted overheads}}{\text{Budgeted machine hours}}$$

$$= \frac{\$85,000}{17,000}$$

$$= \underline{\$5}$$

   (b)   The overhead for the period was | under | absorbed by $ | 4,250 |

Overhead over-/(under)-absorbed = Overhead absorbed – Overhead incurred

= (21,250 × $5) – $110,500

= $(4,250)

8

	Debit $	Credit $	No entry in this a/c $
Overhead control account		✓	
Work in progress account			✓
Income statement	✓		

Under-absorbed overhead means that the overhead charged to production was too low and so there must be a debit to the income statement.

9   The overhead absorption rate was $ | 5.00 | (to 2 decimal places)

Workings

Actual overheads = $500,000

∴ Absorbed overheads   = $500,000 + $50,000
                  = $550,000

Absorbed overheads = actual production × overhead absorption rate (OAR)

$550,000   = 110,000 units × $OAR

∴ OAR $= \dfrac{\$550,000}{110,000 \text{ units}}$

        = $5.00 per unit

10 Overheads were [over] absorbed by $ [95,000]

Workings

Overhead absorption rate $= \dfrac{\$1,250,000}{500,000 \text{ machine hours}}$

$= \$2.50$ per machine hour

Standard machine hours per unit $= \dfrac{500,000 \text{ hours}}{250,000 \text{ units}}$

$= 2$ machine hours

Standard machine hours produced $= 220,000 \times 2$ machine hours
$= 440,000$ machine hours

	$
Overhead absorbed (440,000 standard hours × $2.50)	1,100,000
Actual overheads incurred	1,005,000
Over-absorbed overhead	95,000

11 $ [6.15] for each [machine hour]

Workings

	Machining $	Assembly $	Main-tenance $	Stores $	Total $
Total overhead	130,000	122,000	39,150	42,000	333,150
Apportion maintenance*	27,600	8,400	(39,150)	3,150	–
Apportion stores	33,150	12,000		(45,150)	–
	190,750	142,400	–	–	333,150

Overhead absorption rate for machining department $= \$190,750/31,000$
$= \$6.15$ per machine hour

* The total maintenance hours for the cost centres receiving a charge = 9,200 + 2,800 + 1,050 = 13,050. Therefore, charge to machining department = 9,200/13,050 × $39,150 = $27,600.

12 (iii) They are based on actual data for each period   [✓]

    (iv) They are used to control overhead costs   [✓]

Overhead absorption rates are determined in advance for each period, usually based on budgeted data. Therefore statement (i) is true and statement (iii) is not true. Overhead absorption rates are used in the final stage of overhead analysis, to absorb overheads into product costs. Therefore statement (ii) is true. Statement (iv) is not true because overheads are controlled using budgets and other management information.

13 (a) The overhead absorption rate for the Casting department was $ [30] per production hour.

Workings

	Casting department
$\dfrac{\text{Production overheads}}{\text{Expected production hours}}$	$\dfrac{\$225,000}{7,500}$
Predetermined overhead absorption rate	= $30/hr

    (b) The overhead in the Dressing department in period 3 was [under] absorbed by $ [875]

Workings

Dressing department overhead absorption rate $= \dfrac{\$175,000}{7,000} = \$25$ per hour

	$
Overhead absorbed (7,280 hours × $25)	182,000
Overhead incurred	182,875
(Under) absorption of overhead	(875)

28 Marginal and absorption costing

1   The absorption costing profit for the period for product M will be:

☑   higher

than the marginal costing profit. The difference between the two profit figures will be
$ [14,400]

Difference in profit = change in inventory level × fixed overhead per unit

$$= (2,400 - 2,700) \times (\$8 \times 6)$$

$$= \$14,400$$

The absorption costing profit will be higher because inventories have increased, and fixed overheads have been carried forward in inventory.

2   The profit using marginal costing would be $ [118,000]

Marginal cost profit   = Absorption cost profit + ((Opening inventory – Closing inventory) ×

Fixed overhead absorption rate)

$$= \$130,000 + ((5,000 - 8,000) \times \$4)$$

$$= \$118,000$$

3   [Lower] $[10,880]

The marginal costing profit will be **lower** than the absorption costing profit because inventories increased during the period. Under the absorption costing method the amount of fixed production overhead carried forward in inventory would have increased.

Difference in profit = 160 units increase in inventory × $68 per unit

$$= \$10,880$$

4   The fixed overhead absorption rate per unit (to the nearest $) is $ [10]

	Units
Opening inventory	825
Closing inventory	1,800
Increase in inventory level	975

	$
Absorption costing profit	60,150
Marginal costing profit	50,400
Difference in profit	9,750

$\therefore$ Overhead absorption rate = $\dfrac{\$9,750}{975}$ = $10 per unit

29 Process costing

1   The quantity of good production achieved was $\boxed{2,625}$ kg.

Good production = input − normal loss − abnormal loss

$$= 3,000 - (10\% \times 3,000) - 75$$
$$= 3,000 - 300 - 75$$
$$= \underline{2,625} \text{ kg}$$

2   (a)   The value credited to the process account for the scrap value of the normal loss for the period will be $\$\boxed{100}$ (to the nearest $)

Normal loss = 10% × input

$$= 10\% \times 5,000 \text{ kg}$$
$$= 500 \text{ kg}$$

When scrap has a value, normal loss is valued at the value of the scrap ie 20p per kg.

Normal loss = $0.20 × 500 kg

$$= \$100$$

(b)   The value of the abnormal loss for the period is $\$\boxed{300}$ (to the nearest $)

	Kg
Input	5,000
Normal loss (10% × 5,000 kg)	(500)
Abnormal loss	(300)
Output	4,200

$$\text{Cost per unit} = \frac{\text{Input costs - scrap value of normal loss}}{\text{Expected output}}$$

$$= \frac{\$4,600^* - \$100}{5,000 - 500}$$

$$= \frac{\$4,500}{4,500} = \$1.00$$

Scrap value of normal loss = 500 kg × $0.20 = $100

Value of abnormal loss = 300 × $1.00 = $300

*	Kg
Materials (5,000 kg × 0.5)	2,500
Labour	700
Production overhead	1,400
	4,600

3   (a)   The cost per equivalent unit of material is $\$\boxed{14.50}$ (to 2 decimal places)

(b)   The cost per equivalent unit of labour is $\$\boxed{8.00}$ (to 2 decimal places)

(c)   The cost per equivalent unit of overheads is $\$\boxed{5.00}$ (to 2 decimal places)

STATEMENT OF EQUIVALENT UNITS

	Total units	Materials	Labour	Overheads
			Equivalent units	
Finished output*	900	900	900	900
Closing WIP	150	(100%) 150	(50%) 75	(30%) 45
	1,050	1,050	975	945

* 750 units input + opening WIP 300 units – closing WIP 150 units

STATEMENT OF COSTS PER EQUIVALENT UNIT

	Materials $	Labour $	Overheads $	Total
Opening inventory	3,600	1,600	400	
Added during period	11,625	6,200	4,325	
Total cost	15,225	7,800	4,725	
Equivalent units	1,050	975	945	
Cost per equivalent unit	$14.50	$8	$5	$27.50

4 (a) ⊡ 1,250 ⊡ equivalent units

STATEMENT OF EQUIVALENT UNITS

	Total Units		Material		Labour		Production overhead
				Equivalent units			
Completed output	800*	(100%)	800	(100%)	800	(100%)	800
Closing WIP	500	(100%)	500	(90%)	450	(40%)	200
	1,300		1,300		1,250		1,000

* Opening WIP 400 + units added 900 – closing WIP 500.

(b) The value of completed output for the period was $ ⊡ 322,400 ⊡ (to the nearest $)

STATEMENT OF EQUIVALENT UNITS

	Total units		Material		Labour		Production overhead
				Equivalent units			
Completed output	800*	(100%)	800	(100%)	800	(100%)	800
Closing WIP	500	(100%)	500	(90%)	450	(40%)	200
	1,300		1,300		1,250		1,000

*Opening WIP 400 + units added 900 – WIP 500

STATEMENT OF COSTS PER EQUIVALENT UNIT

	Total	Material $	Labour $	Production overhead $
Opening stock		49,000	23,000	3,800
Costs incurred		198,000	139,500	79,200
		247,000	162,500	83,000
Equivalent units		1,300	1,250	1,000
Cost per equivalent unit	$403	$190	$130	$83

∴ Value of completed output = $403 × 800 units = $322,400

5   Let   x = material input to process
          0.1x = normal loss
          0.05x = abnormal loss

     ∴ Output = x – 0.1x – 0.05x
     340 litres = x – 0.15x
     340 litres = 0.85x

     x = $\dfrac{340 \text{ litres}}{0.85}$

       = ⎡ 400 ⎤ litres

30 Process costing, joint products and by-products

1   **Common process costs**

	$
Direct materials	120,000
Direct labour	240,000
Prime cost	360,000
Factory overheads (100%)	360,000
Total production cost	720,000
Less: scrap proceeds (16,000 litres × 10% × $20)	(32,000)
Total common costs	688,000

(a)   **Relative sales value method**

Chemical A = $ ⎡ 400,000 ⎤

Chemical B = $ ⎡ 192,000 ⎤

Chemical C = $ ⎡ 96,000 ⎤

Chemical	Output Litres	$ per litre	Sales value $		Total cost $
A	7,200	50	360,000	(÷ 619,200 × $688,000)	400,000
B	4,320	40	172,800	(÷ 619,200 × $688,000)	192,000
C	2,880	30	86,400	(÷ 619,200 × $688,000)	96,000
			619,200		688,000

(b)   **Volume method**

Chemical A = $ ⎡ 344,000 ⎤

Chemical B = $ ⎡ 206,400 ⎤

Chemical C = $ ⎡ 137,600 ⎤

Chemical	Output Litres		Total cost $
A	7,200	(÷ 14,400 × $688,000)	344,000
B	4,320	(÷ 14,400 × $688,000)	206,400
C	2,880	(÷ 14,400 × $688,000)	137,600
	14,400		688,000

31 Job costing and service costing

1   Charge for each hour of writing (to the nearest penny) should be $ | 28.94 |

Weeks worked per year   = 52 – 4 = 48

Hours worked per year   = 48 × 40 hrs

                                   = 1,920

Hours chargeable to clients   = 1,920 × 90% = 1,728

Total expenses = $10,000 + $40,000 = $50,000

Hourly rate = $\dfrac{\$50,000}{1,728}$ = $28.94 per hour

2   ✓   Customer-driven production

        ✓   Complete production possible within a single accounting period

Each job is separately identifiable, according to a customer's requirements. Therefore the first characteristic is correct.

Jobs are usually of comparatively short duration, compared to situations where contract costing is applied. Therefore the second characteristic is correct.

The third characteristic is incorrect because each job is separately identifiable.

3   The price to be quoted for job B124 is $ | 99.60 | (to the nearest penny)

Production overhead absorption rate = $240,000/30,000 = $8 per labour hour

Other overhead absorption rate = ($150,000/$750,000) × 100% = 20% of total production cost

Job B124	$
Direct materials (3 kgs × $5)	15.00
Direct labour (4 hours × $9)	36.00
Production overhead (4 hours × $8)	32.00
Total production cost	83.00
Other overhead (20% × $83)	16.60
Total cost	99.60

4   ✓   High levels of indirect costs as a proportion of total cost

        ✓   Cost units are often intangible

        ✓   Use of composite cost units

In service costing it is difficult to identify many attributable direct costs. Many costs must be treated as **indirect costs** and **shared over several cost units**, therefore the first characteristic does apply. Many services are **intangible**, for example a haircut or a cleaning service provide no physical, tangible product. Therefore the second characteristic does apply. **Composite cost units** such as passenger-mile or bed-night are often used in service costing, therefore the third characteristic does apply. The fourth characteristic does not apply because equivalent units are more often used in **costing for tangible products.**

5   ☑   Patient/day

     ☑   Operating theatre hour

     ☑   Outpatient visit

All of the above would be **measurable** and would be **useful for control purposes.** A ward and an x-ray department are more likely to be used as **cost centres** for the purpose of cost collection and analysis.

6   ☑   Production of the product can be completed in a single accounting period

     ☑   Production relates to a single special order

Job costing is appropriate where each cost unit is **separately identifiable** and is of relatively **short duration**.

32 Budgeting

1   ☑   A factor which limits the activities of an undertaking.

The principal budget factor is also known as the key budget factor or the limiting budget factor.

2   The budgeted labour cost is $ ‎30,800 ‎ (to the nearest $)

Hours to be paid for × 80% = 3,520

∴ Hours to be paid for = 3,520 ÷ 0.8 = 4,400

Budgeted labour cost = $7 × 4,400 hr = $30,800

3   The budgeted labour cost for the job is $ ‎40,800 ‎ (to the nearest $)

Hours to be paid for × 90% = 4,590

∴ Hours to be paid for = 4,590 ÷ 0.9 = 5,100

Budgeted labour cost = $8 × 5,100 hr = $40,800

4   The budgeted number of units of product U to be produced is ‎137,700 ‎ units.

	Units
Budgeted sales	140,000
Less inventory reduction (11,500 units × 20%)	2,300
Budgeted production	137,700

5   The total production cost allowance in a budget flexed at the 83% level of activity would be $ ‎8,688 ‎ (to the nearest $)

Direct material cost per 1% = $30

Direct labour and production overhead:

			$
At	90%	activity	6,240
At	80%	activity	6,180
Change	10%		60

Variable cost per 1% activity = $60/10% = $6

Substituting in 80% activity:

Fixed cost of labour and production overhead   = $6,180 − (80 × $6)
                                                        = $5,700

Flexed budget cost allowance:

	$
Direct material $30 × 83	2,490
Direct labour and production overhead:	
variable $6 × 83	498
fixed	5,700
	8,688

6   Actual $ | 29,760 | (to the nearest $)

     Budget $ | 28,800 | (to the nearest $)

     The actual material cost ($29,760) should be compared with the budget cost allowance for the actual production (4,800 units × $6 = $28,800).

7   The budget cost allowance for selling overhead for a sales level of 2,800 units is $ | 43,000 | (to the nearest $)

			$
Total cost for	3,000	units (× $15.00)	45,000
Total cost for	2,400	units (× $16.25)	39,000
Variable cost of	600	units	6,000

∴ Variable cost per unit = $6,000/600 = $10

∴ Fixed cost = $45,000 − (3,000 × $10) = $15,000

∴ Total cost allowance for 2,800 units:

	$
variable cost (2,800 × $10)	28,000
fixed cost	15,000
	43,000

8   The budgeted level of fixed cost for October was $ | 25,000 | (to the nearest $)

	$
Actual total cost	22,100
Fixed costs below budget	4,500
Budgeted total cost	26,600
Less budgeted variable cost (8,000 passengers × $0.20)	1,600
Budgeted fixed cost	25,000

9   ✓   A budget which is most generally used for planning purposes

       ✓   A budget for a single level of activity

     Fixed budgets are prepared for a single level of activity and do not include any provision for the event that actual volumes may differ from the budget. They are generally used for planning purposes because they use a single level of activity for coordination and resource allocation.

10 | 1,815 | units

	Units
Required for sales	1,800
Plus increase in inventory (150 × 10%)	15
Budgeted production	1,815

11   Materials usage | − | opening inventory of materials | + | closing inventory of materials

     Any opening inventory available at the beginning of the period will **reduce** the quantity to be purchased for a given volume of usage. Any closing inventory required at the end of a period will **increase** the quantity to be purchased in order to satisfy production and leave a sufficient quantity in inventory.

12 ☑ Raw materials inventories are budgeted to increase

Once the material usage budget has been prepared, based on the budgeted production volume, the usage is adjusted for the budgeted change in materials inventories in order to determine the required budgeted purchases. If purchases are greater than production requirements this means that raw material inventories are being increased.

13 ☑ A budget which by recognising different cost behaviour patterns is designed to change as the volume of activity changes.

A flexible budget shows the budgeted costs and revenues at different levels of activity. The budgeted variable costs and revenues are **increased or decreased in line with changes in activity,** and the budgeted fixed cost remains **unaltered**.

14 The usage budget for material Z for the forthcoming year is ⎡ 40,000 ⎤ kgs

Material usage budget = production units × material usage per unit
= 10,000 × 4 kgs
= 40,000 kgs

15 ☑ Budgeted income statement
☑ Budgeted cash flow
☑ Budgeted balance sheet

16 ⎡ 36,750 ⎤ kg

Budgeted production (9,500 + 1,500 − 2,000) = 9,000

Raw materials required: (9,000 × 4) = 36,000 kg

Budgeted raw materials purchases: (36,000 − 12,500 + 13,250) = 36,750 kg

17 The production budget in units for Month 1 will be ⎡ 6,600 ⎤ units

Workings

	12	1	Month 2	3	4
	Units	Units	Units	Units	Units
Production – month 1	3,600	2,400			
Production – month 2		4,200	2,800		
Production – month 3			3,300	2,200	
Production – month 4				3,600	2,400
	3,600	6,600	6,100	5,800	2,400

18 The material cost budget for Month 2 will be $ ⎡ 30,500 ⎤

Workings

6,100 units at $5 per unit = $30,500

Note that the question asks for the **material cost** budget for Month 2 and not the **material purchases** budget.

33 Standard costing

1 (a) $ [98.40]

   Workings

Standard cost per unit	$	$
Materials		
A 1.2 kg × $11 =	13.20	
B 4.7 kg × $6 =	28.20	
		41.40
Labour		
1.5 hours × $8		12.00
Prime cost		53.40
Overheads		
1.5 hours × $30		45.00
Standard cost per unit		98.40

   (b) Attainable work hours per period are [180,000] hours, which represents [90] % of clock hours.

   Attainable work hours = 120,000 units × 1.5 hr = 180,000 hrs

   Clock hours = 500 employees × 400 hr = 200,000 hrs

   ∴ Attainable hours = 90% of clock hours

   (c) (i) $ [20,000 (F)]

        (ii) $ [36,000 (A)]

   Workings

   Labour rate variance

	$
215,000 hrs should cost (× $8)	1,720,000
but did cost	1,700,000
	20,000 (F)

   Labour efficiency variance

126,000 units should take (× 1.5 hrs)	189,000	hrs
but did take (215,000 hrs × 90%)	193,500	hrs
	4,500	hrs (A)
Standard rate per hour	× $8	
	$36,000	(A)

34 Basic variance analysis

1

   (a)

		Favourable	Adverse
The fixed production overhead expenditure variance is	$ [29,750]	[ ]	[✓]

	$
Budgeted fixed production overhead expenditure	380,000
Actual fixed production overhead expenditure	409,750
Fixed production overhead expenditure variance	29,750 (A)

(b)

		Favourable	Adverse
The fixed production overhead volume efficiency variance is	$ 10,000		✓

	$
74,500 units should take (× 1 hour)	74,500 hours
but did take	76,500 hours
Fixed overhead volume efficiency variance in hours	2,000 hours (A)
× standard fixed overhead absorption rate per hour *	$ 5
Fixed production overhead volume efficiency variance	10,000 (A)

* Standard fixed overhead absorption rate per hour =

$$\frac{\text{Budgeted fixed production overhead cost}}{\text{Budgeted labour hours}} = \frac{\$380,000}{76,000} = \$5 \text{ per labour hour}$$

(c)

		Favourable	Adverse
The fixed production overhead volume capacity variance is	$ 2,500	✓	

	$
Budgeted hours of work	76,000 hours
Actual hours of work	76,500 hours
Fixed overhead volume capacity variance in hours	500 hours (F)
× standard fixed overhead absorption rate per hour	$ 5
Fixed production overhead volume capacity variance	2,500 (F)

(d)

		Favourable	Adverse
The fixed production overhead volume variance is	$ 7,500		✓

The fixed production overhead volume variance

= Efficiency variance + capacity variance

= $10,000 (A) + $2,500 (F)

= $7,500 (A)

2   ✓   Actual quantity purchased at actual cost with the actual quantity purchased at standard cost.

3   (a)

		Favourable	Adverse
The direct labour rate variance for June was	$ 1,200	✓	

	$
2,400 hours should have cost (× $9)	21,600
but did cost	20,400
Direct labour rate variance	1,200 (F)

(b)

		Favourable	Adverse
The direct labour efficiency variance for June was	$ 1,800		✓

Standard hours per unit of production = $18/$9 = 2 hours

1,100 units should have taken (× 2 hours)	2,200 hours
but did take	2,400 hours
Efficiency variance in hours	200 hours (A)
× standard rate per hour	× $9
Efficiency variance in $	$1,800 (A)

4

	Favourable	Adverse
The variable production overhead expenditure variance for last period is		
$ ☐ 2,990	☐	☑

Standard variable production overhead cost per hour = $\frac{\$13,475}{3,850}$ = $3.50

	$
2,990 hours of variable production overhead should cost (× $3.50)	10,465
but did cost	13,455
Variable production overhead expenditure variance	2,990 (A)

5   The variable overhead expenditure variance was $ ☐ 8,500

☑ Adverse

Working

Variable overhead absorption rate = $\frac{\text{Budgeted variable overheads}}{\text{Budgeted labour hours}}$

= $2 per labour hour

	$
Actual variable overheads	173,800
Absorbed variable overheads (82,650 hours × $2)	165,300
Variable overhead expenditure variance	8,500 (A)

6

	Favourable	Adverse
The volume variance for last month was $ ☐ 4,755	☐	☑

The volume variance is the increase in cost resulting from a change in the volume of activity, ie the difference between the original budget and the flexed budget.

Volume variance	= $126,100 – $130,855
	= $4,755 (A)

7

	Favourable	Adverse
The expenditure variance for last month was $ ☐ 2,725	☐	☑

The expenditure variance is the difference between the flexed budget and the actual results.

Expenditure variance	= $130,855 – $133,580
	= $2,725 (A)

8   Standard hours per unit = [7]

$$\text{Actual hours worked} = \frac{\$294,800}{\$8}$$
$$= 36,850 \text{ hours}$$

$$\text{Adverse efficiency variance, in hours} = \frac{\$26,000}{\$8}$$
$$= 3,250 \text{ hours}$$

$$\therefore \text{ Standard hours for 4,800 units} = 36,850 - 3,250$$
$$= 33,600 \text{ hours}$$

$$\text{Standard hours per unit} = \frac{33,600}{4,800}$$
$$= 7 \text{ hours}$$

9   The number of units produced in the period was [1,600]

Labour efficiency variance (in $)	=	$27,000
$\therefore$ Labour efficiency variance (in hours)	=	$27,000 ÷ $6 per hour
	=	4,500 hours

Let x = number of units actually produced

	Hours
Actual hours worked	52,500
× units should have taken (30 × x)	×
Labour efficiency variance (in hours)	4,500 (A)

Actual hours worked were therefore 4,500 more than expected (due to an adverse labour efficiency variance).

$$\therefore \text{ x units should have taken} = (52,500 - 4,500) \text{ hours}$$
$$= 48,000 \text{ hours}$$
$$30x = 48,000 \text{ hours}$$
$$x = \frac{48,000 \text{ hours}}{30} = 1,600 \text{ units}$$

10   The standard price per kg was $ [4.50] (to the nearest cent)

Standard cost of material purchased – actual cost of material purchased = price variance

Standard cost   = $32,195 – $1,370 = $30,825

$$\text{Standard price per kg} = \frac{\$30,825}{6,850} = \$4.50$$

11
- ✓ A favourable sales volume variance
- ✓ A favourable labour efficiency variance
- ✓ A favourable material usage variance
- ✓ A favourable sales price variance

The improvement in quality may mean that more units are sold, leading to a favourable sales volume variance.

The more expensive material may be easier to work with, leading to a favourable labour efficiency variance.

There may be less waste with the more expensive material, leading to a favourable material usage variance.

The improvement in quality may mean that a higher price can be charged, leading to a favourable sales price variance.

35 Further variance analysis

1   The budgeted variable cost per unit was $ [4] (to the nearest $)

	$
Budgeted total expenditure = $(140,000 − 10,000)	130,000
Budgeted fixed costs	42,000
Budgeted variable costs	88,000

Budgeted variable cost per unit = $\dfrac{\$88,000}{22,000}$ = $4 per unit

2

(a)

			Favourable	*Adverse*
Material price	$	4,860	✓	
Material usage	$	1,040		✓

Direct materials price variance

	$
9,720 kg should have cost (× $13)	126,360
but did cost	121,500
	4,860 (F)

Direct materials usage variance

	$
4,820 units should have used (× 2 kg)	9,640 kg
but did use	9,720 kg
Materials usage variance in kg	80 kg (A)
× standard price per kg	$13
Materials usage variance (in $)	$1,040 (A)

(b)

			Favourable	*Adverse*
Labour rate	$	3,160		✓
Labour efficiency	$	424	✓	

Direct labour rate variance

	$
15,820 units should have taken (× 3.3 hrs)	63,200
but did cost	66,360
	3,160 (A)

Direct labour efficiency variance

	$
4,820 units should have used (× 3.3 kg)	15,906 hrs
but did use	15,800 hrs
Labour efficiency variance in hrs	106 hrs (F)
× standard rate per hour	× $4
Labour efficiency variance in $	424 (F)

(c)

	Favourable	Adverse
The total fixed production overhead variance is	6,500	✓	

	$
Overhead incurred	41,700
Overhead absorbed (4,820 units × $10 per unit)	48,200
	6,500 (F)

3   (a)   The selling price variance for January was $ ⎣1,600 (A)⎦

Workings

Since there was no change in inventories, production = sales = 100 units

	$
100 units should sell for (× $140)	14,000
but did sell for	12,400
Selling price variance	1,600 (A)

(b)   The sales volume variance for January was $ ⎣1,275 (A)⎦

$$\text{Budgeted sales volume per month} = \frac{\text{Budgeted material cost of sales}}{\text{Standard material cost per unit}}$$

$$= \frac{\$4,600}{\$40}$$

$$= 115 \text{ units}$$

$$\text{Budgeted profit margin per unit} = \frac{\text{Budgeted monthly profit margin}}{\text{Budgeted monthly sales volume}}$$

$$= \frac{\$9,775}{115}$$

$$= \$85 \text{ per unit}$$

Budgeted sales volume	115	units
Actual sales volume	100	units
Sales volume variance in units	15	units (A)
× standard profit per unit	$85	
Sales volume variance in $	$1,275	(A)

4   The favourable sales volume variance using marginal costing is $ ⎣54,000⎦

Workings

Standard contribution per unit = Selling price – variable costs
= $75 – $30*
= $45

*Variable costs

	$ per unit
Direct materials	10
Direct labour	15
Variable production overheads	2
Variable selling costs	3
	30

Budgeted sales volume		7,200 units
Actual sales volume		8,400 units
Sales volume variance in units		1,200 units (F)
× Standard contribution per unit		× $45
Sale volume variance		$54,000 (F)

5

(a)

		Favourable	Adverse
The selling price variance for last period is	$ 80		✓

Workings

	$
Sales revenue from 830 units should have been (× $32)	26,560
but was	26,480
Selling price variance	80 (A)

(b)

		Favourable	Adverse
The sales volume profit variance for last period is	$ 550	✓	

Workings

	$
Budgeted sales volume	780 units
Actual sales volume	830 units
	50 units (F)
× standard profit per unit	× $11
Sales volume profit variance	550 (F)

6

		Favourable	Adverse
Direct material price variance	$18,400	✓	
Direct material usage variance	$17,000		✓

The direct material price variance

This is the difference between what 11,700 kgs should have cost and what 11,700 kgs did cost.

	$
11,700 kgs of Y should have cost (× $10)	117,000
but did cost	98,600
Material Y price variance	18,400 (F)

The variance is favourable because the material cost less than it should have.

The direct material usage variance

This is the difference between how many kilograms of Y should have been used to produce 1,000 units of X and how many kilograms were used, valued at the standard cost per kilogram.

1,000 units should have used (× 10 kgs)	10,000 kgs
but did use	11,700 kgs
Usage variance in kgs	1,700 kgs (A)
× standard cost per kilogram	× $10
Usage variance in $	$17,000 (A)

The variance is adverse because more material than should have been used was used.

7

	Material price variance	Material usage variance
Material A	$ 0	$ 13,200 (F)
Material B	$ 60,000 (A)	$ 13,200 (F)

Workings

Material A

	$
150,000 kg should cost (× $11)	1,650,000
but did cost	1,650,000
Price variance	0

126,000 units should use (× 1.2 kgs)	151,200	kgs
but did use	150,000	kgs
	1,200	kgs (F)
× standard price per kg	× $11	
Usage variance	$13,200	(F)

Material B

	$
590,000 kgs should cost (× $6)	3,540,000
but did cost	3,600,000
Price variance	60,000 (A)

126,000 units should use (× 4.7 kgs)	592,200	kgs
but did use	590,000	kgs
	2,200	kgs (F)
× standard price per kg	× $6	
Usage variance	$13,200	(F)

8   The number of units produced in the period was   1,600

Labour efficiency variance (in $)   = $27,000
∴ Labour efficiency variance (in hours) = $27,000 ÷ $6 per hour
                                        =   4,500 hours

Let x = number of units actually produced

	Hours
Actual hours worked	52,500
x units should have taken (30 × x)	30x
Labour efficiency variance (in hours)	4,500 (A)

Actual hours worked were therefore 4,500 more than expected (due to an adverse labour efficiency variance).

∴ x units should have taken	=	(52,500 – 4,500) hours
	=	48,000 hours
30x	=	48,000 hours
x	=	$\dfrac{48,000 \text{ hours}}{30}$
	=	1,600 units

9   The number of labour hours actually worked was $\boxed{24{,}780}$

4,920 units should have taken (× 6.5 hrs)   31,980
but did take   x

The variance in hours is therefore (31,980 − x) hrs × standard rate ($5)

$$
\begin{aligned}
\text{Labour efficiency variance} &= 159{,}900 - 5x \\
\text{or } 36{,}000 &= 159{,}900 - 5x \\
5x &= 159{,}900 - 36{,}000 \\
x &= \frac{123{,}900}{5} \\
&= 24{,}780
\end{aligned}
$$

10

		Favourable	Adverse
The variable overhead expenditure variance	$\boxed{\$90}$	☐	☑
The variable overhead efficiency variance	$\boxed{\$60}$	☑	☐

(i)

760 hours of variable overhead should cost (× $1.50)	1,140	
but did cost	1,230	
Variable overhead expenditure variance	90	(A)

(ii)

400 units should take (× 2 hours)	800	hrs
but did take (active hours)	760	hrs
Variance in hours	40	hrs (F)
× standard rate per hour	× $1.50	
Variable overhead efficiency variance in $	$60	(F)

36 Cost-volume-profit (CVP) analysis

1   The margin of safety is $\boxed{20\%}$

Workings

$$
\text{P/V ratio} = \frac{\text{Contribution}}{\text{Selling price}}
$$

$$
= \frac{125{,}000}{300{,}000} = 0.4167
$$

$$
\text{Sales revenue at breakeven point} = \frac{\text{Fixed costs}}{\text{P/V ratio}}
$$

$$
= \frac{\$100{,}000}{0.4167} = \$240{,}000
$$

$$
\text{Margin of safety} = \frac{\text{Budgeted sales - breakeven sales}}{\text{Budgeted sales}}
$$

$$
= \frac{300{,}000 - 240{,}000}{300{,}000} \times 100\%
$$

$$
= 20\%
$$

2   The breakeven point (to the nearest whole unit) is $ ⎣3,125⎦ units

    Working

    Breakeven point = $\dfrac{\text{Fixed cost}}{\text{Contribution per unit}}$

    $= \dfrac{50,000}{26 - 10}$

    $= \dfrac{50,000}{16}$

    = 3,125 units

3   Distance ⎣ C ⎦.

    The contribution is equal to the profit plus the fixed costs.

4   (a)   The number of units to be produced and sold annually would reduce by ⎣10.9⎦ %.

          Current profit = total contribution − fixed costs

                        = (8,000 × $8) − $24,400

                        = $39,600

          ∴ **Required profit** = $39,600

          If the new production methods are implemented the required contribution will be:

          Required contribution = revised fixed costs + required profit

                        = $31,720 + $39,600

                        = $71,320

          Required sales = $\dfrac{\text{Contribution required}}{\text{Contribution per unit (revised)}}$

          $= \dfrac{71,320}{10}$

          = 7,132 units

          Percentage reduction = (8,000 − 7,132)/8,000

                        = 10.9%

    (b)   Margin of safety as a percentage of budgeted annual sales would be ⎣60.4⎦ % (to one decimal place)

	$
Selling price per unit	15
Variable cost per unit	5
Contribution per unit	10
Fixed costs ($24,400 × 1.3)	$31,720

          ∴ Breakeven point = $\dfrac{31,720}{\$10}$ =   3,172 units

          Budgeted sales =   8,000 units
          ∴ Margin of safety =   4,828 units

          Margin of safety % = $\dfrac{4,828}{8,000}$ × 100% = 60.4%

BPP
LEARNING MEDIA

5   The budgeted fixed costs = $ $\boxed{300,000}$

Working

$$\frac{\text{Margin of safety}}{\text{Budgeted sales}} = 25\%$$

∴ Margin of safety = 25% × 10,000 units

= 2,500 units

Margin of safety	= budgeted sales volume – breakeven sales volume
2,500 units	= 10,000 units – breakeven sales volume
∴ Breakeven sales volume	= 10,000 units – 2,500 units
	= 7,500 units

$$\text{Breakeven sales volume} = \frac{\text{Budgeted fixed costs}}{\text{Contribution per unit}}$$

$$\therefore 7,500 \text{ units} = \frac{\text{Budgeted fixed costs}}{£40}$$

∴ Budgeted fixed costs = 7,500 units × $40 per unit
= $300,000

6   In order to make a profit of $400,000, Twenty Co will need to sell $\boxed{750,000}$ units.

Working

Total contribution required for a target profit of $400,000	= Target profit + fixed costs
	= $400,000 + $200,000
	= $600,000

Target profit is achieved by earning $\dfrac{\$600,000 \text{ (required contribution)}}{0.8 \text{ (P/V ratio)}} = \$750,000$ sales revenue.

7   If the selling price and variable cost per unit increase by 10% and 7% respectively, the sales volume will need to $\boxed{\text{decrease}}$ to $\boxed{16,515}$ units in order to achieve the original budgeted profit for the period.

Current contribution per unit = $(108 – 73) = $35

$$\text{Current sales volume} = \frac{\$(196,000 + 476,000)}{\$35}$$

= 19,200 units

Revised contribution per unit:

	$ per unit
Selling price $108 × 1.10	118.80
Variable cost $73 × 1.07	78.11
Contribution	40.69

$$\text{Required sales volume} = \frac{\$(196,000 + 476,000)}{\$40.69}$$

= 16,515 units

37 Relevant costing and decision-making

1   (a)   The relevant cost of labour is $ ☐ 2,250

      Working

      Relevant cost of labour

	$
Skilled workers	
Cost	900
Contribution lost from Product P ($7 × 100/2)	350
Semi skilled workers	
Cost	1,000
	2,250

  (b)   The relevant cost of materials is $ ☐ 2,000

      Working

      Relevant cost of materials

	$
Material N	
100 litres × $4	400
Material T	
Cost of purchasing material (100 kg × 8)	800
Lost scrap proceeds (200 kg × $4)	800
	2,000

2   The relevant cost of using the material for a special job is $ ☐ 12,500

The original cost of $45,000 is a non-relevant sunk or past cost. The material would not be reworked, since its value would increase by only $5,000 ($17,500 – $12,500) for a cost of $7,500.

The relevant cost of using the material for the special job is therefore the opportunity cost of the $12,500 scrap sale forgone.

3   (a)   ☐ 13,000 hours

      Working

	Product A	Product B	Product C	Total
Machine hours required per unit	6	4	7	
Maximum demand (units)	3,000	2,500	5,000	
Total machine hours required	18,000	10,000	35,000	63,000
Machine hours available				50,000
Deficiency in machine hours for next period				13,000

  (b)   (i)   Contribution per machine hour (Product A) = $ ☐ 7.67

      (ii)   Contribution per machine hour (Product B) = $ ☐ 11.50

      (iii)   Contribution per machine hour (Product C) = $ ☐ 6.57

      Workings

	Product A	Product B	Product C
	$ per unit	$ per unit	$ per unit
Selling price per unit	200	158	224
Variable cost per unit	154	112	178
Contribution per unit	46	46	46
Machine hours per unit	6	4	7
Contribution per machine hour	$7.67	$11.50	$6.57

(c) $ 115,000

   Working

   2,500 units × $46 = $115,000

4   The relevant cost (deprival value) of the machine is:

   ☑ $180,000

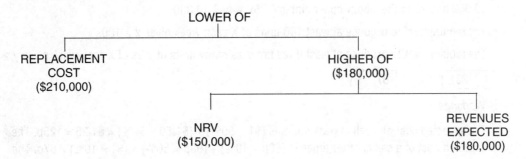

38 Linear programming

1   (a)   The line cuts the x axis at   X =   1.5

   (b)   The line cuts the y axis at   Y =   1.2

   Workings

   (a)   If 4X + 5Y = 6, then if Y = 0, 4X = 6 and hence X = 6/4 = 1.5
   (b)   If 4X + 5Y = 6, then if X = 0, 5Y = 6 and hence Y = 6/5 = 1.2

2   (a)   a ≥   50

   (b)   b ≥   2   a

   (c)   b $ 5   a

   (d)   a + b $ 1,000

   Workings

   The minimum weight of 50 kg of A per hectare gives a ≥ 50.

   The requirement that the weight of B per hectare be between 2 and 5 times the weight of A per hectare gives:

   b ≥ 2a

   b $ 5a

   The maximum total weight of 1,000 kg per hectare gives a + b $ 1,000.

3   Most profitable product   S

   Least profitable product   M

	Product M	Product F	Product S
Contribution per unit	$57	$73	$69
Hours required per unit	5	6	4
Contribution per hour of labour	$11.40	$12.17	$17.25
Ranking	3rd	2nd	1st

4   (a) $\boxed{0.75}$ x + $\boxed{4}$ y $\$$ 10,000

$x \geq \boxed{100}$

$y \geq \boxed{3}$ x

The total labour usage per week in hours is 0.75x + 4y, since each unit of X uses 45 minutes (three quarters of an hour) of labour and each unit of Y uses 4 hours of labour. This must not exceed 10,000 hours, so the labour constraint is 0.75x + 4y $\$$ 10,000.

The requirement to produce at least 100 units of X each week gives x $\geq$ 100.

The requirement to produce at least three times as many units of Y as of X each week gives y $\geq$ 3x.

(b) $\boxed{125}$ x + $\boxed{87}$ y

Workings

The expected cost of a call in peak hours is ($\$$1 × 50%) + ($\$$1.50 × 50%) = $\$$1.25 = 125p. The expected cost of a call at other times is (80p × 40%) + (90p × 50%) + ($\$$1 × 10%) = 87p. The objective is therefore: minimise 125x + 87y.

Mixed Bank answers

Mixed Bank 1

1 C

	$ per unit
Material	20.00
Labour	69.40
Production overhead (14 hours × $12.58)	176.12
Total production cost	265.52
General overhead (8% × $265.52)	21.24
	286.76

2 A

		Process 1		Process 2
		kg		kg
Input		47,000		42,000
Normal loss	(× 8%)	3,760	(× 5%)	2,100
Expected output		43,240		39,900
Actual output		42,000		38,915
Abnormal loss		1,240		985

3 C The actual sales revenue is higher than the flexed budget sales revenue. Since the effect of a sales volume change has been removed from this comparison the higher revenue must be caused by a higher than standard selling price.

A comparison of the original budget volume with the volume shown in the flexed budget and actual result shows that option A is incorrect.

The direct labour cost per unit is different in the two budget figures for labour, therefore option B is incorrect.

The actual material cost ($57,000) was higher than the flexed budget cost allowance ($47,500), therefore option D is incorrect.

4 A Variable costs are conventionally deemed to increase or decrease in direct proportion to changes in output. Therefore the correct answer is A. Descriptions B and D imply a changing unit rate, which does not comply with this convention. Description C relates to a fixed cost.

5 C Above the breakeven point, contribution = fixed costs + profit, therefore distance C indicates the contribution at level of activity L.

Distance A indicates the profit at level of activity L, B indicates the fixed costs and D indicates the margin of safety.

6 The standard allowed weight of material for the period was $\boxed{28,929}$ kg

Standard price per kg of material = $\dfrac{\$114,576}{28,644}$ = $4 per kg

∴ Material usage variance in kg = $\dfrac{\$1,140}{\$4}$ = 285 kg (F)

Standard allowed weight of material for period = (28,644 + 285) kg = 28,929 kg

7

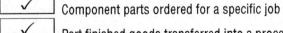

✓   Component parts ordered for a specific job

✓   Part finished goods transferred into a process from an earlier process

The component parts can be identified with a **specific cost unit** therefore they are a direct materials cost. The input from a previous process is classified as direct materials **in the subsequent process**.

Cleaning materials and maintenance materials are classified as **indirect materials costs,** to be absorbed into product costs as a part of the overhead absorption rate.

8   ☑   Hire of a delivery vehicle

        ☑   A piecework scheme with a guaranteed day rate

Both of these costs contain a **fixed element which is incurred regardless of the level of activity.** In addition a variable element is incurred which **fluctuates with the level of activity.**

The rental scheme described for the photocopier is a **step cost.**

9   TC = \$ ⌊ 2,800 ⌋ + \$ ⌊ 0.20 ⌋ L

	Items laundered L	Total cost \$
Period 2	11,650	5,130
Period 1	10,400	4,880
	1,250	250

∴ Variable cost per item laundered = \$250/1,250
                                       = \$0.20

Substituting in period 2,

Fixed cost = \$5,130 – (11,650 × \$0.20) = \$2,800

10   ☑   Realistic apportionment of expenses to responsible departments

       ☑   Improved information for the budget process

Refer to your Study Text for more information on this area.

11   The bonus would be \$ ⌊ 9.00 ⌋.

Standard time allowed for 60 enquiries = 60 × 10/60
                                       = 10 hours

Time saved = 10 hours – 8 hours = 2 hours

Bonus payable = 2 hours × 30% × \$15
              = \$9.00

12   \$

      ☑   Debit work-in-progress account   60,000

      ☑   Credit material stores account   60,000

Inventories of material are recorded at standard price therefore the material price variance would have been transferred to the variance account at the time of purchase. The transfer from inventory of 20,000 kg issued to work-in-progress on 28 June is made at the standard price of \$3 per kg.

13 The profit reported for period 1 using marginal costing principles is $ $\boxed{62,300}$

Income statement for period 1 under marginal costing

			Period 1	
			$	$
Sales:	Alpha (2,300 × $90)			207,000
	Beta (1,600 × $75)			120,000
				327,000
Opening inventory	Alpha		0	
	Beta		0	
			0	
Variable costs:	Alpha (2,500 × $45)		112,500	
	Beta (1,750 × $32)		56,000	
			168,500	
Less:				
Closing inventory	Alpha (200 × $45)		(9,000)	
	Beta (150 × $32)		(4,800)	
Variable cost of goods sold				154,700
Contribution				172,300
Fixed costs				(110,000)
Profit				$\boxed{62,300}$

14 **C** Lowering the selling price by 15% is best described as a short term tactical plan.

15 **B** Relative cell referencing.
Absolute cell referencing keeps one cell in a formula constant when the formula is copied.
A macro is a short program that automates a series of commands.
An IF statement allows a conditional formula to be written

16 **C** Total purchase costs = annual demand × purchase price

$$= 20,000 \times \$40 \text{ per unit}$$

$$= \$800,000$$

Order costs

$$\text{Number of orders} = \frac{\text{Annual demand}}{\text{EOQ}} = \frac{20,000 \text{ units}}{500 \text{ units}} = 40 \text{ orders per annum}$$

Cost per   = 40 orders × $25 per order

Total order costs = $1,000

Holding costs

Average inventory held = EOQ/2= 500/2= 250 units

It costs $4 to hold each unit of inventory

∴ Holding costs = average inventory held × $4 per unit

$$= 250 \text{ units} \times \$4 \text{ per unit} = \$1,000$$

Total annual costs of inventory

	$
Purchase costs	800,000
Order costs	1,000
Holding costs	1,000
Total	802,000

17   **D**   None of the criticisms apply in *all* circumstances.

Criticism (i) has some validity but even where output is not standardised it may be possible to identify a number of standard components and activities whose costs may be controlled effectively by the use of standard costs.

Criticism (ii) also has some validity but the use of information technology means that standards can be updated rapidly and more frequently, so that they may be useful for the purposes of control by comparison.

Criticism (iii) can also be addressed in some circumstances. The use of ideal standards and more demanding performance levels can combine the benefits of continuous improvement and standard costing control.

18   **A**

	Recruit $'000	Retrain $'000
4 new employees (4 × $40,000)	160	
Training cost		15
Replacements		100
	160	115

The supervision cost would be incurred anyway and is not a relevant cost, since an existing manager is used. Similarly, the salaries of the existing employees are not relevant.

The lowest cost option is to retrain the existing employees, at a total relevant cost of $115,000. Therefore the correct answer is A.

Option B includes the actual salary cost of the employees, which is not relevant because it would be incurred anyway. **Option C** is the cost of the recruitment option, including the apportionment of the non-relevant supervision cost. **Option D** is the combined relevant cost of both courses of action – but the lowest cost action would be selected.

19 $\boxed{0.17}$

$$r = \frac{n\sum xy - \sum x \sum y}{\sqrt{[n\sum x^2 - (\sum x)^2][n\sum y^2 - (\sum y)^2]}}$$

$$= \frac{(6 \times 14) - (2 \times 15)}{\sqrt{[6 \times 30 - 2^2][6 \times 130 - 15^2]}} = \frac{84 - 30}{\sqrt{176 \times 555}} = \frac{54}{312.54} = 0.172778 = 0.17 \text{ (to 2 dec places)}$$

20   The total cost of the job is $ $\boxed{440}$ (to the nearest $)

	$
Direct materials 10kg × $10	100
Direct labour 20 hours × $5	100
Prime cost	200
Variable production overhead 20 hours × $2	40
Fixed production overhead 20 hours × $10*	200
Total production cost	440
Selling, distribution and administration	50
Total cost	490

* Overhead absorption rate $= \dfrac{\$100,000}{10,000} = \$10$ per labour hour

Mixed Bank 2

1 B

	Cost centre Alpha $ per unit	Cost centre Beta $ per unit	Total $ per unit
Direct material	20.00	10.10	30.10
Direct labour	11.63	7.35	18.98
Production overhead	6.12	4.98	11.10

2 B The only direct costs are the wages paid to direct workers for ordinary time, plus the basic pay for overtime.

$25,185 + $5,440 = $30,625.

If you selected option A you forgot to include the basic pay for overtime of direct workers, which is always classified as a direct labour cost.

If you selected option C you have included overtime premium and shift allowances, which are usually treated as indirect costs. However, if overtime and shiftwork are incurred specifically for a particular cost unit, then they are classified as direct costs of that cost unit. There is no mention of such a situation here.

Option D includes sick pay, which is classified as an indirect labour cost.

3 B A variable cost will result in a constant cost per unit at each activity level. A semi-variable cost will result in a different cost per unit at each activity level, because of the spreading of fixed costs. A fixed cost is the same absolute amount of total cost for each activity level.

Cost type	Cost per unit for 100 units $	Cost per unit for 140 units $	Cost behaviour
W	80.00	75.43	Semi-variable
X	Constant cost for both activity levels		Fixed
Y	65.00	65.00	Variable
Z	67.00	61.29	Semi-variable

4 D A by-product can be defined as being 'output of some value, produced incidentally while manufacturing the main product'.

Option A is incorrect because a by-product has some value.

Option B is incorrect because this description could also apply to a joint product.

Option C is incorrect because the value of the product described could be relatively high, even though the output volume is relatively low

5

☑ Standard material usage per unit

☑ Budgeted production volume

Since there are no production resource limitations, the production budget would be prepared before the material usage budget. The budgeted material usage would then be calculated as:

budgeted production volume × standard material usage per unit

The budgeted change in materials inventory is relevant when preparing the **materials purchases budget.**

The budgeted average lead time for delivery of materials is relevant when determining **inventory control levels**. It does not affect the budgeted material usage.

		Favourable	Adverse
6	Selling price variance	$600	✓	

	$
Sales revenue from 2,000 should be (× $15)	30,000
but was (× $15.30)	30,600
Selling price variance	600 (F)

The variance is favourable because the price was higher than expected.

7 The value of the normal loss is $ 300

Normal loss = 20% × input
= 20% × 5,000 kg
= 1,000 kg

When scrap has a value, normal loss is valued at the value of the scrap ie 30c per kg.

Normal loss = $0.30 × 1,000 kg
= $300

8 The value of the abnormal loss is $ 230 . This value will be ✓ debited to the income statement.

	kg
Input	5,000
Normal loss (20% × 5,000 kg)	(1,000)
Abnormal loss	(200)
Output	3,800

$$\text{Cost per kg} = \frac{\text{Input costs} - \text{scrap value of normal loss}}{\text{Expected output}}$$

$$= \frac{\$4,900^* - \$300}{5,000 - 1,000} = \frac{\$4,600}{4,000} = \$1.15$$

		$
*	Materials (5,000 kg × $0.5)	2,500
	Labour	800
	Production overhead	1,600
		4,900

Abnormal loss = $1.15 × 200 = $230

9 The value of the output from the process is $ 4,370

Output = 3,800 kg

Cost per unit = $1.15 (see workings)

∴ Output = 3,800 × $1.15 = $4,370

Workings

$$\text{Cost per unit} = \frac{\text{Input costs} - \text{input costs scrap value of normal loss}}{\text{Expected output}}$$

$$= \frac{\$4,900^* - \$300}{5,000 - 1,000} = \frac{\$4,600}{400} = \$1.15$$

		$
*	Materials (5,000 kg × $0.5)	2,500
	Labour	800
	Production overhead	1,600
		4,900

10   ✓   under absorbed

Production overhead incurred of $64,000 was $6,000 higher than the $58,000 absorbed into work in progress.

11   The amount payable (to the nearest $) to employee A is $ 235

Workings

	$
500 units at $0.20	100
100 units at $0.25	25
200 units at $0.55	110
	235

12   A $ 90,000

     B $ 54,000

     C $ 25,000

     D $ 62,500

Workings

A: sales revenue = $90,000

B: variable cost for sales of $90,000 = $90,000 × $(0.50 + 0.10) = $54,000

C: fixed cost   = $10,000 cost of sales + $15,000 administration
                = $25,000

D: **Contribution per $ of sales**

	$
Sales price	1.00
Cost of sales	(0.50)
Selling and distribution costs	(0.10)
Contribution per $ (C/S ratio)	0.40

Monthly sales breakeven point $= \dfrac{\text{Fixed costs}}{\text{C/S ratio}} = \dfrac{25,000}{0.4} = \$62,500$

13   ✓   Useful for monitoring output in a standard costing system

     ✓   The quantity of work achievable at standard performance in an hour

     ✓   A basis for measuring output when dissimilar products are manufactured

A standard hour is the quantity of work achievable at standard performance, expressed in terms of a standard unit of work done in a standard period of time. It is a useful measure since it can be used to monitor output in a budgeting or standard costing system. It also overcomes the problem of how to measure output when a number of dissimilar products are manufactured.

14 The total overhead for the Residential cost centre will be $ | 135,318 |

	Resi-dential $	Catering $	House-keeping $	Main-tenance $	Total $
Initial allocation and apportionment	85,333	68,287	50,370	23,010	227,000
Reapportion maintenance (50:30:20)	11,505	6,903	4,602	(23,010)	–
	96,838	75,190	54,972	–	227,000
Reapportion housekeeping (70:30)	38,480	16,492	(54,972)		–
	135,318	91,682	–		227,000

15 A   Y = 50 + 7X

If we increase expenditure on advertising by $1, we replace X with (X + 1)

Y = 50 + 7(X + 1)
Y = 50 + 7X + 7
Y = 57 + 7X

Therefore, sales are now $57 on average, compared with $50 previously. Sales increase by $7 on average. **Option C** is therefore incorrect.

If advertising costs are increased by $7

Y = 50 + 7(X + 7)
Y = 50 + 7X + 49
Y = 99 + 7X

Sales are increased by $49 on average.

Option B is therefore incorrect.

If Y = 50 + 7X

when advertising is zero, X = 0

∴   Y = 50 + (7 × 0)
       Y = 50 + 0
       Y = 50

Therefore **option D** is incorrect.

16 B   Fixed costs per unit   = $16 ÷ 4 = $4

Units in closing inventory   = 17,500 – 15,000 = 2,500 units

Profit difference   = inventory increase in units × fixed overhead per unit
                            = 2,500 × $4 = $10,000

Inventories increased, therefore fixed overhead would have been carried forward in inventory using absorption costing and the profit would be higher than with marginal costing.

If you selected **option A** you calculated the correct profit difference, but misinterpreted the 'direction' of the difference.

If you **selected option C** or **D** you evaluated the inventory difference at variable cost and full cost respectively.

		Hours
17	**D**	
	Active hours required	380
	Add idle time (5/95)	20
	Total hours to be paid	400 @ $6 per hour
	Total labour cost	$2,400

If you selected option A you reduced the active hours by five per cent. However, the hours to be paid must be **greater than** the active hours, therefore the idle hours must be added. If you selected option B you made no allowance for the idle hours, which must also be paid for. If you selected option C you added five per cent to the active hours, but note that the idle time is quoted as a **percentage of the total time to be paid for.**

18   **B**   **Statement (i)** is consistent with a favourable material price variance. If the standard is high then actual prices are likely to be below the standard.

Statement (ii) is consistent with a favourable material price variance. Bulk purchase discounts would not have been allowed at the same level in the standard, because purchases were greater than expected.

Statement (iii) is not consistent with a favourable material price variance. Higher quality material is likely to cost more than standard, resulting in an **adverse** material price variance.

19   **C**   Let x = the number of hours 12,250 units should have taken

12,250 units should have taken	x hrs
but did take	41,000 hrs
Labour efficiency variance (in hrs)	x − 41,000 hrs

Labour efficiency variance (in $) $= \$11,250 \text{ (F)}$

$\therefore$ Labour efficiency variance (in hrs) $= \dfrac{\$11,250 \text{ (F)}}{\$6} = 1,875 \text{ (F)}$

$\therefore 1,875 \text{ hrs} = (x - 41,000) \text{ hrs}$

$\therefore$ standard hours for 12,250 units $= 41,000 + 1,875 = 42,875 \text{ hrs}$

$\therefore$ Standard hours per unit $= \dfrac{42,875 \text{ hrs}}{12,250 \text{ units}} = 3.50 \text{ hours}$

If you selected **option A** you treated the efficiency variance as adverse. **Option B** is the actual hours taken per unit and **option D** is the figure for the standard wage rate per hour.

20   **D**   For product F, costs are 60% of selling price, so profit must be 40% of selling price. Profit per unit of F = $20 × 40% = $8.

For product G, profit is 40% of cost. Profit per unit of G = $15 × 40% = $6.

The objective is therefore: maximise 8f + 6g. Therefore the correct answer is D.

BPP
LEARNING MEDIA

Mock exams

ACCA

Paper F2

Management Accounting

Mock Examination 1

Question Paper	
Time allowed	**2 hours**
ALL 50 questions are compulsory and MUST be attempted	

DO NOT OPEN THIS PAPER UNTIL YOU ARE READY TO START UNDER EXAMINATION CONDITIONS

ALL 50 questions are compulsory and MUST be attempted

1   Four lines representing expected costs and revenue have been drawn on a break-even chart:

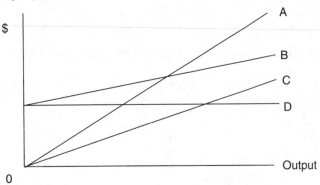

Which line represents variable cost?

A   Line A
B   Line B
C   Line C
D   Line D

(2 marks)

2   Four lines have been labelled as J, K, L and M at different levels of output on the following profit-volume chart:

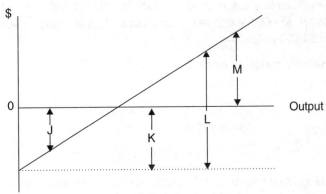

Which line represents the total contribution at the corresponding level of output?

A   Line J
B   Line K
C   Line L
D   Line M

(2 marks)

3   A manufacturing company has four types of cost (identified as T1, T2, T3 and T4)

The total cost for each type at two different production levels is:

Cost type	Total cost for 125 units $	Total cost for 180 units $
T1	1,000	1,260
T2	1,750	2,520
T3	2,475	2,826
T4	3,225	4,644

Which two cost types would be classified as being semi-variable?

A   T1 and T3
B   T1 and T4
C   T2 and T3
D   T2 and T4

(2 marks)

4   A company manufacturers and sells a single product. The following data relate to a weekly output of 2,880 units:

	$ per unit	$ per unit
Selling price		80
Less costs:		
Variable production	30	
Other variable	10	
Fixed	25	
		(65)
Profit		15

What is the weekly breakeven point (in units)?

A   900
B   1,440
C   1,800
D   4,800

(2 marks)

5   An organisation manufactures a single product which is sold for $60 per unit. The organisation's total monthly fixed costs are $54,000 and it has a contribution to sales ratio of 40%. This month it plans to manufacturer and sell 4,000 units.

What is the organisation's margin of safety this month (in units)?

A   1,500
B   1,750
C   2,250
D   2,500

(2 marks)

6   An organisation is using linear regression analysis to establish an equation that shows a relationship between advertising expenditure and sales. It will then use the equation to predict sales for given levels of advertising expenditure. Data for the last five periods are as follows:

Period number	Advertising expenditure	Sales
	$'000	$'000
1	17	108
2	19	116
3	24	141
4	22	123
5	18	112

What are the values of 'Σx', 'Σy' and 'n' that need to be inserted into the appropriate formula?

	Σx	Σy	n
A	$600,000	$100,000	5
B	$100,000	$600,000	5
C	$600,000	$100,000	10
D	$100,000	$600,000	10

(2 marks)

7   Which of the following correlation coefficients indicates the weakest relationship between two variables?

A   + 1.0
B   + 0.4
C   − 0.6
D   − 1.0   (2 marks)

8   Which of the following statements are correct?

(i)   Strategic information is mainly used by senior management in an organisation
(ii)   Productivity measurements are examples of tactical information
(iii)   Operational information is required frequently by its main users

A   (i) and (ii) only
B   (i) and (iii) only
C   (i), (ii) and (iii)   (1 mark)

9   A company manufactures two products P1 and P2 in a factory divided into two cost centres, X and Y. The following budgeted data are available:

	Cost centre	
	X	Y
Allocated and apportioned fixed overhead costs	$88,000	$96,000
Direct labour hours per unit:		
Product P1	3.0	1.0
Product P2	2.5	2.0

Budgeted output is 8,000 units of each product. Fixed overhead costs are absorbed on a direct labour hour basis.

What is the budgeted fixed overhead cost per unit for Product P2?

A $10
B $11
C $12
D $13   (2 marks)

10   A manufacturing company uses a machine hour rate to absorb production overheads, which were budgeted to be $130,500 for 9,000 machine hours. Actual overhead incurred were $128,480 and 8,800 machine hours were recorded.

What was the total under absorption of production overheads?

A $880
B $900
C $2,020
D $2,900   (2 marks)

11   Which of the following would NOT be classified as a service cost centre in a manufacturing company?

A   Product inspection department
B   Materials handling department
C   Maintenance department   (1 mark)

12   A company operates a job costing system. Job number 605 requires $300 of direct materials and $400 of direct labour. Direct labour is paid at the rate of $8 per hour. Production overheads are absorbed at a rate of $26 per direct labour hour and non-production overheads are absorbed at a rate of 120% of prime cost.

What is the total cost of job number 605?

A $2,000
B $2,400
C $2,840
D $4,400

(2 marks)

The following information relates to questions 13 and 14:

A company operates a process costing system using the first in first out (FIFO) method of valuation. No losses occur in the process.

The following date relate to last month:

	Units	Degree of completion	Value
Opening work in progress	100	60%	$680
Completed during the month	900		
Closing work in progress	150	48%	

The cost per equivalent unit of production for last month was $12.

13   What was the value of the closing work in progress?

A $816
B $864
C $936
D $1,800

(2 marks)

14   What was the total value of the units completed last month?

A $10,080
B $10,320
C $10,760
D $11,000

(2 marks)

15   A company's budgeted sales for last month were 10,000 units with a standard selling price of $20 per unit and a contribution to sales ratio of 40%. Last month actual sales of 10,500 units with total revenue of $204,750 were achieved.

What were the sales price and sales volume contribution variances?

	Sales price variance ($)	Sales volume contribution variance ($)
A	5,250 adverse	4,000 favourable
B	5,250 adverse	4,000 adverse
C	5,000 adverse	4,000 favourable
D	5,000 adverse	4,000 adverse

(2 marks)

16   A company operates a standard absorption costing system. The standard fixed production overhead rate is $15 per hour.

The following data relate to last month: Actual hours worked   5,500
Budgeted hours   5,000
Standard hours for actual production   4,800

What was the fixed production overhead capacity variance?

A $7,500 adverse
B $7,500 favourable
C $10,500 adverse
D $10,500 favourable   **(2 marks)**

17   A contract is under consideration which requires 600 labour hours to complete. There are 350 hours of spare labour capacity. The remaining hours for the contract can be found either by weekend overtime working paid at double the normal rate of pay or by diverting labour from the manufacture of product QZ. If the contract is undertaken and labour is diverted, then sales of product QZ will be lost. Product QZ takes three labour hours per unit to manufacture and makes a contribution of $12 per unit. The normal rate of pay for labour is $9 per hour.

What is the total relevant cost of labour for the contract?

A $1,000
B $2,250
C $3,250
D $4,500   **(2 marks)**

18   A company purchased a machine several years ago for $50,000. Its written down value is now $10,000. The machine is no longer used on normal production work and it could be sold now for $8,000.

A one-off contract is being considered which would make use of this machine for six months. After this time the machine would be sold for $5,000.

What is the relevant cost of the machine to the contract?

A $2,000
B $3,000
C $5,000
D $10,000   **(2 marks)**

19   A company has monthly fixed costs of $10,000 and variable costs per unit of production of $15. The equation of the straight line relating productions (P) to costs (C) is:

A   C = 10,000P + 15
B   P = 10,000 + 15C
C   C = 10,000 + 15/P
D   C = 10,000 + 15P   **(2 marks)**

20   A company plans to produce and sell 14,000 units of a product.

Fixed costs absorbed are $20 per unit
Contribution per unit is $24.

What is the margin of safety?

A   14,000 units
B   11,667 units
C   2,800 units
D   2,333 units   **(2 marks)**

21   Reginald is the manager of production department M in a factory which has ten other production departments. He receives monthly information that compares planned and actual expenditure for department M. After department M, all production goes into other factory departments to be completed prior to being despatched to customers. Decisions involving capital expenditure in department M are not taken by Reginald.

Which of the following describes Reginald's role in department M?

A   A cost centre manager
B   An investment centre manager
C   A profit centre manager   (1 mark)

The following information relates to questions 22 and 23.

A company manufacturers and sells two products (X and Y) which have contributions per unit of $8 and $20 respectively. The company aims to maximise profit. Two materials (G and H) are used in the manufacture of each product. Each material is in short supply – 1,000 kg of G and 1,800 kg of H are available next period. The company holds no inventories and it can sell all the units produced.

The management accountant has drawn the following graph accurately showing the constraints for materials G and H.

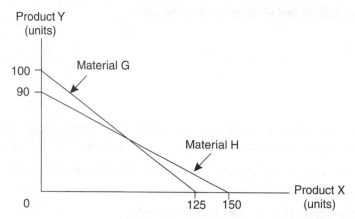

22   What is the amount (in kg) of material G and material H used in each unit of product Y?

	Material G	Material H
A	10	20
B	10	10
C	20	20
D	20	10

(2 marks)

23   What is the optimal mix of production (in units) for the next period?

	Product X	Product Y
A	0	90
B	50	60
C	60	50
D	125	0

(2 marks)

24   A company has two production departments and two service departments with the following fixed overheads:

	Production		Service	
	A	B	C	D
	$'000	$'000	$'000	$'000
	1,000	1,200	1,200	1,600

Service department C divides its time between the other departments in the ratio 3:2:1 (for A, B, and D respectively). Department D spends 40% of its time servicing Department A and 60% servicing Department B. If all service departments' overheads are allocated to production departments, the total fixed overhead cost of Department A is:

A $2,400,000
B $2,200,000
C $1,320,000
D $2,320,000   (2 marks)

25   An abnormal loss would arise when

(i)   Total losses are less than expected
(ii)   Total losses are greater than expected
(iii)   Total output is less than expected
(iv)   Total output is greater than expected

Which one of the following is correct?

A   (i) only
B   (i) and (ii)
C   (ii) and (iii)
D   (iii) and (iv)   (2 marks)

26   Up to a given level of activity in each period the purchase price per unit of a raw material is constant. After that point a lower price per unit applies both to further units purchased and also retrospectively to all units already purchased.

Which of the following graphs depicts the total cost of the raw materials for a period?

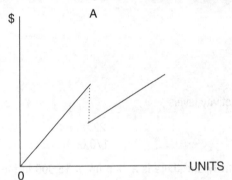

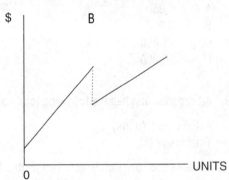

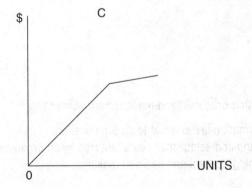

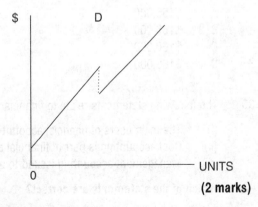

(2 marks)

27 The following breakeven chart has been drawn showing lines for total cost (TC), total variable cost (TVC), total fixed cost (TFC) and total sales revenue (TSR):

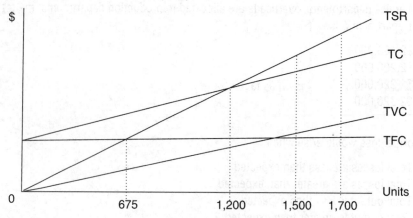

What is the margin of safety at the 1,700 units level of activity?

A 200 units
B 300 units
C 500 units
D 1,025 units

(2 marks)

28 A company manufactures a single product with a variable cost per unit of $22. The contribution to sales ratio is 45%. Monthly fixed costs are $198,000.

What is the breakeven point (in units)?

A 4,950
B 9,000
C 11,000
D 20,000

(2 marks)

29 An organisation has the following total costs at two activity levels:

Activity level (units)	17,000	22,000
Total costs ($)	140,000	170,000

Variable cost per unit is constant in this range of activity and there is a step up of $5,000 in the total fixed costs when activity exceeds 18,000 units.

What is the total cost at an activity level of 20,000 units?

A $155,000
B $158,000
C $160,000
D $163,000

(2 marks)

30 The following statements relate to financial accounting or to cost and management accounting:

(i)   The main users of financial accounting information are external to an organisation.
(ii)   Cost accounting is part of financial accounting and establishes costs incurred by an organisation.
(iii) Management accounting issued to aid planning, control and decision making.

Which of the statements are correct?

A (i) and (ii) only
B (i) and (iii) only
C (ii) and (iii) only

(1 mark)

31 **Fill in the missing words.**

A spreadsheet is an electronic piece of paper divided into .... and .... The point where these intersect is known as a ....

(1 mark)

32 Long term planning is also known as **tactical** planning.

A True
B False

(1 mark)

33 A company uses 9,000 units of a component per annum. The component has a purchase price of $40 per unit and the cost of placing an order is $160. The annual holding cost of one component is equal to 8% of its purchase price.

What is the Economic Order Quantity (to the nearest unit) of the component?

A 530
B 671
C 949
D 1,342

(2 marks)

34 A company determines its order quantity for a component using the Economic Order Quantity (EOQ) model.

What would be the effects on the EOQ and the total annual ordering cost of an increase in the annual cost of holding one unit of the component in stock?

	EOQ	Total annual ordering cost
A	Lower	Higher
B	Higher	Lower

(1 mark)

35 Consider the following statements:

(i) Job costing is only applicable to service organisations.

(ii) Batch costing can be used when a number of identical products are manufactured together to go into finished inventory.

Is each statement TRUE or FALSE?

	Statement (i)	Statement (ii)
A	False	False
B	False	True
C	True	True
D	True	False

(2 marks)

36 An organisation absorbs overheads on a machine hour basis. The planned level of activity for last month was 30,000 machine hours with a total overhead cost of $247,500. Actual results showed that 28,000 machine hours were recorded with a total overhead cost of $238,000.

What was the total under absorption of overhead last month?

A $7,000
B $7,500
C $9,500
D $16,500

(2 marks)

37 The following information relates to a manufacturing company for next period:

	units		$
Production	14,000	Fixed production costs	63,000
Sales	12,000	Fixed selling costs	12,000

Using absorption costing for the profit for next period has been calculated as $36,000.

What would the profit for next period be using marginal costing?

A $25,000
B $27,000
C $45,000
D $47,000

(2 marks)

38 Information relating to two processes (F and G) was as follows:

Process	Normal loss as % of input	Input litres	Output litres
F	8	65,000	58,900
G	5	37,500	35,700

For each process, was there an abnormal loss or an abnormal gain?

	Profess F	Process G
A	Abnormal gain	Abnormal gain
B	Abnormal gain	Abnormal loss
C	Abnormal loss	Abnormal gain
D	Abnormal loss	Abnormal loss

(2 marks)

39 Last month 27,000 direct labour hours were worked at an actual cost of $236,385 and the standard direct labour hours of production were 29,880. The standard direct labour cost per hour was $8.50.

What was the labour efficiency variance?

A $17,595 Adverse
B $17,595 Favourable
C $24,480 Adverse
D $24,480 Favourable

(2 marks)

40 Last month a company's budgeted sales were 5,000 units. The standard selling price was $6 per unit with a standard contribution to sales ratio of 60%. Actual sales were 4,650 units with a total revenue $30,225.

What were the favourable sales price and adverse sales volume contribution variance?

	Sales price	Sales volume contribution
	$	$
A	2,325	1,260
B	2,500	1,260
C	2,325	2,100
D	2,500	2,100

(2 marks)

41 Which of the following is an initial requirement of a management control system?

A Establishing the standard to be achieved
B Measuring the actual performance
C Setting organisational objectives

(1 mark)

42 **Which one of the following would be classified as indirect labour?**

A Assembly workers on a car production line
B Bricklayers in a house building company
C Forklift truck drivers in the stores of an engineering company

(1 mark)

43 The following statements relate to the calculation of the regression line y = a + box using the information on the formulae sheet at the end of this examination paper:

(i) n represents the number of pairs of data items used
(ii) $(\Sigma x)^2$ is calculated by multiplying Σx by Σx
(iii) Σxy is calculated by multiplying Σx by Σy

Which statements are correct?

A   (i) and (ii) only
B   (i) and (iii) only
C   (ii) and (iii) only
D   (i), (ii) and (iii)   **(2 marks)**

44 The correlation coefficient (r) for measuring the connection between two variables (x and y) has been calculated as 0.6.

How much of the variation in the dependent variable (y) is explained by the variation in the independent variable (x)?

A   36%
B   40%
C   60%
D   64%   **(2 marks)**

45 The following statements relate to relevant cost concepts in decision making:

(i) Materials can never have an opportunity cost whereas labour can

(ii) The annual depreciation charge is not a relevant cost

(iii) Fixed costs would have a relevant cost element if a decision causes a change in their total expenditure

Which statements are correct?

A   (i) and (ii) only
B   (i) and (iii) only
C   (ii) and (iii) only   **(1 mark)**

46 A company is evaluating a project that requires 4,000 kg of a material that is used regularly in normal production. 2,500 kg of the material, purchased last month at a total cost of $20,000, are in inventory. Since last month the price of the material has increased by $2\frac{1}{2}\%$.

What is the total relevant cost of the material for the project?

A $12,300
B $20,500
C $32,300
D $32,800   **(2 marks)**

47 In a process where there are no work–in–progress inventories, two joint products (J and K) are created. Information (in units) relating to last month is as follows:

Product	Sales	Opening inventory of finished goods	Closing inventory of finished goods
J	6,000	100	300
K	4,000	400	200

Joint production costs last month were $110,000 and these were apportioned to joint products based on the number of units produced.

What were the joint production costs apportioned to product J for last month?

A $63,800
B $64,000
C $66,000
D $68,200   (2 marks)

48 A company manufactures two products (L and M) using the same material and labour. It holds no inventories. Information about the variable costs and maximum demands are as follows:

	Product L $/unit	Product M $/unit
Material ($4 per litre)	13	19
Labour ($7 per hour)	35	28
	Units	Units
Maximum monthly demand	6,000	8,000

Each month 50,000 litres of material and 60,000 labour hours are available.

Which one of the following statement is correct?

A   Material is a limiting factor but labour is not a limiting factor.
B   Material is not a limiting factor but labour is a limiting factor.
C   Neither material nor labour is a limiting factor.
D   Both material and labour are limiting factors.   (2 marks)

The following information relates to questions 49 and 50.

A company has established the following selling price, costs and revenue equations for one of its products:

Selling price ($ per unit) = $50 - 0.025Q$

Marginal revenue ($ per unit) = $50 - 0.05Q$

Total costs per month ($) = $2,000 + 15Q$

Q represents the number of units produced and sold per month.

49 At what selling price will monthly profits be maximised?

A $15.00
B $17.50
C $25.00
D $32.50   (2 marks)

50 What would be the monthly profit if the selling price per unit was set at $20?

A $1,000
B $4,000
C $6,000
D $12,000   (2 marks)

Answers

DO NOT TURN THIS PAGE UNTIL YOU HAVE
COMPLETED THE MOCK EXAM

1   C   Line C represents total variable cost.

2   C   Line L represents the total contribution at the corresponding level of output.

3   A

Cost type	Total cost for 125 units	Cost per unit @ 125 units	Total cost for 180 units	Cost per unit @ 180 units
	$	$	$	$
T1	1,000	8.00	1,260	7.00
T2	1,750	14.00	2,520	14.00
T3	2,475	19.80	2,826	13.75
T4	3,225	25.80	4,644	25.80

Cost types T1 and T3 have different costs per unit at different activity levels and are therefore most likely to be classified as semi-variable costs.

Cost types T2 and T4 have the same cost per unit at different levels of activity and are therefore wholly variable costs.

4   C   Fixed costs = 2,880 units × $25 per unit

$$= \$72,000$$

Contribution per unit = $80 – (30 + 10)
$$= \$40$$

$$\text{Breakeven point} = \frac{\text{fixed costs}}{\text{contribution per unit}}$$

$$= \frac{72,000}{40}$$

$$= 1,800 \text{ units}$$

5   B $$\text{Breakeven sales revenue} = \frac{\text{fixed costs}}{\text{c/s ratio}}$$

$$= \frac{\$54,000}{0.4}$$

$$= \$135,000$$

$$\text{Breakeven units} = \frac{135,000}{60}$$
$$= 2,250 \text{ units}$$

∴ Margin of safety = (4,000 – 2,250) units
= 1,750 units

6   B

Period number	Advertising expenditure $'000	Sales $'000
1	17	108
2	19	116
3	24	141
4	22	123
5	18	112
	100	600

N = 5 (five pairs of data)

Sales (y) are dependent on the levels of advertising expenditure (x).

7   B   + 0.4 indicates the weakest relationship between two variables.

8   C   Statements (i), (ii) and (iii) are all correct.

BPP
LEARNING MEDIA

9   D

	Cost centre	
	x	*y*
	$	$
Overheads	88,000	96,000

Budgeted direct labour hours

Product P1	24,000 hours	8,000 hours
Product P2	20,000 hours	16,000 hours
	44,000 hours	24,000 hours

Budgeted overhead absorption rate

$$\text{Cost centre X} = \frac{\$88,000}{44,000 \text{ hours}} = \$2 \text{ per direct labour hour}$$

$$\text{Cost centre Y} = \frac{\$96,000}{24,000 \text{ hours}} = \$4 \text{ per direct labour hour}$$

Budgeted fixed overhead cost per unit – Product P2

Cost centre x = 2.5 hours $2 per direct labour hour

      = $5

Cost centre y = 2 hours @ $4 per direct labour hour

      = $8

∴ fixed overhead per unit of Product P2 = $(5+8)

                          = $13

10   A

	$
Overhead absorbed (8,800 machine hours × $14.50*)	127,600
Actual overhead	128,480
Under-absorbed overhead	880

$$* \text{ Budgeted overhead absorption rate} = \frac{\$130,500}{9,000 \text{ machine hours}} = \$14.50 \text{ per machine hour}$$

11   A   The product inspection department would not be classified as a service cost centre in a manufacturing company.

12   C   Total cost – job number 605

	$
Direct materials	300
Direct labour	400
Prime cost	700
Production overheads ($26 × $400/$8)	1,300
	2,000
Non-production overheads (120% × $700)	840
Total cost – job number 605	2,840

13   B   Closing work in progress   = 48% × 150 units × $12

                             = $864

14 C

	$
Opening work in progress	680
Completed in month (800* × $12)	9,600
Opening work in progress (40 × $12)	480
Total value of units completed	10,760

* 900 units − 100 units = 800 units

15 A

	$
Sales revenue from 10,500 units should have been × $20)	210,000
but was	204,750
Sales price variance	5,250 (A)

$$\frac{\text{contribution per unit}}{\$20} = 0.4$$

∴ contribution per unit = 0.4 × $20

= $8

Budgeted sales	10,000 units
Actual sales	10,500 units
Sales volume variance	500 units (F)
× standard contribution per unit	× $8
Sales volume contribution variance	$4,000 (F)

16 B

Budgeted hours of work	5,000 hours
Actual hours of work	5,500 hours
Fixed production overhead capacity variance	500 hours (F)
× standard fixed production overhead rate	× $15
Fixed production overhead capacity variance (in $)	7,500 (F)

17 C **Relevant cost-labour: diverting labour from QZ**

	$	$
350 hours spare capacity (no relevant cost)		
250 hours @ $9	2,250	
Opportunity cost = 250 hours × ($12/3)	1,000	3,250
Total relevant cost of labour for contract		3,250

Relevant cost of labour: weekend work

	$
350 hours spare capacity (no relevant cost)	–
250 hours at $(9×2) = $18	4,500
Total relevant cost of labour	4,500

The weekend work option should be disregarded as it is too expensive.

18 B

	$
Sales proceeds now	8,000
Sales proceeds – six months	5,000
Relevant cost of machine	3,000

19 D C = 10,000 + 15P

20 **D** 2,333 units

$$\text{Breakeven sales} = \frac{14,000 \times 20}{24}$$

= 11,667 units

Margin of safety = 14,000 − 11,667

= 2,333 units

21 **A** Reginald's role in department M is as cost centre manager.

22 **A** 1,000 kg of Material G produces 100 units of Product Y

∴ each unit of Product Y uses $\dfrac{1,000\,\text{kg}}{100\,\text{units}}$ = 10 kg per unit

1,800 kg of Material H produces 90 units of Product Y

∴ each unit of Product Y uses $\dfrac{1,800\ \text{kg}}{90\ \text{units}}$ = 20 kg per unit

23 **A**

Option			Total contribution
			$
A (0, 90)	(0 × $8) + (90 × $20)	=	1,800
B (50, 60)	(50 × $8) + (60 × $20)	=	1,600
C (60, 50)	(60 × $8) + (50 × $20)	=	1,480
D (125,0)	(125 × $8) + (0 × $20)	=	1,000

The company aims to maximise profits therefore the optimal mix of production is that which maximises contribution, ie Option A, zero units of Product X and 90 units of Product Y.

24 **D**

	A	B	C	D
	$'000	$'000	$'000	$'000
Fixed overheads	1,000	1,200	1,200	1,600
C (3:2:1)	600	400	(1,200)	200
				1,800
D (40:60)	720	1,080		(1,800)
	2,320			

25 **C** (ii) If more losses have been incurred than expected, the loss is abnormally high.

(iii) If output is less than expected, losses must be higher than expected.

26 **A**

27 **C** Breakeven is at 1,200 units where TC = TSR
Margin of safety = 1700 − 1200 = 500 units

28 **C** Contribution per unit = $22/0.55 × 0.45 = $18
Breakeven point = Fixed costs/contribution per unit
= 198,000/18
= 11,000 units

29 **C** Variable cost per unit = $\dfrac{(170,000 - 5,000) - 140,000}{22,000 - 17,000}$

= $5

At 22,000 units, fixed costs = $170,000 − (22,000 × $5)
= $60,000

Total cost at an activity level of 20,000 units = $60,000 + (20,000 × $5)
= $160,000

30	B	Cost accounting is not part of financial accounting.

31   A spreadsheet is an electronic piece of paper divided into **rows** and **columns**. The point where these intersect is known as a **cell**.

32	B	Long-term planning is **strategic** planning. Tactical planning is medium term.

33   C $EOQ = \sqrt{2 \times C_o \times D / C_h}$

$C_o = \$160$
$D = 9,000$ units
$C_h = 8\% \times \$40 = \$3.20$

$EOQ = \sqrt{2 \times 160 \times 9,000 / 3.2}$

$= 949$ units

34   A   Holding cost is part of the denominator in the formula so any increase will reduce EOQ. This will mean that less will be ordered each time so there will be more orders each year, increasing the annual ordering cost.

35   B   Job costing can also be used in manufacturing organisations.

36   A   Overhead absorption rate = $247,500/30,000 = \$8.25$
Absorbed overheads = $28,000 \times \$8.25 = \$231,000$
Actual cost = $\$238,000$
Under absorption = $238,000 - 231,000 = \$7,000$

37   B   The fixed overhead absorbed into the inventory valuation is the difference in the marginal costing profit.

Inventory = $14,000 - 12,000 = 2,000$ units

Value of fixed production costs absorbed into inventory

$= 2,000 \times 63,000/14,000$

$= \$9,000$

Marginal costing profit = $36,000 - 9,000 = \$27,000$

38   C   Process F: Expected output = $92\% \times 65,000 = 59,800$ litres

                 Actual output = 58,900 litres

                 There is an abnormal loss

        Process G: Expected output = $95\% \times 37,500 = 35,625$ litres

                 Actual output = 35,700 litres

                 There is an abnormal gain

39   D

Actual hours @ standard rate	$27,000 \times \$8.50 = \$299,500$
Standard hours @ standard rate	$29,880 \times \$8.50 = \$253,980$
Labour efficiency variance	$\$24,480$ F

40   A   Sales price variance:

Actual sales @ standard rate	$4,650 \times \$6 = \$27,900$
Standard sales at actual price	$= \$30,225$
Labour efficiency variance	$\$2,325$ F

Sales volume contribution variance:
Standard contribution = $\$6 \times 60\% = \$3.60$ per unit
Volume variance = $5,000 - 4,650 = 350$ units A
@ $\$3.60$ = $\$1,260$ A

41	C	Objectives for the organisation need to be set before further steps in establishing a management control system can be taken.

41   C   Objectives for the organisation need to be set before further steps in establishing a management control system can be taken.

42   C   The drivers are not working directly on engineering projects

43   A Σxy is calculated by multiplying x and y for each data item and then adding all of the results.

44   A   The variation is given by the coefficent of determination, r^2

$r^2 = 0.6 \times 0.6 = 0.36$

45   C   Materials can have an opportunity cost if they could have been used for something else.

46   D   Purchase cost per kg = 20,000/2,500 = \$8

Updated cost per kg = \$8 × 1.025 = \$8.20

Relevant cost of 4,000 kgs   = 4,000 × \$8.20

= \$32,800

47   D   Production in units:

J: 6,000 – 100 + 300 =   6,200
K: 4,000 – 400 + 200 =   3,800
                    10,000

Joint costs apportioned to J:
6,200/10,000 × \$110,000 = \$68,200

48   D

	Product L	Product M	Total	Available
Material in litres	6,000 × 13/4 = 19,500	8,000 × 19/4 = 38,000	57,500	50,000
Labour in hours	6,000 × 35/7 = 30,000	8,000 × 28/7 = 32,000	62,000	60,000

Both material and labour are limited factors.

49   D   Profits are maximised when marginal revenue = marginal cost

Marginal revenue = 50 – 0.05Q

Marginal cost = 15

50 – 0.05Q = 15

$Q = \dfrac{50 - 15}{0.05}$

Q = 700

Selling price = 50 – 0.025Q
= 50 – (0.025 × 700)
= \$32.50

50   B   When selling price is \$20:

20 = 50 – 0.025Q

$Q = \dfrac{50 - 20}{0.025}$

= 1,200

At 1,200 units:

Total revenue = 1,200 × \$20 = \$24,000

Total costs = 2,000 + (15 × 1,200) = \$20,000

Profit = 24,000 – 20,000 = \$4,000

ACCA

Paper F2

Management Accounting

Mock Examination 2

Question Paper	
Time allowed	**2 hours**
ALL 50 questions are compulsory and MUST be attempted	

DO NOT OPEN THIS PAPER UNTIL YOU ARE READY TO START UNDER EXAMINATION CONDITIONS

ALL 50 questions are compulsory and MUST be answered

1   An organisation has found that there is a linear relationship between production volume and production costs.

It has found that a production volume of 400 units corresponds to production costs of $10,000 and that a production volume of 800 units corresponds to production costs of $12,000. The production costs for a production volume of 1,000 units are

$ [_____]   **(2 marks)**

2   Two variables are said to be **correlated** if the both change by the same amount.

Is this statement: (tick one)

[ ]   True

[ ]   False   **(1 mark)**

3   If high levels of inventory are maintained this increases the .... costs.

Which word correctly completes this sentence?

[ ]   Holding

[ ]   Ordering

[ ]   Stockout   **(1 mark)**

4   A company absorbs production overhead in the assembly department on the basis of direct labour hours. Budgeted direct labour hours for the period were 200,000. The production overhead absorption rate for the period was $2 per direct labour hour.

Actual results for the period were as follows.

Direct labour hours worked	220,000
Production overheads incurred	$480,000

Under-absorbed overhead = $ [_____]   **(2 marks)**

The following information relates to questions 5, 6 and 7

An organisation sells one product for which data is given below:

	$ per unit
Selling price	10
Variable cost	6
Fixed cost	2

The fixed costs are based on a budgeted level of activity of 5,000 units for the period.

5   The organisation wishes to earn a profit of $6,000 for one period, the number of units that must be sold =

[_____]   **(2 marks)**

6   The organisation's margin of safety for the budget period if fixed costs prove to be 20% higher than

budgeted is [_____] %   **(2 marks)**

7   If the selling price and variable cost increase by 20% and 12% respectively by how much must sales volume change compared with the original budgeted level in order to achieve the original budgeted profit for the period?

☐   24.2% decrease
☐   24.2% increase
☐   39.4% decrease
☐   39.4% increase   **(2 marks)**

8

Which of the following descriptions best suits the above graph?

Cost/unit falls due to:

☐   A learning curve effect
☐   Overtime being worked
☐   The availability of discounts for materials
☐   Actual overheads being more than expected   **(2 marks)**

9   A company pays its employees a guaranteed weekly wage of $160, plus $1 per piecework hour produced. In a certain week an employee produces the following output.

	Piecework time allowed per unit
15 units of product Alpha	2.0 hours
20 units of product Beta	0.8 hours
Hours worked	40 hours

The employee's pay for the week is $ ☐   **(2 marks)**

The following information relates to questions 10, 11 and 12

A company reported an annual profit of $47,500 for the year ended 31 March 2000. The company uses absorption costing. One product is manufactured, the Heath, which has the following standard cost per unit.

	$
Direct material (2 kg at $5/kg)	10
Direct labour (4 hours at $6.50/hour)	26
Variable overheads (4 hours at $1/hour)	4
Fixed overheads (4 hours at $3/hour)	12
	52

The normal level of activity is 10,000 units although actual production was 11,500 units. Fixed costs were as budgeted.

Inventory levels at 1 April 1999 were 400 units and at the end of the year were 600 units.

10   The profit under marginal costing would be $[   ]   **(2 marks)**

11   The budgeted fixed overheads for the year ended 31 March 2000 were $[   ]   **(2 marks)**

12   The actual under or over absorption was $[   ]   **(2 marks)**

[ ]   Under absorbed

[ ]   Over absorbed

13   The pharmacy in a busy hospital uses pre-determined rates for absorbing total overheads, based on the budgeted number of prescriptions to be handled. A rate of $7 per prescription has been calculated, and the following overhead expenditures have been estimated at two activity levels.

Total overheads	Number of prescriptions
$	
97,000	13,000
109,000	16,000

During a particular period fixed overheads were $45,000.

Based on the data above, what was the budgeted level of activity in prescriptions to be handled during the period in question?

[ ]   13,000

[ ]   15,000

[ ]   16,000

[ ]   33,333   **(2 marks)**

14   An organisation has 1,400 units of Product XX in inventory and 2,550 units on order with suppliers. If the free inventory is 1,950 the number of units of Product XX that have been requisitioned but not yet issued is

[   ]   **(2 marks)**

15   A company produces a product called the Kiwi. The cost of the raw material used to make the Kiwi is $10 per kg. During a typical year 15,000 kgs of the raw material are used. The cost of placing a typical order for the raw material is $250 and the annual cost of holding inventory as a percentage of cost is 10%. The

company's EOQ is [   ] kgs.   **(2 marks)**

16   The following information relates to a management consultancy organisation.

Overhead absorption rate per consulting hour	$25.00
Salary cost per consulting hour (senior)	$40.00
Salary cost per consulting hour (junior)	$30.00

The organisation adds 35% to total cost to arrive at the selling price.

Assignment number 3036 took 172 hours of a senior consultant's time and 440 hours of junior time.

The price that should be charged for assignment number 3036 is $[   ] (to the nearest $).

(2 marks)

17   Wages = units produced × rate of pay per unit.

Does this refer to: (tick one)

[ ]   A day rate system

[ ]   A piecework scheme   **(1 mark)**

18   'The objective of .... costing is to include in the total cost of a product an appropriate share of the organisation's total overhead.'

Which word completes this sentence? (tick one)

☐   Marginal

☐   Absorption   **(1 mark)**

19   An organisation uses linear programming to establish the optimal production plan for the production of its two products, V and W, given that it has the objective of minimising costs. The following graph has been established bearing in mind the various constraints of the business. The clear area indicates the feasible region.

The optimal solution is most likely to be at [＿＿＿＿] or [＿＿＿＿＿]   **(2 marks)**

20   A company has 500 units of material K in inventory for which it paid $2,000. The material is no longer in use in the company and could be sold for $1.50 per kg.

The company is considering taking on a single special order which will require 800 units of material K. The current purchase price of material K is $5 per kg.

In the assessment of the relevant cost of the decision to accept the special order, the cost of material K is

$ [＿＿＿＿]   **(2 marks)**

21   A company makes one product, which passes through a single process.

Details of the process for last period are as follows:

Materials   5,000 kg at 50c per kg
Labour $800
Production overheads   200% of labour

Normal losses are 20% of input in the process, and without further processing any losses can be sold as scrap for 30p per kg.

The output for the period was 3,800 kg from the process.

There was no work in progress at the beginning or end of the period.

The value of the abnormal loss is $ [＿＿＿＿]   **(2 marks)**

22 Over and under absorption of overheads occurs because: (tick one)

☐ The wrong absorption rates are used

☐ The absorption rates are based on estimates

☐ The overheads are incorrectly allocated   **(1 mark)**

23 Complete this sentence.

Marginal cost is the .... cost of one unit of product or service.   **(1 mark)**

24 A removals company operates with three vehicles. The following estimated data are available:

During week 30 it is expected that all three vehicles will be used, 560 tonnes will be loaded and a total of 7,900 kilometres travelled (including return journeys when empty) as shown in the following table:

Journey	Tonnes carried (one way)	Kilometres (one way)
1	68	360
2	56	530
3	80	780
4	64	230
5	52	440
6	80	960
7	58	180
8	52	200
9	50	270
	560	3,950

The number of tonne-kilometres achieved during week 30 was ☐.   **(2 marks)**

25 The following graph shows total costs and total revenues at various output levels.

Profits are maximised along line ☐   **(2 marks)**

26 Complete this sentence:

Inventory values using absorption costing are .... than those calculated using marginal costing.   **(1 mark)**

27 A secondary product arising from a process and of less value than the principal product is known as: (tick one)

☐ A joint product

☐ A by-product   **(1 mark)**

28 An organisation manufactures various products and uses CVP analysis to establish the minimum level of production to ensure profitability.

Fixed costs of $75,000 have been allocated to a specific product but are expected to increase to $150,000 once production exceeds 40,000 units, as a new factory will need to be rented in order to produce the extra units. Variable costs are a stable $7.50 per unit over all levels of activity. Revenue from this product will be $11.25 per unit.

The total cost equation when production is less than or equal to 40,000 units is

C = ☐ + ☐ Q

where C = total cost

Q = quantity   **(2 marks)**

29 A company operates a continuous process producing three products and one by-product. Output from the process for a week was as follows.

Product	Selling price per unit	Units of output from process
	$	Units
A	16	5,000
B	50	10,000
C	40	10,000
D (by-product)	4	1,750

Total output costs were $138,500.

The unit valuation for product C using the sales revenue basis for allocating joint costs was $ ☐ per unit (to the nearest cent).   **(2 marks)**

30 The management accountant of a company has already allocated and apportioned the fixed overheads for the period although he has yet to reapportion the service centre costs. Information for the period is as follows.

	Production departments		Service departments		Total
	1	2	Stores	Maintenance	
Allocated and apportioned overheads	$35,000	$65,500	$12,600	$16,900	$130,000
Work done by:					
Stores	50%	40%	–	10%	
Maintenance	75%	20%	5%	–	

The total overheads included in production department 1 if the reciprocal method is used to reapportion service cost centre costs is $ ☐ (to the nearest $).   **(2 marks)**

The following information relates to questions 31 and 32

An organisation has recorded the following sales information for the past five months.

Month	Advertising expenditure	Sales revenue
	$'000	$'000
1	20	82
2	16	70
3	24	90
4	22	85
5	18	73

The following has also been calculated (all figures in $'000):

Σ(Advertising expenditure)	=	100
Σ(Sales revenue)	=	400
Σ(Advertising expenditure × Sales revenue)	=	8,104
Σ(Advertising expenditure^2)	=	2,040
Σ(Sales revenue^2)	=	32,278

31 The value of b in the regression equation is ⬚ (to 1 decimal place). **(2 marks)**

32 The value of a in the regression equation is ⬚ **(2 marks)**

33 A costing method applied where work is undertaken to customers special requirements for each order is known as: (tick one)

☐ Job costing
☐ Batch costing
☐ Service costing **(1 mark)**

34 A company is building a model in order to forecast total costs based on the level of output. The following data is available for last year.

20X2 Month	Output '000 units (X)	Costs $'000 (Y)
January	16	170
February	20	240
March	23	260
April	25	300
May	25	280
June	19	230
July	16	200
August	12	160
September	19	240
October	25	290
November	28	350
December	12	200

The correlation coefficient, r, is calculated using the following formula.

$$r = \frac{n\Sigma xy - \Sigma x \Sigma y}{\sqrt{[n\Sigma x^2 - (\Sigma x)^2][n\Sigma y^2 - (\Sigma y)^2]}}$$

The correlation coefficient, r, between output and costs for the company is ⬚ (to 3 decimal places).
(2 marks)

35 The following information relates to a company.

Actual overheads	$496,980
Actual machine hours	16,566
Budgeted overheads	$475,200

Based on the above information and assuming that the budgeted overhead absorption rate was $32 per hour, the overhead for the period was ⬚ absorbed by $ ⬚ **(2 marks)**

36   The following information relates to a company.

Budgeted overheads $690,480
Budgeted machine hours   15,344
Actual machine hours   14,128
Actual overheads $679,550

Overhead for the period was ☐ absorbed by $ ☐   **(2 marks)**

37   The following information is available for part LP42.

Minimum usage per day   300 units
Average usage per day   400 units
Maximum usage per day   600 units
Lead time for replenishment   3-4 days
Reorder quantity   1,900 units

The maximum level of inventory is ☐ units.   **(2 marks)**

38   A company absorbs overheads on machine hours which were budgeted at 14,400 with budgeted overheads of $316,800. Actual results were 14,100 hours with overheads of $338,400.

Overheads were ☐ absorbed by $ ☐   **(2 marks)**

39   A company has decided to paint its factory and has asked the premises maintenance department for details on the overheads associated with painting 13,800 square metres. The following data show the overhead expenditure associated with two activity levels.

Square metres painted   12,750   15,100
Overheads $73,950 $83,585

The estimate of the overheads if 13,800 square metres are to be painted is $ ☐   **(2 marks)**

40   Product W is made from material P. There are 5,824 units of material P in inventory and 10,608 units on order with suppliers. If the free inventory is 8,112 units, how many units of material P have been requisitioned but not yet issued from stores?

Write your answer here: ☐ units   **(2 marks)**

41   A company absorbs overheads on labour hours. In one period 8,200 hours were worked, actual overheads were $109,000 and there was $14,000 over absorption.

The overhead absorption rate per hour was $ ☐ (to the nearest $)   **(2 marks)**

42   An employee is paid according to the following schedule.

No of units produced Units	Rate of pay per unit in this band $
Up to and including 50	4.10
51 to 60	4.30
61 to 70	4.40
71 and above	4.50

The employee's remuneration for an output of 68 units in a period would be $ ☐ .   **(2 marks)**

43   In the context of reporting the profit for a given period, tick the statements which is/are true?

☐   If inventory levels reduce, absorption costing will report a lower profit than marginal costing.

☐   If inventory levels reduce, marginal costing will report a lower profit than absorption costing.

☐   If production and sales volumes are equal, marginal costing and absorption costing will report the
     same profit figure.   **(2 marks)**

44   The following data is available for period 9.

Opening inventory	10,000 units
Closing inventory	18,000 units
Absorption costing profit	$280,000

Which of the following additional items of information is needed to calculate the marginal costing profit for
period 9?

☐   The sales volume in units

☐   The budgeted total fixed overhead

☐   The total cost per unit

☐   The fixed overhead absorption rate per unit   **(2 marks)**

45   A company uses a special machine in order to manufacture these three products. The machine cost
$140,000 ten years ago. It is expected that the machine will generate future revenues of $100,000.
Alternatively the machine could be scrapped for $80,000. An equivalent machine in the same condition
would cost $90,000 to buy now.

The relevant cost of the machine is $ ⬚   **(2 marks)**

46   Fill in the missing words:

Fixed budgets remain unchanged regardless of the level of ....

Flexible budgets are prepared using .... costing and so mixed costs must be split into
their .... and.. components   **(2 marks)**

47   A principal budget factor is:

☐   The factor on which total annual expenditure is highest

☐   The factor with the highest unit cost

☐   A factor which limits the activities of an undertaking

☐   A factor common to all budget centres

☐   A factor controllable by the manager of the budget centre   **(2 marks)**

48   Which of the following would not help to explain an adverse direct material usage variance?

☐   The material purchased was of a lower quality than standard

☐   Inexperienced employees led to high levels of losses due to spillage

☐   Activity levels were higher than budget therefore more material was used   **(1 mark)**

Extracts from a company's records from last period are as follows.

	Budget	Actual
Production	1,925 units	2,070 units
Variable production overhead cost	$13,475	$13,455
Labour hours worked	3,850	2,990

The variable production overhead efficiency variance for last period is

	Favourable	Adverse
$ ☐	☐	☐

(2 marks)

50   A company manufactures a single product. An extract from a variance control report together with relevant standard cost data is shown below.

Standard direct material cost (10kg × $4 per kg) $40 per unit

Actual results for January

Total direct material cost	$4,800
Direct material price variance	$1,600 adverse
Direct material usage variance	$800 favourable

The actual production in January was ☐ units.

(2 marks)

Answers

DO NOT TURN THIS PAGE UNTIL YOU HAVE
COMPLETED THE MOCK EXAM

1   The production costs for a production volume of 1,000 units are $ [13,000]

Using the high-low method

	Units	Total costs $
High	800	12,000
Low	400	10,000
	400	2,000

Variable cost per unit $= \dfrac{\$2,000}{400} = \$5$

Substituting in high activity:

Fixed costs $= \$12,000 - (800 \times \$5)$
$= \$12,000 - \$4,000$
$= \$8,000$

For a production volume of 1,000 units

Total costs $=$ fixed costs $+$ variable costs
$= \$8,000 + (1,000 \times \$5)$
$= \$8,000 + \$5,000 = \$13,000$

2   ☑   False. Variables are correlated if a change in one causes a change in the other. It does not have to be by the same amount.

3   If high levels of inventory are maintained this increases the **holding** costs.

4   Under-absorbed overhead $= \$$ [40,000]

	$
Overhead absorbed 220,000 hours × $2	440,000
Overhead incurred	480,000
Overhead under absorbed	40,000

5   The number of units that must be sold $=$ [4,000]

Workings

	$
Target profit	6,000
Fixed costs (5,000 × $2)	10,000
Target contribution	16,000

Contribution per unit ($10 – $6)	$4
Units required to achieve target profit	4,000

6   [40] %

Workings

Fixed costs ($10,000 × 120%)	$12,000
Units required now to break even (÷ $4 contribution)	3,000
Budgeted units of sales	5,000
Margin of safety (units)	2,000

In percentage terms, margin of safety $= \dfrac{2,000}{5,000} \times 100\% = 40\%$

7 ☑ **24.2% decrease.**

	$
Original budgeted profit:	
Contribution (5,000 × $4)	20,000
Fixed costs	10,000
Profit	10,000

	$ per unit
New sales price ($10 × 1.20)	12.00
New variable cost ($6 × 1.12)	6.72
New contribution	5.28

Contribution required (as above)	$20,000
Sales volume now needed (÷ $5.28)	3,788 units

This is 1,212 units or 24.24% **less than** the original budgeted level of 5,000 units of sales.

8 ☑ The availability of discounts for materials

9 Philip's pay for the week is $ 206

Workings

Piecework hours produced

	Piecework hours
Product Alpha 15 × 2 hours	30
Product Beta 20 × 0.8 hours	16
	46

Philip's pay = $160 + (46 × $1) = $206

10 The profit under marginal costing would be $ 45,100

Working

	$
Absorption costing profit	47,500
Add: fixed overhead included in opening inventory ($12 × 400)	4,800
Less fixed overhead included in closing inventory ($12 × 600)	(7,200)
Marginal costing profit	45,100

Remember that if closing inventory is greater than opening inventory then absorption costing will give the higher profit figure and the value of the additional fixed overhead included in inventory should be deducted from the absorption costing profit in order to obtain the marginal costing profit.

11 The budgeted fixed overheads for the year ended 31 March 2000 were $ 120,000

Working

Budgeted production = 10,000 units

Budgeted fixed overheads per unit = $12

Budgeted fixed overheads = 10,000 × $12 = $120,000

12 The actual under or over absorption was $ 18,000

☑ Over absorbed

Working

	$
Actual fixed overheads = budgeted fixed overheads	120,000
Absorbed overheads (11,500 × $12)	(138,000)
Over-absorbed overheads	18,000

13 ☑ 15,000

Variable overhead + fixed overhead = total overhead

∴ Fixed overhead per prescription = $7 – $4 = $3

Total fixed overheads = $45,000

∴ Budgeted activity level = $\dfrac{\$45{,}000}{\$3}$ = 15,000 prescriptions

14 ⬚ 2,000

Working

Free inventory balance = units in inventory + units on order - units requisitioned but not yet issued (R)

$$1{,}950 = 1{,}400 + 2{,}550 - R$$
$$R = 1{,}400 + 2{,}550 - 1{,}950$$
$$R = 2{,}000$$

15 The company's EOQ = ⬚ 2,739 ⬚ kg

Working

$$EOQ = \sqrt{\frac{2C_o D}{C_h}} = \sqrt{\frac{2 \times \$250 \times 15{,}000}{\$10 \times 10\%}} = 2{,}739 \text{ kg}$$

16 $ ⬚ 47,763 ⬚

Working

	$
Salary costs: Senior consultant (172 × $40)	6,880
Junior time (440 × $30)	13,200
Overhead absorbed (612 × $25)	15,300
Total cost	35,380
Mark up (35%)	12,383
Selling price	47,763

17 ☑ A piecework scheme

18 ☑ Absorption

19 ⬚ 4 ⬚ or ⬚ 5 ⬚

Badger plc has an objective of minimising costs and therefore the potential optimal solutions will be closest to the origin, ie 4 or 5.

20 $ ⬚ 2,250 ⬚

Relevant cost of material K

		$
500 units in inventory:	If not used on this order, would be sold ($1.50 × 500)	750
300 units extra required:	Need to be purchased at current price ($5 × 300)	1,500
		2,250

21   The value of the abnormal loss is $ $\boxed{230}$

	Kg
Input	5,000
Normal loss (20% × 5,000 kg)	(1,000)
Abnormal loss	(200)
Output	3,800

Cost per kg $= \dfrac{\text{Input costs} - \text{scrap value of normal loss}}{\text{Expected output}}$

$= \dfrac{\$4,900^* - \$300}{5,000 - 1,000}$

$= \dfrac{\$4,600}{4,000} = \$1.15$

Value of abnormal loss = $1.15 × 200 kg = $230

	$
*Materials (5,000 kg × 0.5)	2,500
Labour	800
Production overhead	1,600
	4,900

22   ☑   The absorption rates are based on estimates

23   Marginal cost is the **variable** cost of one unit of product or service.

24   The number of tonne-kilometres achieved during week 30 was $\boxed{265,300}$.

Workings

Journey	Tonnes	Km	Tonne km
1	68	360	24,480
2	56	530	29,680
3	80	780	62,400
4	64	230	14,720
5	52	440	22,880
6	80	960	76,800
7	58	180	10,440
8	52	200	10,400
9	50	270	13,500
	560	3,950	265,300

25   Profits are maximised along line $\boxed{AB}$

(Profits are defined as total revenue minus total costs at any level of output. Profits are therefore at a maximum where the vertical distance between the total revenue and total cost curve is the greatest, ie line AB.)

26   Inventory values using absorption costing are **greater** than those calculated using marginal costing.

27   ☑   A by-product

28   The total cost equation when production is less than or equal to 40,000 units is

$$C = \boxed{75{,}000} + \boxed{7.5} \, Q$$

Fixed costs = $75,000 at production levels of 40,000 or less.

Variable costs are a constant $7.50 per unit.

29    $ $\boxed{5.37}$ per unit (to the nearest cent)

Total sales revenue = ($16 × 5,000) + ($50 × 10,000) + ($40 × 10,000)

$$= \$(80{,}000 + 500{,}000 + 400{,}000)$$

$$= \$980{,}000$$

Joint costs to be allocated = Total output costs – revenue from by-product

$$= \$138{,}500 - (\$4 \times 1{,}750)$$

$$= \$131{,}500$$

Costs to product C = $131,500 × $\dfrac{(\$40 \times 10{,}000)}{\$980{,}000}$

$$= \$53{,}674 \text{ (to the nearest \$)}$$

Cost per unit of product C = $\dfrac{\text{Total costs}}{\text{Total units}}$

$$= \dfrac{\$53{,}674}{10{,}000}$$

$$= \$5.37 \text{ (to the nearest cent)}$$

30    $ $\boxed{55{,}445}$ (to the nearest $)

S = Stores overhead, after apportionment from maintenance

M = Maintenance overhead, after apportionment from stores

S = 12,600 + 0.05M

M = 16,900 + 0.1S

S = 12,600 + 0.05 (16,900 + 0.1S)

S = 12,600 + 845 + 0.005S

0.995S = 13,445

$$\therefore \quad S = \dfrac{13{,}445}{0.995}$$

$$= \$13{,}513$$

If S   = $13,513

M   = 16,900 + (0.1 × 13,513)

= $18,251

For production department 1, the total overheads are

$35,000 + ($13,513 × 50%) + ($18,251 × 75%)

= $35,000 + $6,756.50 + $13,688.25

= $55,444.75

= $55,445 (to the nearest $)

31 | 2.6 | (to 1 decimal place)

Workings

Let   x = Advertising expenditure (in $'000)

y = Sales revenue (in $'000)

n = 5

b $= \dfrac{n\Sigma\Sigma x - \Sigma x\Sigma y}{n\Sigma\Sigma^2 - (\Sigma\Sigma x^2}$

$= \dfrac{(5 \times 8,104) - (100 \times 400)}{(5 \times 2,040) - 100^2}$

$= \dfrac{40,520 - 40,000}{10,200 - 10,000}$

$= \dfrac{520}{200} = 2.6$

32 | 28 |

Workings

a $= \dfrac{\Sigma y}{n} - b\dfrac{\Sigma x}{n}$

$= \dfrac{400}{5} - (2.6 \times \dfrac{100}{5})$

$= 28$

33   ✓   Job costing

34   The correlation coefficient, r, between output and costs for Birdsall is | 0.946 | (to 3 decimal places).

Workings

The correlation coefficient, r, is calculated using the following formula.

r $= \dfrac{n\Sigma xy - \Sigma x\Sigma y}{\sqrt{[n\Sigma x^2 - (\Sigma x)^2]\ [n\Sigma y^2 - (\Sigma y)^2]}}$

$= \dfrac{37,200}{\sqrt{3,720 \times [12 \times 745,200 - (2,920)^2]}}$

$= \dfrac{37,200}{\sqrt{3,720 \times 416,000}}$

$= \dfrac{37,200}{39,338.531}$

$= 0.946$

35   The overhead for the period was | over | absorbed by $ | 33,132 |

	$
Overheads absorbed (16,566 × $32)	530,112
Actual overheads	496,980
Over-absorbed overheads	33,132

36   Overhead for the period was ⎣ under ⎦ absorbed by $ ⎣ 43,790 ⎦

Overhead absorption rate = $\dfrac{\$690,480}{15,344}$ = $45 per machine hour

Overhead absorbed = $45 × 14,128 hrs =	$635,760
Overhead incurred	$679,550
Overhead under absorbed	$43,790

37   The maximum level of inventory is ⎣ 3,400 ⎦ units.

Reorder level	= maximum usage × maximum lead time
	= 600 × 4 = 2,400 units
Maximum level	= reorder level + reorder quantity − (min. usage × min. lead time)
	= 2,400 + 1,900 − (300 × 3)
	= 3,400 units

38   Overheads were ⎣ under ⎦ absorbed by $ ⎣ 28,200 ⎦

Overhead absorption rate $= \dfrac{\text{Budgeted overheads}}{\text{Budgeted machine hours}}$

$= \dfrac{\$316,800}{14,400}$

= $22 per machine hour

Overhead absorbed = $22 × 14,100	$310,200
Overhead incurred =	$338,400
Under absorption	$28,200

39   The estimate of the overheads if 13,800 square metres are to be painted is $ ⎣ 78,255 ⎦

Variable overhead	$= \dfrac{\$83,585 - \$73,950}{15,100 - 12,750} = \dfrac{\$9,635}{2,350}$
	= $4.10 per square metre
Fixed overhead	= $73,950 − ($4.10 × 12,750)
	= $73,950 − $52,275 = $21,675

Overheads on 13,800 square metres

therefore	= $21,675 + ($4.10 × 13,800)
	= $21,675 + $56,580
	= $78,255

40   ⎣ 8,320 ⎦ units

Free inventory balance	=	units in inventory	+	units on order	−	units requisitioned but not yet issued (x)

8,112	=	5,824 + 10,608 − x
x	=	8,320

41 The overhead absorption rate per hour was $\boxed{15}$ (to the nearest $)

Overheads absorbed	=	Actual overheads + overheads over-absorbed
	=	$109,000 + $14,000
	=	$123,000

$$\text{Overhead absorption rate} = \frac{\text{Overheads absorbed}}{\text{Hours worked}}$$

$$= \frac{\$123,000}{8,200}$$

$$= \$15 \text{ per hour}$$

42 The employee's remuneration for an output of 68 units in a period would be $\boxed{283.20}$.

Workings

			$
First 50 units =	50	× $4.10	205.00
Units 51 to 60 =	10	× $4.30	43.00
Units 61 to 68 =	8	× $4.40	35.20
	68		283.20

43 ✓ If inventory levels reduce, absorption costing will report a lower profit than marginal costing.

✓ If production and sales volumes are equal, marginal costing and absorption costing will report the same profit figure.

If inventories reduce, fixed overheads are 'released' from inventory using absorption costing, and the absorption costing profit will be lower than the marginal costing profit.

A difference in reported profits arises only when inventory volumes change, therefore the other statement is also correct.

44 ✓ The fixed overhead absorption rate per unit

We know that the profit using marginal costing would be lower than the absorption costing profit, because inventories are increasing. However, we cannot calculate the value of the difference without the fixed overhead absorption rate per unit.

Difference in profit	=	8,000 units inventory increase	×	fixed overhead absorption rate per unit

45 The relevant cost of the machine is $\boxed{90,000}$

Workings

Cost of machine = $140,000 = past/sunk cost

Future revenues = $100,000 = expected revenue

NRV = $80,000 = scrap proceeds

Replacement cost = $90,000

The relevant cost can be calculated using the following diagram.

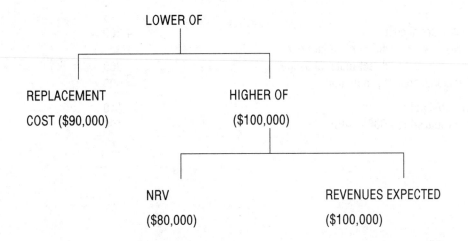

The relevant cost of the machine is the lower of the replacement cost and $100,000, ie $90,000.

46   Fixed budgets remain unchanged regardless of the level of **activity**.

Flexible budgets are prepared using **marginal** costing and so mixed costs must be split into their **fixed** and variable components.

47   ✓   A factor which limits the activities of an undertaking.

The principal budget factor is also known as the key budget factor or the limiting budget factor.

48   ✓   Activity levels were higher than budget therefore more material was used

The first statement would help to explain an adverse material usage variance, because lower quality material may lead to higher wastage.

The second statement would also help to explain an adverse material usage variance, because higher losses would increase material usage.

The third statement would not necessarily help to explain an adverse material usage variance. If activity levels were higher than budget this would not affect the quantity of materials used **per unit** of production. The usage variance would be calculated based on the **standard usage for the actual output**.

49
		Favourable	Adverse
The variable production overhead efficiency variance for last period is	$ 4,025	✓	

Standard variable production overhead cost per hour = $\dfrac{\$13,475}{3,850}$ = $3.50

Standard time allowed for one unit = 3,850 hours ÷ 1,925 units = 2 hours

2,070 units should take (× 2 hours)	4,140 hours
but did take	2,990 hours
Efficiency variance in hours	1,150 hours (F)
× standard variable production overhead per hour	× $3.50
	$4,025 (F)

50   The actual production in January was [100] units

Workings

		$
Total actual direct material cost		4,800
Add back variances:	direct material price	(1,600)
	direct material usage	800
Standard direct material cost of production		4,000
Standard material cost per unit		$40
Number of units produced ($4,000 ÷ $40)		100

ACCA

Paper F2

Management Accounting

Mock Examination 3

Pilot paper

Question Paper	
Time allowed	**2 hours**
ALL 50 questions are compulsory and MUST be attempted	

DO NOT OPEN THIS PAPER UNTIL YOU ARE READY TO START UNDER EXAMINATION CONDITIONS

Please go to the ACCA's website at http://62.254.188.145/main.html, where you can practise this exam on a computer.

ALL 50 questions are compulsory and MUST be attempted

1   The following break-even chart has been drawn showing lines for total cost (TC), total variable cost (TVC), total fixed cost (TFC) and total sales revenue (TSR):

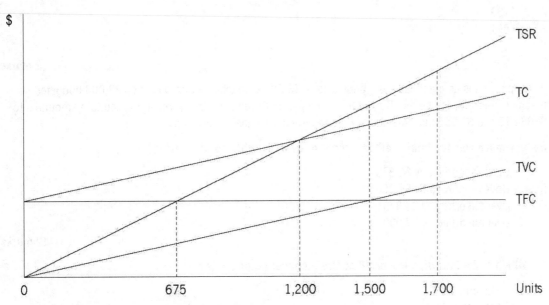

What is the margin of safety at the 1,700 units level of activity?

A   200 units
B   300 units
C   500 units
D   1,025 units   (2 marks)

2   The following assertions relate to financial accounting and to cost accounting:

(i)   The main users of financial accounting information are external to an organisation.

(ii)   Cost accounting is that part of financial accounting which records the cash received and payments made by an organisation.

Which of the following statements are true?

A   Assertions (i) and (ii) are both correct.
B   Only assertion (i) is correct.
C   Only assertion (ii) is correct.   (1 mark)

3   Regression analysis is being used to find the line of best fit (y = a + bx) from eleven pairs of data. The calculations have produced the following information:

$\Sigma x = 440$, $\Sigma y = 330$, $\Sigma x^2 = 17,986$, $\Sigma y^2 = 10,366$, $\Sigma xy = 13,467$ and $b = 0.69171$

What is the value of 'a' in the equation for the line of best fit (to 2 decimal places)?

A   0.63
B   0.69
C   2.33
D   5.33   (2 marks)

4   The purchase price of a stock item is $25 per unit. In each three month period the usage of the item is 20,000 units. The annual holding costs associated with one unit equate to 6% of its purchase price. The cost of placing an order for the item is $20.

What is the Economic Order Quantity (EOQ) for the stock item to the nearest whole unit?

A   730
B   894
C   1,461
D   1,633

(2 marks)

5   A company uses an overhead absorption rate of $3.50 per machine hour, based on 32,000 budgeted machine hours for the period. During the same period the actual total overhead expenditure amounted to $108,875 and 30,000 machine hours were recorded on actual production.

By how much was the total overhead under or over absorbed for the period?

A   Under absorbed by $3,875
B   Under absorbed by $7,000
C   Over absorbed by $3,875
D   Over absorbed by $7,000

(2 marks)

6   **For which of the following is a profit centre manager responsible?**

A   Costs only
B   Revenues only
C   Costs and revenues.

(1 mark)

7   An organisation has the following total costs at two activity levels:

Activity level (units)	16,000	22,000
Total costs ($)	135,000	170,000

Variable cost per unit is constant within this range of activity but there is a step up of $5,000 in the total fixed costs when the activity exceeds 17,500 units.

What is the total cost at an activity of 20,000 units?

A $155,000
B $158,000
C $160,000
D $163,000

(2 marks)

8   A company manufactures and sells a single product. In two consecutive months the following levels of production and sales (in units) occurred:

	Month 1	Month 2
Sales	3,800	4,400
Production	3,900	4,200

The opening inventory for Month 1 was 400 units. Profits or losses have been calculated for each month using both absorption and marginal costing principles.

Which of the following combination of profits and losses for the two months is consistent with the above data?

	Absorption costing profit/(loss)		Marginal costing profit/(loss)	
	Month 1	Month 2	Month 1	Month 2
	$	$	$	$
A	200	4,400	(400)	3,200
B	(400)	4,400	200	3,200
C	200	3,200	(400)	4,400
D	(400)	3,200	200	4,400

9   **Which of the following best describes a flexible budget?**

A   A budget which shows variable production costs only.

B   A monthly budget which is changed to reflect the number of days in the month.

C   A budget which shows sales revenue and costs at different levels of activity.

D   A budget that is updated halfway through the year to incorporate the actual results for the first half of the year.   **(2 marks)**

10   Information relating to two processes (F and G) was as follows:

Process	Normal loss as %of input	Input litres	Output litres
F	8	65,000	58,900
G	5	37500	35,700

For each process, was there an abnormal loss or an abnormal gain?

	Process F	Process G
A	Abnormal gain	Abnormal gain
B	Abnormal gain	Abnormal loss
C	Abnormal loss	Abnormal gain
D	Abnormal loss	Abnormal loss

(2 marks)

11   An organisation manufactures a single product which is sold for $80 per unit. The organisation's total monthly fixed costs are $99,000 and it has a contribution to sales ratio of 45%. This month it plans to manufacture and sell 4,000 units.

What is the organisation's margin of safety this month (in units)?

A   1,250
B   1,750
C   2,250
D   2,750   **(2 marks)**

12   **Which one of the following should be classified as indirect labour?**

A   Assembly workers on a car production line
B   Bricklayers in a house building company
C   Machinists in a factory producing clothes
D   Forklift truck drivers in the stores of an engineering company.   **(2 marks)**

13   A company is evaluating a project that requires 400kg of raw material X. The company has 150kg of X in stock that were purchased six months ago for $55 per kg. The company no longer has any use for X. The inventory of X could be sold for $40 per kg. The current purchase price for X is $53 per kg.

What is the total relevant cost of raw material X for the project?

A $17,950
B $19,250
C $21,200
D $21,500   **(2 marks)**

14   **Which of the following is NOT a feasible value for the correlation coefficient?**

A   +1.4
B   +0.7
C   0
D   −0.7   **(2 marks)**

15   The following statements relate to aspects of budget administration:

Statement (1): An important task of a budget committee is to ensure that budgets are properly coordinated.

Statement (2): A budget manual is the document produced at the end of the budget setting process.

Which of the following is true?

A   Only statement (1) is correct.
B   Only statement (2) is correct.
C   Both statements are correct.   **(1 mark)**

16   Up to a given level of activity in each period the purchase price per unit of a raw material is constant. After that point a lower price per unit applies both to further units purchased and also retrospectively to all units already purchased.

Which of the following graphs depicts the total cost of the raw materials for a period?

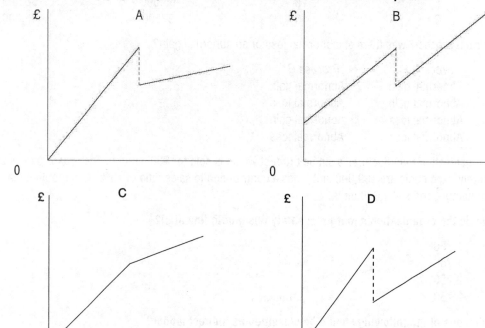

                                                                                          (2 marks)

17   A manufacturing organisation incurs costs relating to the following:

(1)   Commission payable to salespersons.

(2)   Inspecting all products.

(3)   Packing the products at the end of the manufacturing process prior to moving them to the warehouse.

Which of these costs are classified as production costs?

A   (1) and (2) only
B   (1) and (3) only
C   (2) and (3) only
D   (1), (2) and (3)   **(2 marks)**

18   **Which of the following is correct with regard to expected values?**

A   Expected values provide a weighted average of anticipated outcomes.
B   The expected value will always equal one of the possible outcomes.
C   Expected values will show the decision maker's attitude to risk.
D   The expected value will never equal one of the possible outcomes.   **(2 marks)**

19   There is a 60% chance that a company will make a profit of $300,000 next year and a 40% chance of making
      a loss of $400,000.

      What is the expected profit or loss for next year?

      A $120,000 Loss
      B $20,000 Loss
      C $20,000 Profit
      D $120,000 Profit   **(2 marks)**

20   A company's budgeted sales for last month were 10,000 units with a standard selling price of $20 per unit
      and a standard contribution of $8 per unit. Last month actual sales of 10,500 units at an average selling
      price of $19.50 per unit were achieved.

      What were the sales price and sales volume contribution variances for last month?

	Sales price variance ($)	Sales volume contribution variance ($)
A	5,250 Adverse	4,000 Favourable
B	5,250 Adverse	4,000 Adverse
C	5,000 Adverse	4,000 Favourable
D	5,000 Adverse	4,000 Adverse

                                                                                              (2 marks)

21   A company manufactures and sells one product which requires 8 kg of raw material in its manufacture. The
      budgeted data relating to the next period are as follows:

	Units
Sales	19,000
Opening inventory of finished goods	4,000
Closing inventory of finished goods	3,000

	Kg
Opening inventory of raw materials	50,000
Closing inventory of raw materials	53,000

      What is the budgeted raw material purchases for next period (in kg)?

      A   141,000
      B   147,000
      C   157,000
      D   163,000   **(2 marks)**

22   The following statements refer to spreadsheets:

      (i)   A spreadsheet is the most suitable software for the storage of large volumes of data.

      (ii)   A spreadsheet could be used to produce a flexible budget.

      (iii) Most spreadsheets contain a facility to display the data in them within them in a graphical form.

      Which of these statements are correct?

      A   (i) and (ii) only
      B   (i) and (iii) only
      C   (ii) and (iii) only
      D   (i), (ii) and (iii)   **(2 marks)**

23   A company always determines its order quantity for a raw material by using the Economic Order Quantity (EOQ) model.

What would be the effects on the EOQ and the total annual holding cost of a decrease in the cost of ordering a batch of raw material?

	EOQ	Annual holding cost
A	Higher	Lower
B	Higher	Higher
C	Lower	Higher
D	Lower	Lower

(2 marks)

24   **Which one of the following is most likely to operate a system of service costing?**

A   A printing company
B   A hospital
C   A firm of solicitors.

(1 mark)

25   The following budgeted information relates to a manufacturing company for next period:

	Units		$
Production	14,000	Fixed production costs	63,000
Sales	12,000	Fixed selling costs	12,000

The normal level of activity is 14,000 units per period.

Using absorption costing the profit for next period has been calculated as $36,000.

What would the profit for next period be using marginal costing?

A $25,000
B $27,000
C $45,000
D $47,000

(2 marks)

26   A company manufactures a single product which it sells for $20 per unit. The product has a contribution to sales ratio of 40%. The company's weekly break- even point is sales revenue of $18,000.

What would be the profit in a week when 1,200 units are sold?

A $1,200
B $2,400
C $3,600
D $6,000

(2 marks)

27   The following graph relates to a linear programming problem:

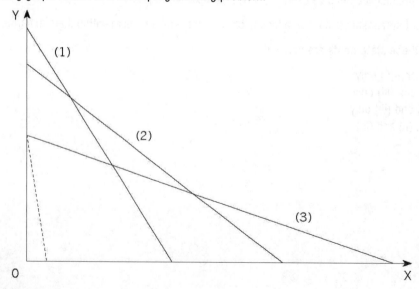

The objective is to maximise contribution and the dotted line on the graph depicts this function. There are three constraints which are all of the "less than or equal to" type which are depicted on the graph by the three solid lines labelled (1), (2) and (3).

At which of the following intersections is contribution maximised?

A   Constraints (1) and (2)
B   Constraints (2) and (3)
C   Constraints (1) and (3)
D   Constraint (1) and the x-axis   **(2 marks)**

28   In an organisation manufacturing a number of different products in one large factory, the rent of that factory is an example of a direct expense when costing a product.

Is this statement true or false?

A   True
B   False   **(1 mark)**

29   A company operates a process in which no losses are incurred. The process account for last month, when there was no opening work-in-progress, was as follows:

Process account

	$		$
Costs arising	624,000	Finished output (10,000 units)	480,000
		Closing work-in progress (4,000 units)	144,000
	624,000		624,000

The closing work-in-progress was complete to the same degree for all elements of cost.

What was the percentage degree of completion of the closing work-in-progress?

A   12%
B   30%
C   40%
D   75%   **(2 marks)**

30   A company manufactures and sells two products (X and Y) both of which utilise the same skilled labour. For the coming period, the supply of skilled labour is limited to 2,000 hours. Data relating to each product are as follows:

Product	X	Y
Selling price per unit	$20	$40
Variable cost per unit	$12	$30
Skilled labour hours per unit	2	4
Maximum demand (units) per period	800	400

In order to maximise profit in the coming period, how many units of each product should the company manufacture and sell?

A   200 units of X and 400 units of Y
B   400 units of X and 300 units of Y
C   600 units of X and 200 units of Y
D   800 units of X and 100 units of Y   **(2 marks)**

31   The following statements refer to organisations using job costing:

(i)   Work is done to customer specification.
(ii)   Work is usually completed within a relatively short period of time.
(iii) Products manufactured tend to be all identical.

Which two of these statements are CORRECT?

A   (i) and (ii)
B   (i) and (iii)
C   (ii) and (iii)   **(1 mark)**

The following information relates to questions 32 and 33:

A company uses standard costing and the standard variable overhead cost for a product is: 6 direct labour hours @ $10 per hour

Last month when 3,900 units of the product were manufactured, the actual expenditure on variable overheads was $235,000 and 24,000 hours were actually worked.

32   What was the variable overhead expenditure variance for last month?

    A $5,000 Adverse
    B $5,000 Favourable
    C $6,000 Adverse
    D $6,000 Favourable   **(2 marks)**

33   What was the variable overhead efficiency variance for last month?

    A $5,000 Adverse
    B $5,000 Favourable
    C $6,000 Adverse
    D $6,000 Favourable   **(2 marks)**

34   When a manufacturing company operates a standard marginal costing system there are no fixed production overhead variances.

    Is this statement true or false?

    A   True
    B   False   **(1 mark)**

35   A company operates a standard costing system. The variance analysis for last month shows a favourable materials price variance and an adverse labour efficiency variance.

    The following four statements, which make comparisons with the standards, have been made:

    (1)   Inferior quality materials were purchased and used.
    (2)   Superior quality materials were purchased and used.
    (3)   Lower graded workers were used on production.
    (4)   Higher graded workers were used on production.

    Which statements are consistent with the variance analysis?

    A   (1) and (3)
    B   (1) and (4)
    C   (2) and (3)
    D   (2) and (4)   **(2 marks)**

36   Which of the following best describes a principal budget factor?

    A   A factor that affects all budget centres.
    B   A factor that is controllable by a budget centre manager.
    C   A factor which limits the activities of an organisation.
    D   A factor that the management accountant builds into all budgets.   **(2 marks)**

37 Four vertical lines have been labelled G, H, J and K at different levels of activity on the following profit-volume chart:

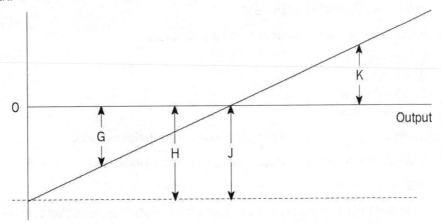

Which line represents the total contribution at that level of activity?

A   Line G
B   Line H
C   Line J
D   Line K   (2 marks)

38 Data is information that has been processed in such a way as to be meaningful to its recipients.

Is this statement true or false?

A   True
B   False   (1 mark)

39 Two products G and H are created from a joint process. G can be sold immediately after split-off. H requires further processing into product HH before it is in a saleable condition. There are no opening inventories and no work in progress of products G, H or HH. The following data are available for last period:

	$
Total joint production costs	350,000
Further processing costs of product H	66,000

Product	Production	Closing inventory
G	420,000	20,000
HH	330,000	30,000

Using the physical unit method for apportioning joint production costs, what was the cost value of the closing inventory of product HH for last period?

A $16,640
B $18,625
C $20,000
D $21,600   (2 marks)

40 A company purchased a machine several years ago for $50,000. Its written down value is now $10,000. The machine is no longer used on normal production work and it could be sold now for $8,000.

A project is being considered which would make use of this machine for six months. After this time the machine would be sold for $5,000.

What is the relevant cost of the machine to the project?

A $2,000
B $3,000
C $5,000
D $10,000   (2 marks)

41 A company operates a standard absorption costing system. The standard fixed production overhead rate is $15 per hour. The following data relate to last month: Actual hours worked 5,500 Budgeted hours 5,000 Standard hours for actual production 4,800

What was the fixed production overhead capacity variance?

A $7,500 Adverse
B $7,500 Favourable
C $10,500 Adverse
D $10,500 Favourable

(2 marks)

42 The following statements relate to relevant cost concepts in decision-making:

(i) Materials can never have an opportunity cost whereas labour can.

(ii) The annual depreciation charge is not a relevant cost.

(iii) Fixed costs would have a relevant cost element if a decision causes a change in their total expenditure

Which statements are correct?

A (i) and (ii) only
B (i) and (iii) only
C (ii) and (iii) only
D (i), (ii) and (iii)

(2 marks)

43 A contract is under consideration which requires 600 labour hours to complete. There are 350 hours of spare labour capacity for which the workers are still being paid the normal rate of pay. The remaining hours for the contract can be found either by weekend overtime working paid at double the normal rate of pay or by diverting labour from other production. This other production makes a contribution, net of labour cost, of $5 per hour. The normal rate of pay is $9 per hour.

What is the total relevant cost of labour for the contract?

A $1,250
B $3,500
C $4,500
D $4,900

(2 marks)

44 An organisation operates a piecework system of remuneration, but also guarantees its employees 80% of a time-based rate of pay which is based on $20 per hour for an eight hour working day. Three minutes is the standard time allowed per unit of output. Piecework is paid at the rate of $18 per standard hour.

If an employee produces 200 units in eight hours on a particular day, what is the employee's gross pay for that day?

A $128
B $144
C $160
D $180

(2 marks)

45 A semi-variable cost is one that, in the short term, remains the same over a given range of activity but beyond that increases and then remains constant at the higher level of activity.

Is this statement true or false?

A True
B False

(1 mark)

46 A factory consists of two production cost centres (P and Q) and two service cost centres (X and Y). The total allocated and apportioned overhead for each is as follows:

P	Q	X	Y
$95,000	$82,000	$46,000	$30,000

It has been estimated that each service cost centre does work for other cost centres in the following proportions:

	P	Q	X	Y
Percentage of service cost centre X to	50	50	–	–
Percentage of service cost centre Y to	30	60	10	

The reapportionment of service cost centre costs to other cost centres fully reflects the above proportions.

After the reapportionment of service cost centre costs has been carried out, what is the total overhead for production cost centre P?

A $124,500
B $126,100
C $127,000
D $128,500 (2 marks)

The following information relates to questions 47 and 48:

A company manufactures and sells two products (X and Y) which have contributions per unit of $8 and $20 respectively. The company aims to maximise profit. Two materials (G and H) are used in the manufacture of each product. Each material is in short supply – 1,000 kg of G and 1,800 kg of H are available next period. The company holds no inventories and it can sell all the units produced.

The management accountant has drawn the following graph accurately showing the constraints for materials G and H.

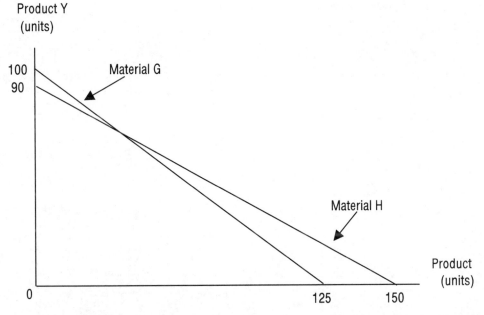

47 **What is the amount (in kg) of material G and material H used in each unit of product Y?**

	Material G	Material H
A	10	20
B	10	10
C	20	20
D	20	10

(2 marks)

48   **What is the optimal mix of production (in units) for the next period?**

	Product X	Product Y
A	0	90
B	50	60
C	60	50
D	125	0

(2 marks)

49   The following statement refers to a quality of good information: The cost of producing information should be greater than the value of the benefits of that information to management.

Is this statement true or false?

A   True
B   False

(1 mark)

50   A company which operates a process costing system had work-in-progress at the start of last month of 300 units (valued at $1,710) which were 60% complete in respect of all costs. Last month a total of 2,000 units were completed and transferred to the finished goods warehouse. The cost per equivalent unit for costs arising last month was $10. The company uses the FIFO method of cost allocation.

What was the total value of the 2,000 units transferred to the finished goods warehouse last month?

A $19,910
B $20,000
C $20,510
D $21,710

(2 marks)

Answers

The examiner's answers to all the questions in Mock Exam 3 are included at the back of this kit.

1   C   The breakeven point is at 1,200 units, so the additional 500 units forms the margin of safety.

2   B   Assertion (i) is correct.
Assertion 2 is incorrect.
Cost accounting is part of management accounting.

3   C $y = a + bx$

$330/11 = a + (0.69171 \times 440)/11$

$30 = a + 27.66$

Therefore $a = 2.33$

4   C $\text{EOQ} = \sqrt{\dfrac{2CoD}{Ch}} = \dfrac{\sqrt{2 \times 20 \times (4 \times 20,000)}}{25 \times 6\%} = \dfrac{\sqrt{3,200,000}}{1.5} = 1,460.59$

5   A

Overhead absorbed (30,000 × $3.5)	105,000
Actual overhead	108,875
Under-absorbed	3,875

6   C

7   C   Variable cost per unit = (170,000 – 135,000 – 5,000)/(22,000 – 16,000) = $5

Fixed cost = 135,000 – (16,000 × 5) = $55,000

Total cost at 20,000 units:

$55,000 + $5,000 + (20,000 × $5) = $160,000

8   C   In month 1 production exceeds sales, therefore absorption costing profit will be higher.

In month 2 sales exceed production, therefore marginal costing will show a higher profit.

9   C

10   C   F: normal loss = 65,000 × 8% = 5,200. Actual loss (65,000 – 58900) = 6,100

G: normal loss = 37,500 × 5% = 1,875. Actual loss (37,500 – 35,700) = 1,800

Therefore F shows an abnormal loss and G shows an abnormal gain.

11   A   Breakeven point = 99,000/(80 × 45%) = 2,750 units

Margin of safety = 4,000 – 2750 = 1,250 units

12   D

13   B   (150 × $40) + (250 × $53) = $6,000 + $13,250 = $19,250

14   A

15   A   Only statement 1 is correct. The budget manual is produced at the **beginning** of the budgeting process.

16   D

17   C   Salesperson's commission would be classified as distribution costs.

18   A   Expected values provide a weighted average of anticipated outcomes.

19   C

Profit: $300,000 × 60%	180,000
Loss: $400,000 × 40%	(160,000)
Expected profit	20,000

			$
20	A	Sales price variance (0.5 × 10,500)	(5,250)
		Sales volume variance (500 × 8)	4,000

21	B	Units needed (19,000 – 4,000 + 3000)	18,000
		Kg needed (18,000 × 8)	144,000
		Purchases (144,000 – 50,000 + 53,000)	147,000

22   C   A spreadsheet is not useful for storing large volumes of data. A database could perform this function.

23   D   A decrease in the ordering cost would reduce the EOQ (as smaller quantities could now be ordered) and also the holding cost (as lower inventories would be kept).

24   B   Printers and solicitors are more likely to use job costing.

25   B   The marginal costing profit will be lower because all of the production costs will have to be attributed to the 12,000 units which were sold, rather than carried forward in inventory.

The difference will be: (63,000/14,000) × 2,000 = $9,000

			$
26	B	Revenue at 1,200 units (1,200 × 20)	24,000
		Breakeven revenue	(18,000)
			6,000
		Profit (6,000 × 40%)	2,400

27   D   Constraint (1) and the x-axis.

28   B   False

29	D	Cost per unit of finished output (480,000/10,000)	$48
		Cost per unit of work-in-progress (144,000/4,000)	$36

Therefore the WIP is 75% completed

			X	Y
30	D	Contribution per labour hour:		
		(20 – 12)/2	4	
		(40 – 30)/4		2.5

Therefore the maximum amount of X should be produced. 800 units will take 1,600 hours, leaving 400 hours in which 100 units of Y can be produced.

31   A   Statement (iii) is incorrect. This refers to batch costing

			$	
32	B	Standard cost of 24,000 hours	240,000	
		Actual expenditure	(235,000)	
			5,000	Favourable

33	C	Standard hours for 3,900 units (3,900 × 6)	23,400
		Hours taken	24,000
		Additional hours	600

Cost = (600 × 10) = $6,000 adverse

34   False

35   A   A favourable materials price variance means cheaper materials, more likely to be inferior.

An adverse labour efficiency variance means less production happened, which would be consistent with lower graded workers.

36	C	The principal budget factor is the limiting factor for the organisation.

37	C	Line J

38	B	This is the wrong way round. Information is data which has been processed in such a way as to be meaningful.

39   C

	$
Cost per unit joint production (350,000/ (420,000 + 330,000)	0.4666
Cost per unit further processing (66,000/330,000)	0.2
Total cost per unit	0.66666
Value of closing inventory (0.66666 x 30,000)	19,999

40	B	The machine could be sold now for $8,000. Following the project it can be sold for $5,000. Therefore use of the machine on the project has a cost of $3,000.

41   B

Budgeted hours	5,000	
Actual hours	5,500	
Capacity variance	500	× $15 = $7,500 Favourable

The variance is favourable because the overhead rate is based on 5,000 hours being worked and more hours were worked for the same total overhead.

42	C	Statement (i) is incorrect. If materials can be used for something else, they have an opportunity cost.

43   B   The 350 hours spare labour capacity has no cost. The remaining 250 hours can be obtained from:

Overtime (250 × 9 × 2)	$4,500
Diverting labour (250 × (9 + 5))	$3,500

Diverting labour is the lower cost.

44   D   Production in one standard hour = 20 units

Pay for 200 units = 200/20 × 18 = $180

This is above the guaranteed rate.

45	B	False. A cost that increases at a certain range and then remains constant is a stepped fixed cost.

46   D

	P	Q	X	Y
Total overhead	95,000	82,000	46,000	30,000
Reallocate Y	9,000	18,000	3,000	(30,000)
			49,000	
Reallocate X	24,500	24,500	(49,000)	
	128,500			

47   A   100 units using 1,000 kg of G = 10kg per unit

90 units using 1,800 kg of H = 20kg per unit

48   A

			$
A	(90 × 20)	=	1,800
B	(50 × 8) + (60 × 20)	=	1,600
C	(60 × 8) + (50 × 20)	=	1,480
D	(125 × 8)	=	1,000

49	B	False. The cost should be **less** than the benefit.

50   A

	$
Opening WIP	1,710
Completion of 300 units (300 × 40% × 10)	1,200
1,700 units @ $10	17,000
Total value 2,000 units	19,910

ACCA examiner's answers:
Pilot paper

Summarised

1	C		26	B
2	B		27	D
3	C		28	False
4	C		29	D
5	A		30	D
6	C		31	A
7	C		32	B
8	C		33	C
9	C		34	False
10	C		35	A
11	A		36	C
12	D		37	C
13	B		38	False
14	A		39	C
15	A		40	B
16	D		41	B
17	C		42	C
18	A		43	B
19	C		44	D
20	A		45	False
21	B		46	D
22	C		47	A
23	D		48	A
24	B		49	Less
25	B		50	A

In detail

1   C

2   B

3   C $a = (\Sigma y \div n) - [(b\Sigma x) \div n] = (330 \div 11) - [(0.69171 \times 440) \div 11]$
      = $(30 - 27.6684)$
      = 2.3316 (2.33 to 2 decimal places)

4   C $\{[2 \times 20 \times (4 \times 20,000)] \div [0.06 \times 25]\}^{0.5} = 1,461$ units

5   A
Actual cost	$108,875
Absorbed cost (30,000 × 3.50)	$105,000
Under absorption	$ 3,875

6   C

7   C   Variable cost per unit: $[(170,000 - 5,000) - 135,000] \div (22,000 - 16,000) = \$5$
      Total fixed cost (below 17,500 units): $[135,000 - (16,000 \times 5)] = \$55,000$
      Total cost for 20,000 units: $55,000 + 5,000 + (20,000 \times 5) = \$160,000$

8   C   Month 1: Production > Sales   Absorption costing profit > Marginal costing profit
      Month 2: Sales > Production   Marginal costing profit > absorption costing profit
      A and C satisfy Month 1, C and D satisfy Month 2. Therefore C satisfies both.

9   C

		Normal loss	Actual loss	Abnormal loss	Abnormal gain
10 C		litres	litres	litres	litres
	Process F	5,200	6,100	900	–
	Process G	1,875	1,800	–	75

11 A　Contribution per unit (CPU): $(80 \times 0.45) = \$36$
　　　Break even point (units): $(99,000 \div 36) = 2,750$
　　　Margin of safety: $(4,000 - 2,750) = 1,250$ units

12 D

13 B　$(150 \times 40) + (250 \times 53) = \$19,250$

14 A

15 A

16 D

17 C

18 A

19 C　$(300,000 \times 0.60) - (400,000 \times 0.40) = +\$20,000$ (profit)

20 A　Price variance: $(0.50 \times 10,500) = \$5,250$ Adverse
　　　Volume variance: $(500 \times 8) = \$4,000$ Favourable

21 B　Budgeted production: $(19,000 + 3,000 - 4,000) = 18,000$ units
　　　Raw materials required for budgeted production: $(18,000 \times 8) = 144,000$ kg
　　　Budgeted raw material purchases: $(144,000 + 53,000 - 50,000) = 147,000$ kg

22 C

23 D

24 B

25 B　Production > Sales　Absorption costing profit > Marginal costing profit
　　　Marginal costing profit: $\{36,000 - [2,000 \times (63,000 \div 14,000)]\} = \$27,000$

26 B　CPU: $(20 \times 0.4) = \$8$
　　　Break even point: $(18,000 \div 20) = 900$ units
　　　Profit when 1,200 units produced and sold: $(300 \times 8) = \$2,400$

27 D

28 False

29 D　Cost per equivalent unit: $(480,000 \div 10,000) = \$48$
　　　Closing work in progress valuation: $(4,000 \times$ Degree of completion $\times 48) = 144,000$
　　　Degree of completion $= (144,000 \div 4,000 \div 48) = 0.75 = 75\%$

30 D

	X	Y
CPU	$8	$10
Contribution per hour	$4	$2.50
Ranking	1st	2nd

Therefore produce and sell the maximum 800 units of X using 1,600 hours and with the remaining 400 hours produce and sell 100 units of Y.

31 A

32 B

	$
Actual expenditure	235,000
Actual hours × standard rate	
(24,000 × 10)	240,000
Expenditure variance	5,000 Favourable

33 C

	$
Actual hours × standard rate	240,000
Standard cost of actual production	
(3,900 × 6 × 10)	234,000
Efficiency variance	6,000 Adverse

34 False

35 A

36 C

37 C

38 False

39 C   Joint costs apportioned to H: [330,000 ÷ (420,000 + 330,000)] × 350,000 = $154,000
Closing inventory valuation (HH): (30,000 ÷ 330,000) × (154,000 + 66,000) = $20,000

40 B   Relevant cost: (8,000 − 5,000) = $3,000

41 B

Budgeted hours	5,000
Actual hours worked	5,500
Capacity variance	500 hours × 15 = $7,500 Favourable

42 C

43 B   Overtime cost for 250 hours: (250 × 9 × 2) = $4,500
Cost of diverting labour: 250 × (9 + 5) = $3,500
Relevant cost (lowest alternative) = $3,500

44 D   200 units × (3 ÷ 60) × 18 = $180

45 False, this is a stepped fixed cost

46 D

Total overhead to cost centre P:	$
Direct	95,000
Proportion of cost centre X [46,000 + (0.10 × 30,000)] × 0.50	24,500
Proportion of cost centre Y [30,000 × 0.3]	9,000
	128,500

47 A
100 units of Y with all of material G (1,000 kg) = 10 kg per unit
90 units of Y with all of material H (1,800 kg) = 20 kg per unit

48 A
Total contributions:
A   [(0 × 8) + (90 × 20)]   = $1,800
B   [(50 × 8) + (60 × 20)] = $1,600
C   [(60 × 8) + (50 × 20)] = $1,480
D   [(125 × 8) + (0 × 20)] = $1,000

49 Less

50 A

	$
Value of 2,000 units transferred:	
1,700 units × 10	17,000
300 units × 0.40 × 10	1,200
Opening work in progress value	1,710
	19,910

Review Form & Free Prize Draw – Paper F2 Management Accounting (01/10)

All original review forms from the entire BPP range, completed with genuine comments, will be entered into one of two draws on 31 July 2010 and 31 January 2011. The names on the first four forms picked out on each occasion will be sent a cheque for £50.

Name: _____   Address: _____

_____

_____

How have you used this Kit?
(Tick one box only)

☐ Home study (book only)

☐ On a course: college _____

☐ With 'correspondence' package

☐ Other _____

Why did you decide to purchase this Kit?
(Tick one box only)

☐ Have used the complementary Study text

☐ Have used other BPP products in the past

☐ Recommendation by friend/colleague

☐ Recommendation by a lecturer at college

☐ Saw advertising

☐ Other _____

During the past six months do you recall seeing/receiving any of the following?
(Tick as many boxes as are relevant)

☐ Our advertisement in *Student Accountant*

☐ Our advertisement in *Pass*

☐ Our advertisement in *PQ*

☐ Our brochure with a letter through the post

☐ Our website www.bpp.com

Which (if any) aspects of our advertising do you find useful?
(Tick as many boxes as are relevant)

☐ Prices and publication dates of new editions

☐ Information on product content

☐ Facility to order books off-the-page

☐ None of the above

Which BPP products have you used?

Text	☐	Success CD	☐	Learn Online	☐
Kit	☑	i-Learn	☐	Home Study Package	☐
Passcard	☐	i-Pass	☐	Home Study PLUS	☐

Your ratings, comments and suggestions would be appreciated on the following areas.

	Very useful	Useful	Not useful
Passing ACCA exams	☐	☐	☐
Revising F2	☐	☐	☐
Questions	☐	☐	☐
Top Tips etc in answers	☐	☐	☐
Content and structure of answers	☐	☐	☐
Mock exam answers	☐	☐	☐
	☐	☐	☐

Overall opinion of this Kit   Excellent ☐   Good ☐   Adequate ☐   Poor ☐

Do you intend to continue using BPP products?   Yes ☐   No ☐

The BPP author of this edition can be e-mailed at: lesleybuick@bpp.com

Please return this form to: Lesley Buick, ACCA Publishing Manager, BPP Learning Media, FREEPOST, London, W12 8BR

Review Form & Free Prize Draw (continued)

TELL US WHAT YOU THINK

Please note any further comments and suggestions/errors below.

Free Prize Draw Rules

1   Closing date for 31 July 2010 draw is 30 June 2010. Closing date for 31 January 2011 draw is 31 December 2010.

2   Restricted to entries with UK and Eire addresses only. BPP employees, their families and business associates are excluded.

3   No purchase necessary. Entry forms are available upon request from BPP Learning Media Ltd. No more than one entry per title, per person. Draw restricted to persons aged 16 and over.

4   Winners will be notified by post and receive their cheques not later than 6 weeks after the relevant draw date.

5   The decision of the promoter in all matters is final and binding. No correspondence will be entered into.